Pick a
Perfect
Wine
...In No Time

Anita LaRaia

DISCARDED

que

800 East 96th Street,
Indianapolis, Indiana 46290

Pick a Perfect Wine In No Time

International Standard Book Number: 0-7897-3326-9

Library of Congress Catalog Card Number: 2004117315

Printed in the United States of America

First Printing: October 2005

08   07   06   4   3   2

Trademarks

Warning and Disclaimer

Bulk Sales

Que Publishing offers excellent discounts on this book when ordered in quantity for bulk purchases or special sales. For more information, please contact

U.S. Corporate and Government Sales
1-800-382-3419
corpsales@pearsontechgroup.com

For sales outside of the United States, please contact

International Sales
international@pearsoned.com

Publisher
Paul Boger

Acquisitions Editors
Candace Hall
Loretta Yates

Development Editor
Lorna Gentry

Managing Editor
Charlotte Clapp

Project Editor
Mandie Frank

Indexer
Lisa Wilson

Proofreader
Lana Christian

Technical Editor
Ophelia Santos

Publishing Coordinator
Cindy Teeters

Book Designer
Ann Jones

Page Layout
Nonie Ratcliff

Contents at a Glance

Table of Contents

I Wine Basics

II Wine Countries

III Buying, Serving, and Cellaring Wine

About the Author

In 1978, **Anita L. LaRaia** established LÉcole du Vin, The Wine School, in Atlanta, GA. Now called Anita LaRaia's Wine School, Inc. (www.anitalaraia.com) it recently celebrated 28 years of continuous operation, with Anita teaching more than 2,000 classes for the public and wine trade. Many of her graduates are still in the wine business today. Anita's wine industry experience began in London, England, where she worked in one of the largest wine stores and received a wine certificate. She has held sales positions at the retail, wholesale, and import levels of the wine business in the U.S. Known as a dynamic public speaker and entertainer—she sings at her events—Anita is much in demand for corporate parties and as a consultant to wine stores, restaurants, hotels, and wine collectors. Anita was the online wine expert for CNN.com in 2000 and answered every email wine question received within 48 hours. Anita has hosted group wine tours of France and Italy. She has a master's degree in social psychology from Cornell University, has written articles for top wine magazines, and will soon publish a wine textbook for culinary and hospitality schools for Que's parent company and global publisher, Pearson, which owns Prentice-Hall and DK in London.

Dedication

To my husband Michael Nickerson: Thanks, honey, for your patience as I worked around the clock and on weekends for a year to finish this book. You know how lucky I am to have Pearson for a publisher because they have already rewarded you and me with working trips to do wine events in Bermuda and Las Vegas. Happily, I have two more books to write for Pearson, but I promise to take time for some fun with my beloved family and friends. God bless you all for enriching my life in so many ways.

Acknowledgments

My sincere gratitude to the two men who first brought me this opportunity with Pearson: Chef Michael Bologna, CEC, director, Chattahoochee College Culinary School, Marietta, GA; and Vernon Anthony, director of development, Pearson/Prentice-Hall, Columbus, OH, who expects, and will get, a great wine textbook from me. Also, best wishes to Candy Hall, who first signed me to write this book for Que, and Ophelia Santos, WSET wine instructor and owner of Ali Oli restaurant in Atlanta, for reviewing my wine facts. And to my new editors at Que: Loretta Yates, Sean Dixon, and Mandie Frank—thank you so very much for your hard work and dedication through the editing process. Finally, I must thank LeeAnne Fisher, Tara Unger, Ami Sponseller, and Cindy Webster, who have been instrumental in selling my book; and Kimberley Rogers and Andrea Bledsoe for their marketing help. A toast to your happiness!

We Want to Hear from You!

As the reader of this book, *you* are our most important critic and commentator. We value your opinion and want to know what we're doing right, what we could do better, what areas you'd like to see us publish in, and any other words of wisdom you're willing to pass our way.

As publisher for Que Publishing, I welcome your comments. You can email or write me directly to let me know what you did or didn't like about this book—as well as what we can do to make our books better.

Please note that I cannot help you with technical problems related to the topic of this book. We do have a User Services group, however, where I will forward specific technical questions related to the book.

When you write, please be sure to include this book's title and author as well as your name, email address, and phone number. I will carefully review your comments and share them with the author and editors who worked on the book.

Email: feedback@quepublishing.com

Mail: Paul Boger
           Publisher
           Que Publishing
           800 East 96th Street
           Indianapolis, IN 46240 USA

For more information about this book or another Que Publishing title, visit our website at www.quepublishing.com. Type the ISBN (excluding hyphens) or the title of a book in the Search field to find the page you're looking for.

Introduction

It all started with serious sales of "Fat B**tard," "Red Truck," and "Stump Jump." Now wine stores are stocked with bottles bearing wild names. Wine classics with classic labels, however, have not disappeared (although many have updated taste profiles and packaging). The classics still represent the majority of wines sold, which is why the savvy wine buyer needs to know them.

As a wine writer, I receive dozens of press releases about new wineries, vineyards, or vintages. As a wine consultant, I attend frequent trade tastings to find the best newcomers to create exciting restaurant wine lists that customers will crave. (It's a tough job; try sampling 50 wines in an afternoon while staying sober and taking notes!) You learn quickly that smoothness (more balance and fruit concentration) is the sign of a great wine and that better winemaking is happening across the globe.

As a wine teacher, I have to make sense of a mountain of information so that I can explain it to my classes. At wine parties, I entertain everyone from novice to collector with stories of my latest wine and food adventure. Now with *Pick a Perfect Wine In No Time* I can be your own personal wine advisor. Whether shopping in a chic wine emporium or a warehouse store, such as Sam's or Costco, I can find great wine bargains and teach you the secret, too.

In no time, I will welcome you into the brotherhood and sisterhood of wine. I promise to introduce you to the very technical, voluminous subject of wine with humor, inside secrets, and accuracy. My wine school graduates have called me a wine evangelist because I raise the wine cup and treat wine with the respect it deserves. True, but the other side of my dual nature is more like Friar Tuck. He was the jolly monk who fought alongside Robin Hood, and like the monks of centuries ago who cared for vineyards and invented liqueurs, he always carried a barrel of wine in his wagon. That's why my students also named me Anita La Riot! I try to live up to this image and my business cards read: Wine Woman Sings (yes, I sing at my bookings in memory of my mother, who had a beautiful voice).

How I Learned What I Know About Wine

Both my parents were born in Italy, so I am a first-generation Italian American. Having been farmers in Italy, my mother's parents made wine each year in Pennsylvania from fresh Zinfandel grapes that were harvested in California and shipped to their home.

My grandmother also had the best garden in the neighborhood and everything that came to our table was fresh. All the cooking was homemade in the Italian tradition by the women or my father, a trained chef and former candy store/soda fountain owner who made all his own products. (Speaking of ice cream, do you know that Merlot is great with cinnamon, caramel, or butter pecan ice cream?) My dad at one time worked in sales for a wine wholesaler, as did I. I also worked for a major wine importer.

Now you know where I get my great passion for food and wine—and my waistline. Truthfully, I know almost as much about food as I do about wine, which is how I know instinctively what food pairs best with what wine. The best sommeliers (wine stewards) have this talent, and I can teach it to you as well.

But grateful as I am for my European lineage, thank God I was educated in the good old U.S. Though I only use my Cornell master's degree in social psychology to help me woo the public, it has made me an assertive, resourceful woman who feels equal to any challenge. Layered on that is my six-year residence in London, England, where I worked in a large wine store, took courses, and passed a wine certification exam. I arrived in London with no money, no job, and no place to live, but I developed considerable intuition and energy to survive. This risky sojourn brought me to wine as a profession.

My experiences made me who I am and taught me never to be a wine snob. Why? First, it's bloody boring as the British would say; second, someone will always be able to trump you (his or her wine or trip were more expensive or rarer); and third, it defeats the real purpose of wine which is to bring joy and companionship into our lives. Now I'm by passing on my love of wine to you.

Someone once teased that I should bathe in wine. Oh horrors no! I would never do that for it would be a waste of good wine (and cold unless it was mulled wine and then it would be too hot). My cheeky advice: If you want the tingle of bathing in Champagne, use Perrier instead! Actually, you should always drink plenty of water—sparkling or non-sparkling—when you drink wine because all alcohol has a dehydrating effect. Then you won't have that morning after headache. If you still get a hangover, don't blame me. You undoubtedly drank too much and most likely it was not good wine. How much is too much and what's "good" wine? For practical answers (admittedly with attitude), please keep reading.

What *Pick a Perfect Wine In No Time* Can Do For You

I wrote this book for busy people who may not have the time or opportunity to take a wine course. Learning about wine can enhance our lifestyle by improving the quality of our lives in so many ways. Wine can act as the shared topic of conversation when meeting new people and as the hobby you can enjoy with friends and loved ones. Some of you may even be inspired to make wine your career.

The book's title really has two meanings. You want to read and understand any wine label quickly (in no time) to find just the right wine among thousands of bottles available in most wine stores, yet you have "no time" to memorize thousands of wine names. This book is the shortcut you need because it allows you to dive in and easily swim to the next level. Skim the topics, jump from chapter to chapter, or take the handy shopping lists (tear cards) and bring them with you to the caterer, party planner, hotel banqueting department, restaurant, grocer, or wine retailer. You can also read this book at a more leisurely pace and enjoy the wit and wisdom that are sprinkled throughout to make wine fun, not overwhelming.

There are lots of fine wine books in print, but many of them are big reference works that intimidate most readers. Other wine books may be less hefty, but they fail to give practical advice about finding the best wine values or labels by price range, current availability in the marketplace, taste profile, and compatibility with your food choices, menus, and recipes. *Pick a Perfect Wine In No Time* is your key to the world of wines. May it open a treasure chest of wonderful bottles for you.

With the information you learn in this book, you will be able to

- Understand how wine acts as a condiment and flavoring agent like lemon, spices, or chocolate.
- Name the major red and white grape varieties and their food partners.
- Determine a wine's style, taste profile, and relative value by its location of origin and vintage year.

- Learn the six basic types of wine and eight types of dessert wine, and how they are made.

- Identify the world's finest wines at the best price from every area (including new releases) and decode their wine labels.

- Plan your own business or personal wine tastings, dinners, parties—whether ordering wine like a pro in restaurants or entertaining at home—to save money and guarantee success.

- Buy wine with confidence, tour wine countries, start your own wine collection and cellar it properly, and surf the Internet to find any wine.

And I will be with you at every step of the journey.

Who Should Read This Book

This streamlined yet comprehensive little wine book is meant for readers who

- Either have no wine training or know just enough to be dangerous to their pocketbooks and palates. Wine knowledge is like sex—you can't believe everything you hear from your buddies, and if you don't keep abreast of current techniques or keep experimenting, it becomes outdated all too quickly.

- Don't want to have to "kiss a lot of frogs to find the prince" of wines among dozens of very similar selections—we do the kissing and sometimes spitting for you.

- Would like to learn how best to negotiate with your wine merchant for discounts, invitations to private tastings, and access to allocated limited supply wine items.

- Need to be able to read any wine list whether from a restaurant, hotel, or caterer to find the best wines for your particular menu and the best wine values since these on-premise (you drink their wine on the premises) accounts tend to have rather high mark-ups on wine.

- Are curious about corkage fees, buying wine from someone's private cellar, wine of the month clubs, shipping wine across state lines, getting wines appraised, temperature-controlled wine units for the home, wine serving temperatures, corkscrews and accessories, travel to wine country, and wine websites.

- Never want to be at the mercy of a snobbish wine steward, wine store consultant, or overbearing wine friend ever again.

This book is filled with exceptionally useful and easy to absorb wine advice. Let me take the myth and mystery out of wine, without taking away its charm. I invite you to sip a glass while you read. Even if you have never found a wine that you liked, I can help you find one or more wine types that you'll rave are "ab fab" (absolutely fabulous). And don't worry about not finding specific wines that I recommend; I'll always give alternatives that are widely distributed.

How This Book Is Organized

The lessons in this book begin at the core of wine understanding and appreciation and build up in layers. As I noted earlier, you can skip through the book to locate specific information. If you read this book from beginning to end as you would a novel, however, you will get the maximum benefit and the whole process of learning wine will be more enjoyable.

There are three parts to the organization of this book:

- In Part I, "Wine Basics," you'll learn wine history and understand that wine is agriculture, not snobbery. This part explores the latest health studies relating to wine and wine's role as a food. You also learn about grape varieties, including blends and clones, and their present day food partners. This part also explains how each vineyard's geography and location influence wine's taste, uniqueness, and price. Part I also describes in detail the six types of wine and eight types of dessert wine, along with their methods of production. Finally, Part I illuminates Mother Nature's role in the rating vintage years receive and provides examples of actual wine labels and captions representing each major wine type. If your retailer does not have these labels or the same type of wine by a different producer, then you can ask your favorite store to order them for you.

- Part II, "Wine Countries," takes you through California, Washington, Oregon, and our other winemaking states. (Actually all 50 states make wine, though sometimes from fruits other than grapes.) You also learn about Canada's popular Niagara Ice Wine. Next you discover why Australian wines have become the #2 import wine in the U.S., and why New Zealand's citrusy Sauvignon Blancs are prized the world over. Part II spotlights South Africa's great wines along with the "Latin lover" wines of Chile, Argentina, and Spain. Then it's "French Me!"—my trademark slogan for the French originals—with Bordeaux, Burgundy, Champagne, Rhône, and so on. In tribute to the 2004 return of the Olympics to its original home in Athens, I feature the breakthrough wines of Greece that were the hit of three top U.S. wine events in the summer of 2004. Next to last, I tantalize you with chapters on German, Austrian, and Italian wines. And finally, you learn my travel-wise tips for wine country tours.

- In Part III, "Buying, Serving, and Cellaring Wine," you learn how to act as your own sommelier when there is no butler to open the bottles, decant them, or serve wine for you. Then my smart buyer retail shopping guide helps make sense of massive wine departments and gives you the tools you need to find what you need for every purpose. In this part, I teach you all about ordering wine in a restaurant. The information you'll learn helps you choose wines from the wine list by cuisine, taste, and value. Whether you're a beginner or a connoisseur, you'll appreciate this part's lists of coveted categories of wine and practical ways to keep them fresh in your home. Entertaining with wine is really easy once you read my secrets for the successful host or hostess.

- I've capped off this book with a series of helpful appendices including a guide to wine terms and their pronunciation. A list of every grape variety and the type of wine made from those varieties in various countries.

Special Elements and Icons

Pick a Perfect Wine in No Time contains a number of useful lists, notes, tips, sidebars, and other "extras" designed to catch your eye and emphasize items of special interest. As you read the book, you'll quickly spot these icons, which I've used to highlight specific types of information in each chapter:

Vintage Values: This icon marks text that teaches you how to find bargain wines and little-known or low-cost labels, and even save money while still getting great wines.

Perfect Partners: Text marked with this icon gives you great advice on pairing wines with an event's theme, food, clientele, and purpose, using flexible common sense, not hard rules.

Wine Wisdom: This icon marks text where we refer you to wine trade organizations and information bureaus that offer the latest information, websites, and free booklets on the type of wine being discussed. It is also where I debunk wine myths and misinformation by referring to relevant books, news stories, articles, or expert opinions.

Curious Connoisseur: This icon marks the spot where you learn how to find wine classes and tastings in your hometown, as well as ideas for planning wine country tours and ways to further your wine education on the Internet.

Wine Is: History, Agriculture, Health, Food, and Joy

Wine is not snobbery. It is agriculture—as well as a multi-billion dollar industry in the U.S. and the world over that puts many people to work. Wine grapes grow in poor soils where no other agricultural crops will usually grow, so wine can make barren land productive. Added to all of these benefits, drinking wine is like poetry—it lifts the soul and brings us pleasure and relaxation in a busy world. In this chapter, you'll learn a short history of winemaking and some of the major benefits wine brings to people throughout the world.

To do list

- ❑ Learn about the world's first winemakers and wine regions
- ❑ Understand winemaking terms and techniques handed down to us from the Greeks and Romans
- ❑ Learn why wine was a part of the rituals of the early Christian church, and why monks used it as medicine during the Middle Ages
- ❑ Understand how the invention of the cork advanced wine quality and preservation
- ❑ Learn about the development of wine in the New World, and its modern history from the nineteenth century to today

Wine Is History: Ancient Dudes Thought Wine Was Cool

Shrouded in the mists of time are the long ago origins of wine. How long ago is anyone's guess because wine grapes probably grew naturally in certain temperate climates. When grapes were accidentally crushed, they automatically began to "ferment" because of the wine yeasts on the grape skins; and thus grape juice was turned into wine. That wine contained alcohol, which must have given the discoverers a buzz and motivated them to learn ways of making better tasting wine by controlling the action of the vinegar bacteria and wild yeasts that were also on the skins of the grapes.

Wine's Ancient Roots

"Noah, a tiller of the soil, was the first to plant the vine." The Bible: Genesis 9–20

The oldest carbon-wine residue found in a clay jar from Ancient Persia—where we think the grape they named "Shiraz" originated—was 7,000 years old. And some claim the ancient Chinese made wine thousands of years before that. Biblical history refers to Noah as the first winemaker because he took grapevines onto his ark before the great world flood to save them along with the animals and mankind. After the flood, Noah is said to have planted the grapevines on Mt. Ararat in the Middle East, and to have made wine from the grape harvests. Evidence that wine was also a part of ancient Hebrew cultures whose own holy book *The Talmud* contains many references to wine.

When I visited London's Vinopolis wine exhibit a few years ago, I saw a timeline of ancient winemaking in the area of the former Soviet Republic of Georgia dating to

6,000 years BC (before Christ, or BCE, before the Christian era). Scientists theorize that this area of Georgia grew the first ancestors of modern *Vitis vinifera* wine grapes, which now include our best European varieties such as Cabernet Sauvignon, Merlot, and Riesling.

note Egyptians made wine from grapes grown along the Nile, and buried it with their Pharaohs to drink on the journey to the afterlife. Wine quality was important to the Egyptians who rated their wines. Even earlier, beginning in 2000 B.C., the sea-faring Phoenicians took the art of grape growing and winemaking around the Mediterranean and eventually introduced it to the Greeks.

Wine in Classical Greece and Rome

Wine has been an important part of Greek culture for 4,000 years. Greek philosophers such as Plato and Socrates participated in "symposia" (symposiums) where they drank wine in moderation to fuel their brainpower. Wine was featured in Homer's *Iliad* and other Greek literature, and the Greek conqueror Alexander the Great brought winemakers with him as he established rule over the known world. Thousands of years before the French wine laws, the Greeks established "Appellations (names) of Origin" for their wines, planted the first vineyards in southern France, and brought grape varieties to southern Italy that are being used even to this day. The economy of the ancient world was based on three items of agriculture: wheat for bread, olives for olive oil, and grapes for wine.

It was the Greeks who brought knowledge of grape growing *(viticulture)* and wine-making *(vinification)* to the Romans. The Romans called their god of wine Bacchus, and used the Latin word "eno" for wine instead of the Greek word "oeno". To this day, we still use the Greek word *oenophile* (spelled *enophile* in American English) to mean a wine lover or literally "friend of wine." Today's trained wine chemists with degrees in winemaking are called *enologists*.

Within the first century A.D., the Romans spread their knowledge of wine to every corner of their empire: from Italy to France, Germany, North Africa, Spain, and England. The Romans also made several winemaking innovations and improved upon the large clay wine jar with pointed ends and curves like a woman called an *amphora*, which Greeks used for wine storage. Examples of these huge ancient amphorae greet visitors at the gates of the lovely Italian wine town of Montalcino in Tuscany.

Tuscany was actually settled by the cultured, wine-loving Etruscans, who pre-dated the Romans. But the Romans are credited with developing wine bottles and barrels and with realizing that burning sulfur in the barrels (which creates sulfur dioxide or *sulfites*) would prevent bacterial spoilage. The Romans also were responsible for establishing some of the greatest French vineyard regions, including the Rhône, Bordeaux, Bourgogne (Burgundy), Loire, and Champagne, as well as the Mosel and Rhein areas of Germany. All these wine regions followed rivers, had vineyards positioned to catch either the rising or setting sun, and provided temperate climates moderated by protective mountains or proximity to the ocean.

The Romans considered wine a civilizing influence on the locals, changing them from hunters/gatherers to farmers. So it is not surprising that Roman armies carried grapevines and planted them as a not-so-subtle symbol of their takeover in town after town first, in their own boot of Italy, and then the rest of Europe. Plus the very practical Romans could tax the wine, drink it, and use it to prevent food poisoning and the spread of water-borne diseases such as cholera. Red wine is a natural anti-septic and antibacterial agent.

Wine During the Time of Christ

During the time of Christ, wine production was extensive in Palestine; and wine was a prominent feature of daily meals and special celebrations. Bible stories tell of Christ's miracle of turning water into wine for the wedding at Cana in Galilee, and of Christ's "Holy Grail" wine cup used at His last supper with the Apostles. Most peo-ple of this era believed wine was special since it could only be made once a year when grapes were harvested. They also felt it assisted their ability to communicate with God (or the divine part of themselves).

Is it any wonder that red wine (which held up better than white wine in the stifling heat of intensely sunny, arid areas) came to represent the "blood of Christ" in Christian religious ceremonies? Now there are some intriguing medical studies that say there may be some truth to the folklore that, in small amounts, red wine can help us improve our mental skills and access our higher minds.

The Role of Wine Through the Middle Ages: Those Jolly Old Monks

"Beer is made by men, Wine by God." Martin Luther

"Wine in itself is an excellent thing." Pope Pius XII

After the fall of the Roman Empire came the Dark Ages. And for those centuries, only the monks and monasteries kept the art of wine-making alive because of their need for sacra-mental wine. By the Middle Ages, or Medieval period in Europe, approximately 500–800 A.D., wine had an important place in Catholic, Jewish, and non-Catholic Christian religious observances. It was during this period of "enlightenment" that the Benedictine and Cistercian monastic orders

note *Wine Wisdom* Liqueurs are high-proof alcohol, based on spirits such as brandy, which is why they are served in tiny cordial glasses (usually after dinner). These liqueurs are dessert in a bottle—even a monk-shaped bottle for Frangelico (Fra "brother monk" Angelico), a hazelnut liqueur from Italy.

(monks and sometimes nuns) of the Catholic Church received donations of important vineyards and became their caretakers.

The mission of these monks was to feed the hungry and heal the sick, so they improved winemaking and invented sweet *liqueurs* based on *brandy* (distilled wine). They mixed potent herbal remedies with sweetened wines, which were much more easily accepted by the patients. The French word *clos* for cloister (the monastery where the monks lived) is in use today in the names of great Burgundy vineyards in France and California wineries.

The Seventeenth Century: Corks Can Save Wine—And Can Kill It, Too

Although Shakespeare recommended wine tasting in moderation, it wasn't until a hundred years later when the cork stopper was invented at the end of the seventeenth century that wines could be aged in the bottle and develop *secondary characteristics*—pleasant aromas and flavors such as chocolate that are related to bottle aging. This was the beginning of the modern era of wine; for without the cork, great long-lived wines were not possible.

Though ancient Roman writers praised some of their vintages for lasting many decades, it was most likely because they slowly cooked their wines to concentrate them to the consistency of syrup. Sugar content in sweet wines can preserve them longer, but dry wines have very little sugar. They depend on other components such as tannin to give them longevity. The majority of modern wines taste dry (with some notable dessert wine exceptions), and they couldn't have been cellared at all without tight fitting corks.

Corks are made from the bark of the Quercus suber "cork oak" trees grown mostly in Spain and Portugal. These trees can be over two hundred years old and are a protected natural resource. After the bark is peeled every decade or so, there are more than a dozen steps involved in processing the bark into wine corks, one of which involves a chlorine bath. If any fungus or mold is present in the cork bark, a chlorine bath will produce a foul, musty/moldy smelling chemical in the cork that will ruin any wine.

These bad corks are one of the sources of the term *corked* (my preference) or *corky* wine. This may happen only 1%–3% of the time, but many winemakers don't want to lose even that much good wine to a bad cork. This is why screwcaps are appearing on more wines; in New Zealand, wineries agreed to use them on all their wines. Some wineries use plastic corks—and are they ever difficult to remove! The great scientist Louis Pasteur studied wine corks, however, and concluded that their micropores and compressibility were ideal. Collectors will probably always want real corks on their investment wines.

The Nineteenth Century to Today: Phylloxera Plague and the Development of Winemaking in the New World

By the 1800s, European countries had begun to rely on wine production for most of their income. How devastating it was for them when the plant aphid *Phylloxera (vastaterix)* was unintentionally brought to Europe on grapevines from America's east coast. Phylloxera attacks the roots and prevents them from drawing water and nutrients from the soil, thereby killing the entire grapevine. American vines were able to heal the damage Phylloxera causes, but the European vines could not. Phylloxera spread easily across the vineyards of France and much of Europe, as far away as the island of Madeira. The European Phylloxera plague began in 1863 and continued to wreak havoc, country by country, through 1898.

It took years for vintners to finally devise a solution to Phylloxera. The solution was to graft the European *Vitis vinifera* grape varieties, such as Chardonnay and Pinot Noir, onto Phylloxera-resistant American root stocks. Decades ago, wine auctions could offer the few remaining pre-Phylloxera bottles of wine such as vintage-dated Madeira, but Madeira wines have not used vintages since the time of the Phylloxera plague.

Some far-away countries such as Chile never got phylloxera. Their vineyards may be growing the descendents of the original un-grafted grapevines. As fate would have it, California's vineyards suffered from Phylloxera in the 1860s, as the aphid attacked the European vines that American vintners ordered to start their industry. But, again, grafting put an end to the problem.

note California's vineyards were attacked by a new Phylloxera biotype starting around 1990. UC Davis (University of California at Davis) had developed new root stocks in the 1960s when pioneers such as Robert Mondavi and Joseph Heitz were beginning their wineries. These rootstocks proved to be susceptible to phylloxera. Vineyards were uprooted and replanted with more resistant rootstocks a little at a time.

Phylloxera aphids become flying insects in their next life stage, and they can fly or be brought to vineyards on muddy truck tires—in any country at any time. So the threat is still there, and no one is really immune. The French had developed their own rootstocks and they did not have to contend with a second plague.

It just so happens that the mid-1800s was also important as the serious starting point of winemaking in California, Chile, South Africa, and Australia. What incredible synchronicity! Completely independently of each other, wine dynasties such as Beringer in California and Penfolds in Australia were born over 150 years ago. We call these countries and wines *new world*, as opposed to Europe, which is called *old world*. European wines can be just as modern in taste and technology as the new world wines; but, as you've learned in this chapter, the origins of old-world winemaking are ancient. And though the winemaking history of the new world (U.S., Chile, Australia, and South Africa) is much younger, these countries benefited from

European immigrant winemakers who brought their wine knowledge and grape-vines to these new lands.

Of further embarrassment to Americans was the enactment of Prohibition. The tee-totalers won, and the production, sale, and distribution of alcohol beverages, includ-ing wine, became illegal. The Roaring Twenties roared in secret speakeasies. The law allowed wine only in limited home production or for use in church services until the repeal of Prohibition in 1933. The effect of Prohibition on the California wine indus-try was worse than Phylloxera, and it was 30 years before men of vision would build significant new California wineries.

Wine Is Good for You: The Role of Wine in Health and Diet

"Wine is considered with good reason as the most healthful and the most hygienic of all beverages." Louis Pasteur

"Sorrow can be alleviated by good sleep, a bath, and a glass of good wine." St. Thomas Aquinas

"Wine makes daily living easier, less hurried, with fewer tensions and more toler-ance." Benjamin Franklin

To do list

☐ Learn why red wines have a greater positive impact on health than white wines

☐ Understand the truth about calories and carbohydrates in wine

☐ Sort fact from fiction in understanding the connection between red wine, sulfites, and lead

In 26 years of teaching wine classes, I've observed that doctors are more knowledge-able about wine than those in any other profession, and I believe that their interest in wine derives directly from their own observations of its positive health benefits and from reading the results of many medical studies on wine. Within the medical profession, I've noticed the most enthusiastic wine supporters are cardiologists (heart doctors). In this section of the chapter, I tell you about some of those studies and explore the many ways that wine can play a positive role in maintaining good health and a good diet.

Red Wine—Good for Your Heart and Longevity

Since the CBS-TV network aired their *60 Minutes* program segment, "The French Paradox," in 1991 (updated and re-broadcast several years later), American consumers have been buying more red wines. The paradox referred to in this program's title is that, even though the French enjoy a diet high in cholesterol and fat, they are only one-third as likely to die of a heart attack as Americans. I interviewed Dr. Curtis Ellison of Boston University Medical Center's department of epidemiology after he appeared on the CBS French Paradox program and learned that French medical studies had already indicated that the French have less heart disease because of the red wine they drink.

Dr. Ellison then quite humorously summarized other medical studies for me by saying that "if you want to eat that big steak (or other fatty foods like fried chicken), you would do well to drink red wine along with it (or shortly thereafter)—not only to help keep the fat from being deposited in your arteries as plaque, and to aid in digesting that much meat or protein, but also because the positive effect of drinking red wine only lasts no longer than a couple days." He went on to say that almost everyone in the field agrees that drinking wine regularly, in small to moderate amounts, is important. Infrequent drinking provided little benefit. (Atkins dieters please pay attention; we'll give more info about "carbs" in wine shortly.)

Cornell University scientists first described *resveratrol* in wine in 1992. Resveratrol—along with flavonoids such as tannin that naturally preserve wine—is one of several phenols in wine that acts as an antioxidant. In the Cornell study and later studies at the University of California, Davis showed that resveratrol appeared to reduce mortality from coronary heart disease. Resveratrol is found in greater amounts in red wines because they have the most grape skin contact during fermentation. Other phenols in red wine, particularly *quercetin*, have also been studied for possible anti-cancer capabilities. A layman's guide to the health benefits of these compounds in red wine can be viewed at **www.red-wine-and-health.com**.

Can you drink red grape juice or eat black grapes to get the same health benefit? Yes, but you will not get the added benefit of alcohol in red wines. Studies and repeat studies of large groups of subjects (published in American and British medical journals) concluded that those

note Dr. Harvey E. Finkel—clinical professor of medicine (hematology/oncology cancer specialties) at Boston University Medical Center—wrote a very comprehensive medical bibliography of virtually every study done on wine and health for the Society of Wine Educators (SWE) called "In Vino Sanitas?" to answer the question "in wine is there health?" Dr. Finkel's booklet contains the source references for medical studies I mention in this and subsequent chapters. I was also able to interview Dr. Finkel for further explanations that were invaluable to writing this section of the chapter. Obtain your copy for $10 by placing an order on the new SWE website: **www.societyofwineeducators.org**.

who drank moderate amounts of alcohol daily (in the form of beer, wine, or spirits) had significantly less likelihood of heart disease than either non-drinkers or heavy drinkers. The city of Copenhagen, Denmark went even further and did a long-term health study comparing differences between wine, beer, and spirits. They summarized their findings as pointing to wine as being the most beneficial of the three.

Taking lifestyle into account, making groups comparable and studying death rates from all causes, other scientists discovered that non-drinkers have higher mortality (death rates) from all causes than moderate drinkers—with those who abuse alcohol having the highest death rates of all.

Although every medical study ends with the caution that more study needs to be done to verify results, the positive health benefits of drinking wine in moderation—no more than one glass per day for women and two glasses per day for men—for the prevention or lowering of heart disease, stroke, high blood pressure, diabetes, certain cancers including precursor polyps in the colon, food poisoning, and degenerative effects of aging such as Alzheimer's (dementia) or cataracts, is documented in multiple studies.

caution

Not everyone can or should drink alcohol, especially pregnant women, underage drinkers, and those with predisposition to or family histories of problem drinking. College students—especially young women—need to be aware that "binge drinking" is most damaging to your health, and makes you look (and feel) old long before your time (much like smoking). Excessive drinking also leads to injuries, accidents, deaths (1,400 deaths per year on American college campuses are due to binge drinking), rapes, and assaults (600,000 U.S. college students are assaulted each year by other students who've been drinking). These statistics were reported in *USA Today*, October 29, 2004, and *Parade* magazine, April 3, 2005.

Wine May Increase Brain Power and Aid Relaxation

As for wine aiding brain power as the ancient Greeks claimed, studies done in Bordeaux (where else since this is one of the greatest red wine regions of France?) concluded that small amounts of red wine increased mental acuity and the ability to do mental tasks in the elderly. In 2003, Dr. Herbert Benson's book, *The Break-Out Principle*, carried the results of Harvard research on *nitric oxide*, which counters stress, lowers heart disease, enhances memory and learning, and contributes to "a-ha!" breakthrough thinking that helps us find creative solutions to tough problems. That same year, WebMD reported that researchers tested French red wines that had quadruple the amount of the enzyme needed to produce nitric oxide compared to other wines and beverages.

Studies of gamma amino-butyric acid, or *GABA*, a protein in wine, found it to be a natural stress reducer and tranquilizer, which is why many nursing homes and hospitals now recommend a glass of wine with meals or after dinner for their patients.

In many cases, wine proved to be a better mood elevator, antidepressant, and sleep aid than prescription drugs. The important caveat is that only wine in moderate amounts is beneficial—heavy drinking actually has the opposite effect, acting as a depressant and interfering with sleep.

Watching CNN television news or reading AP stories in your newspaper will advise you of the latest research into intriguing relationships between moderate wine consumption and reduction in risk of second heart attacks or lung

note Ladies: Why can't women drink as much as men? The answer is not just because women have lower body weight! Dr. Finkel confirms that women have only half as much of the enzyme that metabolizes alcohol in their stomach lining as men. That's why it may take only one oversize cocktail to make you intoxicated.

cancer. I say bravo to these brave medical people who want to help us find good health under the best of circumstances—all things being equal, as doctors would say.

Wine Calories and Carbohydrates

Atkins Diet, South Beach Diet—all the high-protein diets—allow a small amount of alcohol. Distilled spirits such as tequila, vodka, gin, rum, and brandy contain no carbohydrates—as long as you don't mix them in a cocktail with sweet liqueurs or sodas and fruit juices. And every light beer is very low carb. But none of these drinks offer the health benefits of red wines. And, since most red wines are dry with very little sugar left after fermentation, red wines are naturally low in carbs.

At one point, the United States Department of Agriculture added a footnote about moderate consumption of wine to their food pyramid and dietary guidelines. In 2005, the USDA emphasized that our diets needed more fruits and vegetables high in antioxidants—the ones with the most vibrant colors such as red and purple, just like black grapes used for making red wine. But no matter how healthy your eating habits are, you'll completely negate the good if you risk your life and others by drinking and driving!

Dry red wines have approximately 100 calories and 2 grams of carbohydrate per 5 oz. serving, which means they are naturally low in carbohydrates. Calories and carbohydrates go up as wines get increasingly sweeter. Most red wines are fermented dry to taste, with 1 gram of sugar per liter left after fermentation. White wines, even those labeled dry, including Chardonnay, may have slightly more residual sugar to compensate for their higher total acidity. This is particularly true for inexpensive whites.

What about low carb wines? In 2004, Brown-Forman came out with very dry "1.6 Chardonnay" and "1.9 Merlot" wines, which give you the exact carb count per serving—but it's not really necessary to buy special wines. Our newest alcohol regulations specify that any alcohol beverage labeled "low carb" must be less than

7 grams of carbohydrate per serving. Watch those "flavored malt beverages" though—they are loaded with sugar carbs.

ONE DOCTOR'S DIET ADVICE FOR WINE LOVERS

I once interviewed the well-known New York diet guru and psychologist Dr. Stephen Gullo, president of the Institute for Health and Weight Sciences's Center for Healthful Living in New York City. He explained that after helping thousands of people to lose weight in his clinic, he had three recommendations:

1. Eat white meat or fish, green vegetables, and lots of low-fat, calcium-rich dairy products.

2. Drink *robust* red wines because they are more satisfying to sip in small quantities and, therefore, do not increase your appetite like chilled white wines.

3. Stay away from snack foods such as bread, chips, or crackers, especially if salty, and "trigger" foods such as cookies. Dr. Gullo's first book, *Thin Tastes Better: Six Step Weight Loss Program; The Successful Alternative to Dieting*, was a national bestseller. His newest book is *The Thin Commandments Diet: The Ten No-Fail Strategies for Permanent Weight Loss*.

Red Wine, Headaches, Sulfites, and Lead

Though the great majority of migraine sufferers have no problem with red wines, some believe red wine can trigger an attack. British researchers put this to a test and found that red wine did provoke a typical migraine attack in those who had previously reported wine-related migraines, but none in migraine sufferers or healthy people who had never noted diet-related headaches. The authors of the study concluded that the antioxidants in red wine, including anthrocyanins, which give red wine its color, could trigger migraines in sensitive individuals. It was noted that as a red wine ages in the bottle, these tannins and coloring agents precipitate out, which explains why older reds seem to cause fewer headaches in these sufferers.

Another way to combat this sensitivity and to lessen any reaction to the histamines in red wines is to dilute them 50/50 with bottled water, as many Europeans and winemakers do—especially at lunch when they must stay sober enough to return to work, or when the weather is very hot.

Sulfites (sulfur dioxide) in wine do not cause headaches—that's a myth. Grapes have natural sulfites; when they are fermented into wine, enough sulfur dioxide is released (20 parts per million) to require the labeling "Contains Sulfites" on virtually all wines, even most organic wines. Sulfites, which your body's own biochemical reactions produce every day, are used as a preservative in many foods, including processed frozen lean or diet dinners, concentrated or reconstituted lemon or lime juices, and dried fruits such as plums or raisins. However, in sensitive individuals, particularly asthmatics or borderline asthmatics, sulfites can cause an allergic reaction that restricts their breathing passages.

tip Sparkling, non-sparkling, and distilled waters are best to mix with wine because, unlike tap water, they have no smell or taste of chlorine or fluoride.

The sulfur dioxide added to wine is measured in parts per million and has been regulated by our government since 1933. Without a minimum amount of sulfur dioxide, most wines would spoil or oxidize (turn brown) in distribution. Winemakers never want to add too much sulfur dioxide because it creates a burnt match or rotten egg smell of sulfur in the wine. Light body, low alcohol, inexpensive or bulk processed, dry white wines need more sulfur dioxide to prevent oxidation since they age more quickly than any other type of wine.

tip Red wines have the least amount of sulfites added because they already have plenty of natural preservatives from the black grape skins used to make them. Wine coolers have the most sulfur dioxide added because, without it, the fruit juice they contain would re-ferment the wine.

Finally, I would like to discuss lead in wine, which can have two origins: air pollution from leaded gasoline (which grapes can absorb) and old-fashioned lead foil capsules over the cork. Our government tested hundreds of bottles on store shelves and found there was much less lead in wine (parts per billion) than in our drinking water and many canned foods! Wineries the world over agreed years ago to stop using lead capsules over their corks. Capsules on wine bottles are now plastic or alloys of tin or aluminum.

caution Be careful— these new alloy capsules are razor sharp and can cut you when trying to get through them to the cork. My advice is to simply use your corkscrew knife and cut right up the side. Remove the entire capsule before you pull the cork.

Wine Is Food, Joy, Friendship, and Romance

Oliver Wendell Holmes, 1809–1894, said "Wine is food." What this simple equation means to me is three things:

1. Wine is fermented grape juice. Like grape juice itself, wine contains important nutrients such as vitamins C and potassium, without any fat or sodium. It may be mostly water content like all fruit juices, but as Galileo said, "Wine is sunlight held together by water."

   And I'd consider bottled sunshine to be a food.

2. The main acids in grapes/wine include citric acid, so it is not a stretch to think of using white wine as a condiment like lemon juice on fish. Red wines also have incredible berry flavors—blackberry, raspberry, strawberry, and so on—from the natural organic compounds in the skins of black grapes. Red wines can also be spicy or peppery, so drinking them with certain dishes adds a new dimension of taste much like the fruits or herbs we add when cooking.

3. Wine enhances and brings out each layer of flavor in complex foods and sauces. Unlike water, which is neutral in flavor, or beer, which is often used to wash away the heat of very spicy cuisine, a well-chosen red Latin wine from Chile makes it possible for you to taste every ingredient in a hand-crafted Mexican mole sauce containing 11 kinds of chili peppers, 3 kinds of nuts, and dark chocolate. This is why I love wine and food pairing.

Wine is also joy. Champagne is called the wine of celebration. One of the greatest French Champagnes—produced by Pol Roger—is named after Winston Churchill, who said, "In victory you deserve champagne; in defeat you need it." Even the Nazis knew that and stole an absolute mountain of Champagne from the French during World War II. Thank goodness Mr. Churchill's inspiration for victory had more divine backing. So many celebrities have paid tribute to champagne that I can't resist sharing some of their amusing musings. Our own Mark Twain said, "Too much of anything is bad, but too much champagne is just right." And Oscar Wilde exclaimed, "Only people with no imagination can't find a good reason to drink champagne."

Wine is also the stuff of friendship and romance. Wine has brought me so many of the good things in life—including my husband. He took my wine course in 1980, and we've been together ever since. In fact, several couples became couples after meeting in my wine classes. And I have remained friends with several people I trained and helped get started in the wine business back in 1979. What's even more amazing is that they are still working in the wine business. Now I have to laugh when I find out that some of the young women who take my course become so enamored of wine that they decide who they will continue dating on the basis of how much the guy knows about ordering wine in a restaurant!

The real proof of wine's ability to socialize us, make us better people, and help us live life to the fullest for me is in the joy I see in the faces of my students and wine country traveling companions. Our politics, religion, and backgrounds may be very different, but wine levels the playing field and we accept each other with understanding. Years may pass without any contact, but then they call out of the blue to tell me how much I have changed their lives for the better (though I can't take the credit; it belongs to wine). As a teacher, I love it when my students go far beyond me in their study of wine.

Summary

In this chapter, I've given you a brief overview of the history of wine, the results of medical studies of wine in health and diet, resources for your own personal investigations of the latest books and websites, and the ways wine nourishes both our body and spirit. The world of wine keeps changing, expanding, and improving—so you are off the hook because no one, including me, can know everything about wine. So, burn those out-of-date wine books. And let's have fun with wine as the conversation piece and the entertainment.

In the next chapter, we introduce you to the world's best red and white grape varieties, their countries of origin, the types of wine they make, their varietal aromas, their taste profiles, and their food partners. We will also explain how vineyards and their "terroir" determine wine styles and pricing. Until then, get plenty of rest, eat well, and drink wisely.

How Grapes and Vineyards Determine Taste, Style, Value, and Food Affinities

The grape variety used to make the wine determines its taste and food partners. This means that in order to know what a wine will taste like, we must know the grape variety or varieties used to make it.

Our objective for this chapter is to highlight the red grapes. (I'm not switching terms on you: We call black grapes that make red wine simply "red grapes;" and "white grapes" are those which make white wine, even if they have green, golden, or pink skins. Before you can begin wine shopping and matching wines to foods, it's important to learn how to recognize these grapes and understand what they indicate about the color, aroma, taste, and food partners of the wine.

Vineyard conditions of climate, geography, and soil (called *terroir*) determine the style of the resulting wine and its relative price in the market place. It's like Jamaica Blue Mountain coffee or Hawaii Kona chocolate compared to coffee from Columbia or chocolate from Mexico—the same coffee or cocoa beans, but grown in different soils, climates, and geography, resulting in distinctly different tastes. This chapter explores both the grape variety and vineyard quality factors for wine, and begins our practical study of the grape. We begin, however, with a brief guide to wine-tasting, to help you understand some of the tasting terms used to describe the wines in this chapter.

To do list

- ☐ Learn to organize major grape varieties, both white and red, by categories based on origin and similarity in taste, such as the Bordeaux grapes, Burgundy grapes, and so on
- ☐ Understand how both white and red grapes relate to each other from light to medium to full body, so you can find the wines you need for any occasion or purpose
- ☐ Begin learning which grapes suit your own personal taste preferences and menus with our shopping list and tasting homework

Learning to Taste Wine's Many Flavors

In this and other chapters of the book, you'll read terms such as "mouth feel" and "varietal aroma," used to describe the taste of wine. Although I'll teach you a simple procedure for tasting wine in this section of the chapter, I have to tell you that I can't help you learn to taste a specific flavor or smell a specific aroma. There is no way to put the flavor of wine into words, except to tell you what aromas and flavors you might expect to experience when you taste wines.

Others have attempted to relay the experience of specific wine aromas using a variety of tools. The *Aroma Wheel* belongs to the University of California-Davis, but it provides more negative aromas than positive ones and can be counterproductive for our purposes. The *Le Nez* kit provides the essences of wine aromas in little bottles. This kit costs hundreds of dollars, and I don't think it's necessary for learning these aromas. You can actually make your own aroma samples (for smelling purposes only) by adding cherries, green apple, tobacco, anise, and so on to any basic white or red wine.

But the best way to learn about varietal aromas is to sniff and taste lots of different wines. Learn to trust your own memory bank from a lifetime of smelling roses, lemons, green pepper, and other strong aromas. Like any other skill, the secret of learning to taste wine is practice.

You don't need to memorize all the grape aromas described in this chapter. But you *do* have to see, smell, and taste a grape variety to understand its flavor. So I will ask you many times in this book to decide what kind of wines/grapes you think you might like, based on my descriptions, and then buy some to taste. That's the only homework required to develop a good nose for the wines you love.

That said, you can use some tasting techniques to help draw out the maximum flavor from a glass of wine. As complicated as you might have believed this process to be, wine tasting is relatively simple and straightforward. Here are the basic steps for tasting wine (see Figure 2.1):

1. Look at the color of the wine in your glass to judge the age or oxidation, which appears as color separation and a clear lip around the edge of the wine, as well as a slight browning of the color. Very dark red wines have to be held up to the light to see through them and make sure they are crystal clear. The best way to judge a wine's color is to tilt it in the glass away from you against a white background, as you look at the color of the wine at the very edge of its rim. Young red wines can be deeply purple, evolving to a garnet color as they age. White wines can be judged by looking straight down into the glass. The best whites will be the most brilliant and sparkle like diamonds.

2. Vigorously swirl the wine in your glass to release the aroma so that you can take a deep sniff. The first sniff of the wine's *aroma* will tell you if there are any *off-odors*, such as the burnt match smell of too much sulfur dioxide or musty *cellar* smells that often disappear with more swirling. If the wine simply smells grapey, as it should, proceed with more swirling to vaporize the molecules of wine and get them past the soft palate, where receptors are waiting to make the smell connection to the olfactory lobes of the brain. Take an even deeper sniff and try to distinguish the *varietal aromas* of that grape variety, whether strawberry in Pinot Noir or grapefruit in Savignon Blanc. Then judge the *bouquet* of the wine, including raisin or toast, that comes from aging in the barrel and bottle.

    Swirl the wine in your glass a couple of times and then stop. Look for the *legs* or clear "tears" that fall back into the wine once you have stopped swirling. These *legs* are a visual measure of the wine's *body* or viscosity (thickness). Thicker, more slow-forming *legs* indicate fuller body. The *legs* themselves are not water, but rather represent the alcohol in the wine and are a type of glycerol.

3. Sip a small mouthful of the wine, roll it around your tongue, and do the wine "gurgle." To gurgle the wine, hold it in the middle of your tongue while you part your lips very slightly and carefully, and suck in some air. This wine gurgling vaporizes more molecules of the wine so that we get an intense impression of its aroma and flavors. If

tip If you are a starving student or can't afford to eat out or indulge your wine habit, ask a family member or friend with a fabulous wine cellar to open some bottles and help you practice wine tasting. No wine-rich friends? Then you might consider a part-time job in a good wine store or restaurant that offers staff wine training. Or get your wine store to invite you to free trade tastings offered by wholesalers.

the wine has a very high *acidity*, you will feel a "needles and pins" sensation on the sides of your tongue. If the wine has a lot of *tannin*, you will feel a dry sensation on the surface of your tongue and throughout your palate.

4. Swallow the wine to judge the aftertaste or *finish*. Great wines have a long lingering, pleasant finish. This is called the *memory* of the wine.

FIGURE 2.1

The wine tasting process.

#1 Look at the color,

#2 Smell the wine,

#3 Take a mouthful,

#4 Consider the aftertaste.

Grape Varieties and Varietal Wines

Any wine named for the *grape variety* or varieties used is called a *varietal* wine. By some estimates, there are 5,000 grape varieties grown in the world, but only four of them were originally called *"noble"* grapes, meaning the best. These four noble grapes plus about two dozen more are considered the world's finest *wine* grapes. And many of these grapes are blended together to make more complex, interesting wines. It is the grape variety or varieties that help us anticipate how the wine will taste.

All of the noble grapes, plus most of the other two dozen important wine grapes, belong to Europe's famous *Vitis vinifera* species of grapes—whether they are now grown in California or Australia or elsewhere in the world. Non-vinifera grapes were already growing in North America when the Vikings landed; other species of wine grapes, such as Vitis labrusca, which includes Concord and Catawba, are still grown on the east coast of North America.

The Four Noble Grapes

European Vitis vinifera grapes are considered the best for making great wine, especially the two red and two white grapes that comprise the original four noble grapes. The noble grapes include these varieties:

- Cabernet Sauvignon
- Pinot Noir
- Chardonnay
- Riesling

The following sections discuss each of these four grape varieties, their origins, aroma, and food partners.

Cabernet Sauvignon

Cabernet Sauvignon is called a "noble" grape because it makes a truly great, dark, intensely aromatic and very concentrated dry red wine whenever it's planted in an ideal location and properly produced. Here are its basics:

- **Origin:** Bordeaux, France. Red Bordeaux is not only one of the red wine classics, it is also the standard against which all other great dry red wines in the world are judged. And Cabernet Sauvignon (pronounced "cab-air-nay soh-vee-nyon") is the greatest of the five red grapes of Bordeaux.

- **Varietal Aromas:** Berry, *cassis* (meaning black currant, which is a tiny dark blue berry used to make cassis liqueur), black cherry, chocolate, mocha (chocolate coffee), mint, evergreen, cedar, cigar box, pencil shavings, forest berry, licorice, anise, allspice, tea, tobacco, leather, or green pepper. Only the finest versions of Cabernet will have several of these wonderful aromas and flavors in the same wine.

- **Food Partners:** On traditional fine dining menus, Cabernet Sauvignon is most often served with lamb, filet mignon (steak), the cheese course, or a traditional layered chocolate or black forest (with cherries) cake.

Cabernet's incredible intensity showcases each of its many layers of flavor, and contributes to its full body, richness, concentration, and longevity.

Cabernet also has a high tannin content—the same tannin as in strong tea and a good source of those healthy red wine antioxidants—which preserves it and gives it long life in the bottle. This is the reason collectors collect Cabernet Sauvignon. The high tannin content makes Cabernet *tannic* or astringent (dry sensation on your tongue) when it's young; but as it ages over many years in the bottle, this tannin softens and precipitates out as a *sediment*, leaving older Cabernet much smoother, though delicate. Some of the greatest red Bordeaux wines, such as Château Margaux and Château Mouton-Rothschild, are made predominantly from Cabernet Sauvignon grapes. The other source of tannin in great red wines, particularly Cabernet Sauvignon, is wood tannin from aging in oak barrels.

Unlike the softer Merlot red grape from Bordeaux, Cabernet has immense fruit concentration in the "middle range" of the taste process while holding the wine on your tongue just before swallowing. Wine aficionados may call it "Cab" for short because it is so famous that everyone will know which grape they are referring to. I abbreviate it in my tasting notes as CS to distinguish it from the other Cabernet red Bordeaux grape with similar characteristics: for example, Cabernet Franc (CF).

Cabernet Sauvignon prefers a moderately warm, sunny climate (such as the middle of Napa Valley, CA, and Bordeaux, France) and ripens late in the season. It has small *berries* (what winemakers call the individual grapes in the bunch) with thick, deeply colored skins and the same organic compounds found in black currants and black cherries, but little juice. This high *skin to juice ratio* (thick skin, very little pulp or juice) is what gives Cabernet and other great red grapes their dark color and intense flavor.

In Bordeaux and the rest of the wine world, Cabernet Sauvignon is seldom used to make 100% of the wine. Most often it is blended with the other red Bordeaux grapes, such as Merlot, to make a more balanced, harmonious and complex wine. These Cabernet/Merlot *blends* of red Bordeaux grapes make some of the finest dry red wines in the world and can be pricier collectors' items. Read more about the other Bordeaux grapes and their blends in the sections that follow.

Pinot Noir

Pinot Noir ("pee-noh nwah") grapes makes a dry red wine that is substantially lighter in color and body than Cabernet. It has only four red pigments in its grape skins, while Cabernet and most other red grapes have nine pigments. Pinot Noir contains more acid rather than tannin; as a result, it does not usually live as long as Cabernet. Here are the basics about Pinot Noir grapes and wine:

- **Origin:** Burgundy and Champagne, France. Both the Burgundy and Champagne wine regions are very cool (and somewhat rainy), and their native grapes—the red grape Pinot Noir (noir means black in French) and the white grape Chardonnay—develop more complex characteristics when grown in cool weather areas.

- **Varietal Aromas:** Strawberry, red raspberry, violets, roses, nutmeg, stewed tomatoes, earthy (smell of the soil), truffles, or mushroom.
- **Food Partners:** Grilled Salmon is a marriage made in heaven with Pinot Noir. So are duck, game birds such as pheasant, Cornish game hens, mild Chinese or Asian cuisine, and foods such as omelets that are prepared with mushrooms, especially wild mushrooms. If you're looking for an elegant, lighter style red with less tannin, Pinot Noir is for you.

Pinot Noir is described as having a ruby or garnet color with some "color separation" that leaves a clear "lip" at the round edge of the wine as it ages.

Although French Champagne looks like a bubbly white wine, most of it is actually *blanc de noir*—white wine made from black Pinot Noir grapes. More about Champagne—and the fruitier Rosé (rose pink) and blush (blushing pink) wines made from red grapes in Chapter 3, "Winemaking—The Six Basic Types of Wine."

Since the Pinot Noir grape is more genetically mutable than any other red grape, it *clones* easily, as do Chardonnay and Merlot, in that order. After centuries of sharing cuttings from the vineyards, these grape varieties, especially Pinot Noir, mutated and began to show different characteristics of color, aroma, and taste. The best clones of Pinot Noir are said to be the Dijon clones from Dijon in Burgundy, France. (Yes, that's also where they make the popular Grey Poupon mustard.)

The Dijon clones contribute more richness, color, aroma, fruit concentration, and greater longevity to any blend of Pinot Noir clones. Oregon winemakers were the first to bring these Dijon clones of Pinot Noir to the U.S., but now they are grown in California and other cool areas such as Tasmania (an Australian island off the continenet's southern coast), New Zealand and Loire, France. To produce the best wine, several clones of Pinot Noir are usually planted in one winery's vineyard. Even if the clone and vineyard area are perfect, Pinot Noir is still a very difficult grape to grow and make into fine wine.

Chardonnay

Though it is a white grape and, therefore, not as intensely flavored as most red grapes, Chardonnay (pronounced "shar-doh-nay") makes some of the world's biggest, richest types of dry white wine. Here are the basics about Chardonnay grapes:

- **Origin:** Burgundy and Champagne, France. Like Pinot Noir, Chardonnay prefers cool weather climates and clones easily. Again, Dijon clones are considered among Chardonnay's best clones.
- **Varietal Aromas:** Melon, green apple, pineapple, lemon or lime (one or the other, never both), limestone, butter or butterscotch (from malolactic fermentation), cream, vanilla (from new oak barrels), toast, walnut or hazelnut, squash or pumpkin, smoky or flinty (a mineral quality).

- **Food Partners:** Since the best Chardonnays have that lemon butter profile, they partner well with shellfish such as lobster or crab, fin fish such as sea bass, pork, turkey, and other white meats. And if you must have white wine with red meat, Chardonnay is one of the few that can stand up to it. Because it is so rich and high in alcohol, it clashes with vinegar or green herbs such as dill.

Chardonnay is especially rich if it has been *barrel fermented* in oak, adding hints of vanilla from new oak barrels, and lots of toasty, yeasty, creamy *mouth feel* (a wine's complexity and harmony of flavors) which reaches every crevice of your palate.

There is even a second fermentation that could be done for the most expensive types of Chardonnay called *malolactic fermentation*, in which the tart green apple malic acid in the grapes is converted to the softer lactic acid of butter. Chardonnay is also high in *tartaric acid* (the main acid in all grapes) and especially *citric acid*, the citrusy acid of lemons and limes.

Most Chardonnay lovers crave the beautiful butterscotch or lemon butter flavors in the great ones, but they dislike over-oaked Chardonnays that smell and taste burnt like charred wood.

Riesling

When grown in cool areas with enough sunshine to ripen the grapes, Riesling (pronounced "rees-ling") shows perfect, delicate, and exact balance between its acidity and natural grape sugar content. That is why Riesling makes some of the finest sweet white wines in both the Old and New World. However, not all Riesling wines are sweet. On the contrary, the Germans have several levels of natural sweetness, from dry to medium-dry to slightly sweet to sweet and very sweet. The sweetness level for these higher quality wines relate to the ripeness of the white Riesling grapes at harvest. Here are the basics about Riesling:

note Some wine experts claim that older Rieslings could also smell like diesel fuel or gasoline. Sorry, but I have never smelled that in a Riesling, and I've tasted great German Rieslings from different decades going back to 1911. But I did smell diesel fuel, or petrol as the British say, in very sweet white *Muscadine* wine from Georgia. Muscadine grapes are not from the great wine grape species *Vitis vinifera* like Riesling; they are from a completely different species of grapes native to the eastern United States. Remember, *better grape varieties make better wine.*

- **Origin:** Germany.
- **Varietal Aromas:** Green apple, apple blossoms or other white flowers, peaches, white peaches, apricot, honey, nougat candy.
- **Food Partners:** Their incredible range allows Riesling wines to partner with appetizers such as scallops in butter sauce, through main courses such as trout or chicken salad, to desserts such as pumpkin pie.

Riesling wines are light in body and alcohol and taste as if you are sipping fresh, sun-kissed green grapes. They are perfect summer picnic wines or luncheon wines because they contain just enough alcohol to help cool you in summer or relax you at lunch, but not enough (like many Chardonnays) to put you flat on your fanny. Terrific Rieslings are available from the United States (including probably your own home state); Alsace, France; and Australia.

The Bordeaux Grapes

In addition to the original four noble grapes, we must add several more wine grape varieties that are just as prestigious and popular. They are organized for ease of learning by their type or category, which is the place where they originated. The first to be discussed here are the Bordeaux grapes.

As you read earlier, Cabernet Sauvignon grapes are grown in the Bordeaux region of France. But other important wine grapes are grown in that region as well. Let's start with the two best white grapes grown in Bordeaux. The first, Sauvignon Blanc, is most often used to make dry wines but is also a dessert wine (or is included in the blend of other dessert wines). And the second, Sémillon, can be used to make both dry wine or sweet dessert wine. Finally, there are a total of five red grapes growing in Bordeaux: Cabernet Sauvignon, Merlot, Cabernet Franc, Malbec, and Petit Verdot. You'll learn about these other red Bordeaux grapes later in this section.

Sauvignon Blanc

The very popular grape variety Sauvignon Blanc (pronounced "so-vee-nyon blawnk", the "k" sound at the end is pronounced in English but not in French) is the white cousin of Cabernet Sauvignon. When made into dry wine, it is lighter than Chardonnay. It is also not as high in alcohol or as "oaky," since it is not usually barrel fermented like Chardonnay—except in pricier versions. Here are the basics:

- **Origin:** Bordeaux region of France.
- **Varietal Aromas:** Citrus, ruby red grapefruit, gooseberry (a common fruit for pies in England and New Zealand; it looks like a hairy green grape and tastes like a green kiwi), grass, and herbal.
- **Food Partners:** Sauvignon Blanc is terrific with tangy goat cheeses, from soft, crumbly Chevre to saltier feta to addictively delightful Arina Goat Gouda from Holland.

Some of the lightest and most citrusy, non-oaked (meaning fermented in stainless steel, as opposed to fermenting or aging in oak barrels) Sauvignon Blanc wines are from New Zealand; these wines have received rave reviews. Sauvignon Blanc (I abbreviate it SB) also originates from the Loire region of France where it is used to make the famous *Pouilly-Fumé*. That's where California winemaker Robert Mondavi got the idea of calling Sauvignon Blanc by the alternate name of *Fumé Blanc*.

Sémillon

Sémillon ("sem-meel-yon"), the other well-known white grape of Bordeaux, is either blended with Sauvignon Blanc to produce a richer, more flavorful dry, white wine or a golden sweet dessert wine called Sauternes. Both Sauvignon Blanc and Sémillon grapes can be shriveled to raisins by the rare and natural *Botrytis (cinerea)* or *noble rot* fungus. Other areas of the world, especially Australia, California, and Chile, also make their own version of the two sweet white dessert wines: Botrytis Sémillon or Late-Harvest Sauvignon Blanc. We'll discuss dessert wines in our next chapter, so let's move on by looking at some of the basics about Sémillon grapes and wine:

- **Origin:** Bordeaux region of France.
- **Varietal Aromas:** Fig, honey, beeswax or lanolin.
- **Food Partners:** Blended with Sauvignon Blanc in a top-of-the-line dry white Graves from Bordeaux or Meritage White from California, the dry Sémillon blend marries well with roast chicken cooked with tarragon or rosemary, pork loin stuffed with figs and grilled or fried oysters, vegetarian dishes, or Cajun cuisine. As sweet dessert wine Sauternes or Botrytis Sémillon, its honeycomb flavor is divine with apple tart or apple pie.

Contrary to French wine rules, Australians even dare to blend Sémillon into Chardonnay to lighten it. These "Sem-Chards" are perfect with the Pacific Rim/Asian influenced cuisine that's so important in Australia.

The Bordeaux Red Grapes

As I mentioned earlier, the five red grapes grown in Bordeaux include Cabernet Sauvignon, Merlot, Cabernet Franc, Malbec, and Petit Verdot. These grapes are so similar that they are usually blended together in any combination, not only in Bordeaux but the rest of the world as well. The French let three other red Bordeaux grape varieties—Carmenère, St. Macaire, and Gros Verdot—die out in the vineyards, so California is the only place now growing all three.

Merlot

We talked about the most important of the Bordeaux red grapes, Cabernet Sauvignon, earlier in this chapter. The most popular and well-known of the other four red Bordeaux grapes is Merlot (pronounced "mair-loh"). Merlot shares some of Cabernet Sauvignon's berry or mint flavors, but it is more one-dimensional. Merlot is called the grape "with the hole in the middle" because it becomes bland or watery, rather than concentrated and jammy with fruit like Cabernet, in the middle range of the taste process just before you swallow it.

Because it varies so much in style, you have to taste a lot of Merlots in the moderate price ranges before you find the good ones. Look for smoothness, balance, and harmony between the acidity, alcohol, and tannin—and for berry flavors (not just mint or evergreen). Since Merlot is softer and less tannic than Cabernet Sauvignon, it can partner a wide variety of foods from turkey to grilled meats or barbecue.

MERLOT BARGAINS FROM AROUND THE WORLD

Among moderate priced Merlots from $10 to $15, I prefer California Merlots— such as Sterling "VINTNERS Collection" Merlot 2003 Central Coast (suggested retail $12.99). Sterling Vineyards winery is in Napa Valley where some of the very best (pricier) Merlots originate, so this is a bargain by taste even if the grapes are grown much further south of Napa on the Central Coast. I also recommend fine Chile Merlots from "cut above" but undervalued wineries, such as Morandé, and even a new style Greek Merlot, such as Tselepos, which won against all other Merlots entered from around the world in the prestigious 2004 Star Wine tasting competition in Philadelphia. I've also had great Merlots from Washington, Australia, South Africa, Argentina, and (of course) France, Merlot's home country.

That's why Merlot can transition from fish, such as thick grouper or tuna, to roast chicken, burgers or pizza, and even to cinnamon or butter pecan ice cream. Merlot even marries well with semi-sweet chocolate, and brownies.

Other Red Bordeaux Grapes

Cabernet Franc (pronounced "cab-air-nay frawnk") is much sought after as a separate varietal wine in California. It can be pricey, but very elegant. It's also grown in the Loire region of France.

Malbec (pronounced "mal-beck") is used to make Argentina's most famous red wine, and is known for its mint chocolate aftertaste, affinity for beef, and bargain price tag.

Petit Verdot ("peh-teet vair-doh") is the rarest of all the five red Bordeaux grapes because it is seldom used on its own in a wine—except in Australia where some wonderful examples are made.

An American woman—Karen Melander Magoon, co-owner of Guenoc winery in Lake County, California—spent 10 years getting our government's approval for the most important of the final three Bordeaux red grapes: Carmenère (pronounced "car-men–air"). Carmenère was often mis-identified as Merlot in Chile, but now it is bottled under its own name there and is very popular with Latin cuisine. It can have a distinct minty or green pepper flavor, but the best Carmenères have a tart red fruit character.

The other two red blending grapes originally from Bordeaux are St. Macaire and Gros Verdot. These grapes are important only because in California and the rest of the U.S., a *Meritage Red* wine made by a bona fide winery member of the Meritage trade association is an upscale blend of any combination (even just two or three) of the eight red Bordeaux grapes.

> **note** Meritage reds are collector's items, but within reach for special occasions. *Meritage White* wines are richer and more expensive than wines labeled Sauvignon Blanc, because they are blends of both the major white Bordeaux grapes: Sauvignon Blanc and Sésmillon. The other white grape of Bordeaux, Muscadelle or Sauvignon Vert, is also allowed in the blend for Meritage Whites as it is for several types of white Bordeaux wines.

The Rhône Grapes

The Rhône River Valley in the south of France is known for its hot, sunny weather, very rocky vineyard soil, the robust Syrah grape and its spicy, deep red wines such as Hermitage. It comes as a surprise to most people that there are also white Rhône wines, such as the 100% Viognier wine called Condrieu from the northern Rhône. So we will discuss and describe the most important white and red Rhône grapes and the styles of wine made from them.

Viognier

Viognier ("vee-oh–nyay") is the most important of the three white Rhône grapes because it makes a spectacularly fruity but very dry white wine. The other two white Rhône grapes, Marsanne and Rousanne, share Viognier's power and perfume, but to a lesser degree. Marsanne is very popular in Australia, and Rousanne is being grown in California's Napa Valley. Here are some facts about Viognier grapes and wine:

- **Origin:** Originally from the Rhône River valley in southern France where the climate is very hot and sunny, Viognier is incredibly popular in the USA as a very chic alternative to Chardonnay.
- **Varietal Aromas:** Tangerines, mandarin oranges, or tropical fruit and flowers. Some of this intense orange and tangerine citrus is carried into the taste, but it is the opposite of light—being very full-bodied and high in alcohol.

- **Food Partners:** Thanksgiving turkey with all the trimmings, Thai duck, pork with raisins and cloves, mild Indian dishes with fruit chutney, and any fish served with fruit salsa.

In Rhône, France, Viognier and the other white Rhône grapes—Marsanne and Rousanne—are used to make dry, full-bodied, tangerine scented white wines such as the rare white *Châteauneuf-du-Pape.* I'll bet you didn't know Châteauneuf-du-Pape could be a white wine as well as a famous red! Of the three white Rhône grapes, Viognier is the most coveted, especially in California. It's even grown in Georgia, and can be purchased inexpensively as a varietal wine from the Languedoc region of southern France.

Syrah

Syrah ("sear-ahh"), the greatest red grape of Rhône, France, is also called Shiraz ("sheer-azz")—an ancient Persian name. This is especially true in Australia, where Shiraz has become the country's universal red grape planted in virtually all its wine areas. Here are a few facts about these grapes and wines:

- **Origin:** Rhône, France
- **Varietal Aromas:** Black raspberry, plum, black pepper, peppercorns (which can be black, white, green, pink), cayenne pepper, spices, or bacon (frying or cooking). Syrah has the deepest, inky black-red color of any red wine, with soft but noticeable tannins and good acidity.
- **Food Partners:** Syrah or Shiraz is a perfect partner for stews, casseroles, venison, pork tenderloin, cheddar cheeses, dark chocolate confections, and very spicy or peppery dishes including Creole and Indian.

The more Syrah in the wine's blend (as opposed to the other red Rhône grapes named below) the more costly the wine. This is why the minimum 80% Syrah, Côte Rôtie is considered a much better wine and costs much more than the everyday dry, red blend called Côtes-du-Rhône that made throughout the Rhône region. This is also true for Californian and South African wines that carry Syrah as the varietal name on the bottle. Syrah is a premium wine for *cellaring* (aging in a temperature controlled wine cellar).

However, most Shiraz imported to our country from Australia is inexpensive and could even be box wine, so California wineries who use the name Shiraz do so for their less expensive versions. But the best and most ageworthy Australian Shiraz wines, such as Penfolds "Grange," can cost hundreds of dollars a bottle.

THE NICER THE NICE, THE HIGHER THE PRICE

Not sure what kind of Shiraz from Australia you have encountered in the wine store? That's easy. Look at the price. If it makes you swoon, put the bottle back—carefully! Your wine store might keep its premium wines in a locked *wine vault* or temperature-controlled cellar, where the wine is stored at ideal serving temperature (45 degrees F. for white wines, 55 degrees F. for reds). The best Australian Shiraz wines will no doubt be in there. Ask if you can respectfully and gingerly browse among the wine gems to familiarize yourself with the brand names and labels.

The Other Rhône Grapes

The Rhône is also the source of other important red grapes. Here are the other Rhône red grapes:

- Grenache (pronounced "gren-ahsh") is used in southern France's Rhône, Languedoc-Roussillon, and Provence areas to make everything from rose-pink, dry but fruity Provence rosé, to inky black, spicy dry or sweet reds in Languedoc-Roussillon. Grenache is called *Garnacha* in Spain, where it is used to make top-of-the-line reds. It is also grown in California and is part of Australia's famous red Rhône-style blend called GSM (after three of the red Rhône grapes: Grenache, Syrah, and Mourvèdre).

- Mourvèdre ("moor-ved-reh") is a fantastic find. Look for it as the varietal name on the label of wines from France, Spain (where it's called *Monastrell*), and California.

- Carignan (pronounced "car-ee-nyan") is a blending grape grown in many parts of the world where Rhône-style reds are produced.

- Cinsault ("san-soh") is the red Rhône grape that was crossed with Pinot Noir to make South Africa's famous hybrid variety Pinotage.

All of these red Rhône grapes are very similar to Syrah, and are usually blended with it.

In fact, red Chateauneuf du Pape from Rhône, France, is really what is called a *GSM blend* of Grenache, Syrah, and Mourvèdre—and that's where the Aussies got the idea. Australia has popularized the term GSM because it makes so many of them. That's another example of New World (Australia) taking Old World (European) classics and giving them an interesting winemaking and marketing spin.

Petite Sirah and Zinfandel: Two Unique California Red Grapes

Only a few California wineries specialize in Petite Sirah (pronounced "peh–teet sear-ah"), but they are certainly worth finding. Petite Sirah is not the true Syrah grape of the Rhône. Some wine experts think it is a clone of Syrah, while others insist it is a completely different grape variety. What is important is that Petite Sirah looks, smells, and tastes like a less complex Syrah. Petite Sirah has the same inky black color, spice, pepper, and black raspberry flavors as Syrah, but the overall effect is of a simpler, more one-dimensional wine. That's fine with me, since Petite Sirah is also much less expensive than Syrah in California. The best examples I've tasted cost no more than $13 or $18 retail. Now I have your attention!

Zinfandel ("zin-fan-dell") deserves to be in anyone's list of the world's finest red grapes. Yet it is really only grown under that name in California. As Shiraz is to Australia, Zinfandel is to California—its universal black grape. It is made in every style:

- White Zinfandel—A blush pink wine that's low alcohol and slightly sweet.
- Red Zinfandel—A big, dry, rich wine with concentrated fruit but high alcohol.
- Zinfandel Port—A red dessert wine.

Here are some of the Zinfandel basics:

- **Varietal Aromas:** Blackberry, grape jelly, and spices.
- **Food Partners:** Barbecue ribs, turkey or bacon sandwiches, bean dishes and chili, risotto or paella, fish or fish stew with marinara tomato sauce, veal, wild boar, blue cheese, and dark chocolate mousse.

The most luscious California Zinfandels are labeled *Old Vines*, which means the grapevines that are harvested to make the wine are more than 35 years old, are often more than 80 years old, and in rare instances, are well over 100 years old. These ancient vines provide the grapes with the most intense flavors and fruit concentration. Lucky for us, they are not that much more expensive.

Anyone tasting them side by side will discover that Zinfandel is probably related to or the same grape as *Primitivo* from Puglia (the heel of the boot) in Italy. But genetic testing has now proven that the true ancestor of Zinfandel is a grape from Croatia, which is across the Adriatic Sea east of Italy.

MERLOT AND SHIRAZ: WORLD-CLASS FAVORITES

More Merlot grapes are planted in the world than any other grape variety—white or red. Because of popular demand, about 25% of the world's grape acreage is now Merlot. Merlot is the most popular red varietal wine in America.

The second most popular red wine in the U.S. is Shiraz (the other name for the Syrah grape) from Australia. In fact, Australia became the #2 importer of wines to the U.S. for the first time in 2004 by overtaking French wines in sales. Not to be outdone, some California wineries have begun labeling some of their wines as Shiraz. (They were already growing Syrah anyway.) Italy remains the #1 importer of wines to the U.S.

Gamay: The Other Burgundy Grape

We have already discussed Pinot Noir and Chardonnay, the two noble grapes of Burgundy (and Champagne), France. We must add another useful red grape to this list.

Gamay (pronounced "gam–may") is the red grape of Beaujolais in the southernmost part of Burgundy. It is a very juicy, large red grape that makes fruity, yet dry, red wine with very little tannin. This makes it the perfect introduction to red wine for people who have no experience with or do not like heavier, more tannic reds. Gamay is also available in California, where it makes the same type of yeasty (bottled right after fermentation), cherry-berry red wine.

In France, Gamay makes an even grapier version called *Beaujolais Nouveau* (new Beaujolais wine) made in record time at harvest every year. We get it around Thanksgiving time in the U.S., and it's great with Thanksgiving turkey as well as many contemporary main course salads. But do not keep it for years—it is meant to be used soon after purchase.

Muscadet and Chenin Blanc: White Grapes of the Loire

France's Loire Valley is home to some important white grape varieties, including the Sauvignon Blanc grape we discussed earlier in this chapter. Muscadet and Chenin Blanc are other important white grapes of the Loire Valley.

Muscadet (pronounced "moose-kah-day") is the name of both a grape and one of France's favorite light, dry white wines. Native to the Loire river valley of France, Muscadet (also called the "melon grape") is also grown in Oregon. The best type of French Muscadet is aged *sur lie* (on the lees of yeast that fall to the bottom of the barrel during and after fermentation), and is creamy but never "oaky." Its price tag is a real bargain. Muscadet partners well with seafood, and it is sublime with oysters, clams, and mussels.

> **note** Don't confuse Muscadet with sweet Muscadine grapes and wine from Georgia (refer to the section on Riesling for more information on Muscadine).

Chenin Blanc ("shen-on blawnk") is the grape variety used to make *Vouvray* and sparkling wines in the Loire. Once more widely planted on our west coast, it is still produced by some notable California wineries. The typical drier style of Chenin Blanc is described as medium-body and medium-dry rather than bone-dry. In the Loire, Chenin Blanc (and its famous wines, including Vouvray) can also be made in sweeter versions, from slightly sweet to very sweet dessert style. In South Africa, Chenin Blanc is a huge favorite as the crisp, yet fruity white varietal wine called Steen.

- **Varietal Aromas:** Chenin Blanc has a distinct floral and even candy bar aroma that foretells some fruitiness. And it is living proof that not all French white wines are too austere.

- **Food Partners:** Shrimp salad, Malaysian mango chicken, macaroni and cheese, and creamy soups or sauces.

Grapes of Germany, Alsace, and Austria

All of the grapes we discuss in this section are white varieties. Gewürztraminer, Pinot Gris (or Pinot Grigio), and Pinot Blanc grape varieties come from both Germany and Alsace, France. (Pinot Grigio is also native to Italy.) The fourth and last white grape variety we discuss in this section, Grüner Veltliner, is native to Austria.

Gewürztraminer (pronounced "guh-verts-trah-mee-ner") is perhaps the second most important grape after Riesling. Here are some basics:

- **Origin:** Germany and Alsace, France.

- **Varietal Aromas:** *Gewürz* is a German word for "spicy." This grape is very spicy, with the strongest perfume aroma of tropical fruits and flowers of any white grape. It is one of only three pink-skinned wine grapes—the other two being Pinot Gris (called Pinot Grigio in Italian; see the next item in this list) and Moschofilero from Greece. It's the pink skin that gives spiciness to the wines, but Gewürztraminer is the spiciest of all white wines. Alsace style is drier, while German style Gewürztraminer is slightly sweeter, lighter, and lower in alcohol.

- **Food Partners:** Ginger snaps, ham and pineapple, mild Indian chicken korma, quiche, and mild sausages.

Pinot Gris ("pee-noh gree") means the "gray pinot" in French because it is a pink-skinned grape, and pink (gray) is halfway between white and red (black). Pink or rosé wines are also called *vin gris* (gray wines) in French because they are between white and red wines in color.

Pinot Grigio ("pee-noh gree-gee-oh") is Italy's name for Pinot Gris—they're the same grape. Pinot Grigio from Italy is one of the most popular white varietal wines in U.S. restaurants. But no matter where Pinot Gris or Grigio is planted, it's a slightly spicy wine, never as spicy as Gewürztraminer. Here are some basics about these grapes and wines:

- **Origin:** Germany; Alsace, France; and Italy.
- **Varietal Aromas:** The Alsace, France version of Pinot Gris is more full-bodied and richer than most Italian Pinot Grigios, except the expensive ones.
- **Food Partners:** Italian Pinot Grigio is great with *antipasti* (appetizers before the main course) platters of salami, prosciutto, cheese, peppers, olives, and artichokes. Pinot Gris or Grigio is also terrific with vegetarian cuisine.

Oregon has really adopted Pinot Gris and now makes some excellent examples of this grape. And like very modern Moschofilero from Greece, Pinot Gris from New Zealand can have a very pale pink-gold color if its pink skins are kept in contact with the juice for a longer period of time.

Pinot Blanc ("pee-noh blawnk") is similar to a light Chardonnay. It makes a perfect *aperitif* (before dinner) dry white wine. Though it is very famous in Alsace, it also originated in Burgundy, like Chardonnay. Oregon has become a specialist in Pinot Blanc. Oregon wineries achieve a pinnacle of perfection with this grape that will make you beg for more.

Grüner Veltliner ("groo-ner velt-lee-ner") is Austria's most popular white varietal wine. It is dry and light in body, with a distinctive white pepper edge. In Austria, it is served even with deli meats and sausages, which proves you can have white wine with meat—although today's sausages can be turkey or chicken as well as pork.

The Italian Grapes

There are many white grapes to love from Italy besides Pinot Grigio. Be adventurous in a good Italian restaurant and learn about the citrusy Fiano from Sicily, the delicately dry *Gavi* (Cortese grape) of the Piedmont, the slightly nutmeg flavor of

Soave (Garganega grape) in Veneto, and the very elegant dry white *Vernaccia* of Tuscany and the superb *Vermentino* of Sardinia and Tuscany.

And we must not forget the bargain-priced, dry sparkling *Prosecco* made from the grape of the same name north of Venice or the lush, slightly sweet Muscat (Moscato in Italian) grape of *Asti Spumante* and the non-bubbly version *Moscato d'Asti*. All of these wines and more will be detailed in future chapters. So if the clam sauce on your linguine is white, order dry white wines from Italy. If your clam sauce is red, order red.

Sangiovese ("san-gee-oh-vay-zay") is the great red grape of Tuscany, Italy, used in all of their great red wines from *Chianti* to *Super Tuscan* (the very finest collector's items that are blends of Sangiovese with Cabernet Sauvignon and Merlot). The best bargains from Italy simply say Sangiovese on the label. Even if they are only $7 or $8 a bottle, they will be very decent drinking. Most inexpensive Sangiovese wines are medium-bodied dry reds that share the

note Other Italian red grapes, such as the red *Corvina* grape of Amarone and Valpolicella in Veneto, will be covered in Chapter 5, "The Wine Label Decoder." And a complete list of Italy's greatest red (and white) grapes and wines, such as the robust Nebbiolo grape of Barolo in the Piedmont, the smooth Montepulciano grape of Abruzzi and Marche, the Aglianico grape of Taurasi wines in Campania, and the sweet red sparkling wine made from Brachetto, will be given in Chapter 12, "Italy's Splendor in the Glass."

same weight and structure as Merlot, without the watery middle. Here are some other basic characteristics of Sangiovese wine:

- **Varietal Aromas:** Cherry brandy, violets and licorice, or anise. Sangiovese is always a very smooth wine, with soft tannins, which is appreciated.

- **Food Partners:** Italian or Mediterranean cuisine including pasta (red sauce or porcini mushroom sauce), pizza (white or red), chicken cacciatore, veal chop, pecorino cheese, and even biscotti.

The Great Grapes of Spain

My favorite white grapes from Spain are Albariño and Verdejo. Albariño is the apricot-flavored, dry white wine of Galicia on the Atlantic, where seafood meets its match in this wine. Verdejo is a modern-style, light, citrusy dry white that everyone will love. Another white grape of Spain, Torrontes, is quite popular now in Australia. And Spain's white sparkling wine grape, Macabeo (also called Viura), can also be made as a *still* or non-sparkling dry white.

As for red Rhône grapes, Grenache, called Garnacha, and Mourvèdre, called Monastrell, are both spectacular dry reds in Spain, whether mid-priced or expensive collector's items. Any Spanish Garnacha or Monastrell will be a prize-worthy robust dry red, especially from the Priorat or Jumilla regions. And all Spanish reds, including Tempranillo, are excellent with tapas, paella, grilled meats, and Manchego sheep's milk cheese from Spain.

Tempranillo ("tem-pran-ee-yo") is Spain's signature, native red grape. It is used to make Spain's renowned Rioja and popular Ribera del Duero red wines. Tempranillo can be made into a mid-priced varietal wine, simply labeled Tempranillo in the $10 price range, or create top-of-the-line wines for cellaring. My advice is to buy younger vintages. Some of the best examples are chocolatey or raisiny, with a somewhat woody finish. Another medium-bodied red wine, Tempranillo will definitely suit Merlot lovers. Tempranillo also makes prime-time wines, some at very reasonable prices. Rioja reds can be quite "oaky" if made in the traditional style, but modern Spanish reds are more international in style, that is, dry, but fresher and more *fruit forward* (grapier), with softer tannins and less wood in the aftertaste, like the best New World wines.

The Red Grape South Africa Invented

Pinotage ("pee-noh-taj") is a cross between Pinot Noir and the Rhône grape Cinsault, as was explained earlier in the section titled "The Rhône Grapes." To me, Pinotage is like Pinot Noir pumped up on vitamins. It has a very earthy, spicy aroma and exotic flavor that is the aura of Africa. Pinotage is a medium-bodied dry red with relatively high acidity and some tannin. It is made to go with South African spicy meat stew and grilled meats. South Africa also produces world-class Chardonnay, Cabernet Sauvignon, Merlot, Chenin Blanc, and especially Syrah.

Four Native Greek Grapes

Greece grows more than 300 indigenous (native) wine grapes. Greece also produces excellent international grape varieties such as Syrah and Merlot.

The 2003 wine vintage turned out to be the best in modern memory. I heartily recommend you try just four native grape varieties: one white, one pink-skinned, and two reds. Assyrtiko grapes make delicious, bone-dry, lemony, yet full-bodied and high acidity white wines from the lovely island of Santorini. Moschofilero pink-skinned grapes make absolutely fabulous dry white wine with aroma of roses and citrus. Xinomavro makes medium-red wines of intense flavor and full body. And Agiorghitiko (St. George) makes more traditional, but elegant reds. Any wine retailer wise enough to know about these newest of the new imported wines has just proved to you that they are truly wine knowledgeable.

GREEK DINING: THE BEST OF SUN, SEA, AND LAND

New Greek fine dining restaurants—using only the purest of ingredients from Greece such as capers, olive oil, and fish flown in from the Aegean Sea—have revolutionized the way Americans view Greek food and wines. With so many beautiful islands and coastlines, the Greeks are seafood experts. Greece is also famous for its sheep. Greek restaurants offer great lamb and thick sheep's milk yogurt that is an after-dinner treat when drizzled with Greek thyme honey made by bees that feed only on thyme flowers. More about Greek wines in Chapter 10, "All Greek to Me."

North American Grape Varieties

There are many more grape varieties that deserve some recognition, including Tannat (yes, its name comes from tannin) a red grape from France that's now a hit in South America; Touriga Nacional, the red grape of Portugal used to make dry reds or sweet red Porto; the sweet white Malvasia grape of Malmsey, Madeira; and French-American hybrids grown on our east coast and in Canada, such as the light, dry white Seyval, and Vidal, which also makes some of the rare and costly "Ice Wines" from Niagara, Canada. We will cover Ice Wine and fortified wines such as Port, Sherry, and Madeira in Chapter 3, "Winemaking—The Six Basic Types." This is more than enough for now—like me, you will probably begin dreaming in grape varieties.

> **tip** Don't try to memorize all of the grapes you've learned about in this chapter, or their wines and countries of origin, because we will give you a summary "Table of Varietal Wines" in Appendix C at the back of this book. We will also cover many wine and food partners in throughout the book, including in Chapter 5, "Wine Label Decoder," and Chapter 18, "Entertaining with Wine."

Vineyards Determine a Wine's Style and Price

Great grapes are worthless unless you plant them in the right areas. Each grape variety requires ideal growing conditions of climate, weather, sunshine, rainfall, soil, and geography to produce the best fruit. And without great grapes, you cannot make great wine. Perhaps the most often asked question of wine novices is, "Why does one Riesling or Chardonnay or Cabernet cost so much more than another?" The answer is terroir. As you read previously about terroir in this chapter, the French first coined the term in Burgundy, where a mosaic of vineyards produce unique flavors from the same grape.

The most expensive, and the best, wines in the world are *single vineyard* wines labeled by the name of the tiny individual vineyard where the grapes were grown. The more specific they are about this exact growing location on the label, the greater the wine's value.

When I first began learning about wine, I thought it was amazing that the finest single vineyards had some of the rarest geological conditions on earth. It was wondrous to realize that the highest rated "Grand Cru" vineyards in Chablis in Burgundy, France, had Kimmeridgian limestone soil, made up of rocks with the fossil imprints of ancient seashells from primordial oceans that once covered the land. Of course the Chardonnay grapes grown in those seven Grand Cru Chablis vineyards will deliver exceptional and extremely unique tasting qualities of limestone and flint that amply explain the cost.

Another mineral that creates supremely good soil conditions is *chalk*. The chalk goes 60 feet deep in Champagne, France, which greatly enhances the crisp taste of real Champagne. Chalk also is an important component of the soils of the finest vineyards for making Sherry in Spain and Cognac brandy in France.

Slate, just like the slate on an expensive house roof, is found in the vineyard soil of the fabulous Mosel area of Germany where Riesling is king in single vineyards such as Wehlener Sonnenuhr. And very deep gravel graces Bordeaux's prestigious red wine areas where elite chateaux such as Haut-Brion in Graves produce their treasured wines. No other agricultural crops can be grown in the very rocky, stony ground of these nutrient poor vineyards.

Certain high-ranking red wine vineyards in Beaujolais have rare minerals such as manganese, which the roots of the grapevine pick up and place in the grapes. So the soil may be poor, but the resulting wine is rich in trace minerals.

Centuries ago, the monks who settled in Priorat, Spain, south of Barcelona, noticed the breathtaking "tiger's eye" striated cliffs which are now the landmark for great Garnacha (Grenache) red wines.

The New World also has one-of-a-kind vineyard areas, such as Australia's exclusive Cabernet viticultural appellation Coonawarra, known for its red "terra rossa" soil. And Diamond Creek Vineyards in Napa, CA, has been making three distinctly different Cabernet Sauvignon wines for decades from their Gravelly Meadow, Red Rock Terrace, and Volcanic Hill single vineyards. Controlling for vintage year, grape variety, and winemaker, the Gravelly Meadow is bursting with black currant, while the Red Rock Terrace is almost as light as a fine red Burgundy (though it is all Cab). And Volcanic Hill has the licorice or anise of a great Italian red.

Once I had the pleasure of sitting next to Bruno Ceretto, who produces outstanding single vineyard Barolos at his family's Piedmont, Italy, estate. He took a paper napkin and drew a hillside of grapes to explain that each part of a hillside not only has different exposure to the sun (east, southeast, and so on) and soil conditions, but it also gets differing amounts of wind, rain, and fog, which affects vineyard climate and temperature. This is what terroir means to a winemaker who understands the personalities of his vineyards and wines. If I do my job, you will too.

Things You'll Need

- ❑   Two bottles of red wine, made from two different red grape varieties, or
- ❑   wo bottles of white wine, made from two different white grape varieties

Summary

In this chapter I have tried to inspire you to make a small investment of time, money, and effort in your wine education. We embark on this great adventure together as we begin with the world's great grapes, their origins, varietal aromas, taste profiles, and food partners. Every trip to the wine store will be a safari for us, a hunting expedition where the "big game" is the next great-tasting bottle of wine, complete with bragging rights. Here's your homework for this chapter:

1. If you think you prefer red wine, visit your favorite liquor store and choose two red wines made from any two different red grape varieties for a comparison tasting. White wine lovers choose any two white (or even pink) wines. Read the grape descriptions in this chapter for choices. Buy from different countries, and buy only recent vintage years from 2000–2004 so that the wines will be young, fresh, and grapey. Shop in a moderate price range from $10–$15 per bottle because lower-end wines will not have much varietal aroma and flavor and will not be good teaching examples.

2. Meet the store's wine consultant and ask if they have tasted the wines you selected. If they have better alternatives, let them suggest other brands.

3. Taste both of the varietal wines you purchased with the same food for contrast. This is how you begin learning what wines improve the taste of your favorite foods. Use the suggested food pairings you read about earlier in this chapter for the wines you've purchase, or try seafood such as scallops with the white wines, and pasta with red sauce or beef with the reds.

If you don't want to cook, either taste the wines with good cheeses, such as cheddar or Asiago; or go to a restaurant with a good wine list and order two different varietal wines by the glass. Don't pay more than, say, $8 each. Meet the *sommelier* or wine steward if they have one. The *sommelier* creates the wine list and handles the purchasing and inventory. He (or she) may also present the wine to you at the table. Feel free to ask questions. If the sommelier is wearing one, ask him about his *tastevin*, a silver wine cup worn around the neck to taste wine and verify that it's good (at the same time the host or hostess is tasting it).

In the next chapter, we learn winemaking and the six basic types of wine, plus eight ways to make dessert wines.

Winemaking—The Six Basic Types of Wine

3

The winemaker has many options once he or she decides what type of wine to produce. The decisions made in the winery will determine how dry or sweet, fruity, aromatic, complex, concentrated, oaky, and high in alcohol and body the finished wine will be.

As you learned in Chapter 2, "How Grapes and Vineyards Determine Taste, Style, Value, and Food Affinities," the key to a wine's taste and style will depend on the grape variety or blend of grapes used, where the grapes were grown, and the quality of the harvest each vintage year. However, a wine's *type* or category, such as dry red or sparkling wine, is determined by the winemaking techniques used to produce it.

The six basic types of wine are dry red, dry white, rosé or blanc de noir, sparkling, fortified, and dessert wines. In this chapter, you learn how these six basic types of wine are made and, as a result, what to expect in the taste of each. Along the way, I will dispel some of the wine misinformation that may have been handed down to you by well-meaning friends. For example, there may be some truth to the tale that wine may act as an aphrodisiac—but too much of a good thing will certainly defeat that purpose!

To do list

- ☐ Study the role and origin of yeasts, grape sugar, and sulfites in the fermentation of wine
- ☐ Understand the definitions and difference between free run and press wines, brandy, and liqueurs

Winemaking Basics

Wine is defined as the alcohol beverage obtained from the fermentation of freshly harvested grapes. The basic process of *winemaking* has remained unchanged—yeasts that grow on all grape skins automatically ferment grape juice into wine when the grapes are crushed. We call this mixture of grape skins immersed in their juice the *must*, and we call the period they are in contact *maceration*. Skin contact or maceration is particularly important for the production of red wines, because the juice inside all grapes is clear. The deep color of red wines must be extracted from the black grape skins.

During the alcohol fermentation, natural fruit sugar in the grapes is converted into equal parts of alcohol and carbon dioxide by the yeasts. Heat is released in the process, which is why most delicate white wines are fermented in stainless steel temperature-controlled fermenters—so they don't "cook."

The level of alcohol produced during fermentation depends on the ripeness or sugar content of the grapes and when the yeast or winemaker stops fermentation. *Table wines* (suitable for drinking at the table with meals), by definition, receive their alcohol from fermentation only. They have 7% alcohol by volume (such as some German wines or Italian Lambrusco) to 15% alcohol by volume (such as some California Zinfandels). This is the upper limit for fermentation because the yeasts die when they produce this level of alcohol. Most dry wines average 11% to 12% alcohol, but many full-bodied dry red or white wines, including Cabernet Sauvignon or Syrah and Chardonnay, typically have 13% to 14% alcohol content.

Yeasts are what give grapes their dusty look, called the *bloom*, which consists of the wine yeasts (best for fermenting wine), and *wild yeasts* (which are hard to control and may produce unpleasant odors and flavors). Commercial yeasts, cultured and freeze-dried from famous wine areas such as Montrachet in Burgundy, France, are added to begin fermentation in modern wineries. In addition, grape skins contain *Acetobacter* or "vinegar bacteria" (discussed in the following section).

Sulfites in Wine

Unfortunately, the vinegar bacteria on grape skins will immediately spoil the new wine once it is exposed to the air, and wild yeasts must also be eliminated before they can ruin the aroma or taste of the wine. Modern winemakers follow a centuries-old tradition of using *sulfur dioxide* and other *sulfites* to kill the wild yeasts and vinegar bacteria and inhibit the growth of other molds or bacteria in the finished wine. Sulfites also stop *oxidation* (browning) of the wine and preserve the wine's flavor during aging and distribution. Without some added sulfur dioxide, we'd have a lot more spoiled bottles of wine on the market.

> **note** People who are asthmatic or sensitive find that sulfites can restrict their nasal passages and breathing. Sulfites do not cause headaches.

The amount of sulfur dioxide added is very small—usually no more than 60–125 parts per million for fine cork-finished dry red and white wines—and strictly regulated by our federal government. Even if no sulfur dioxide is added to a wine, fermenting yeasts will automatically produce it from the inorganic sulfates in all grape juices; so virtually all wines sold in the U.S. are labeled "Contains Sulfites."

Free Run Wine, Press Wine, Brandy, and Liqueurs

Making wine begins with the grapes, which are usually planted in areas where other crops wouldn't grow. Grapes like to struggle in poor soils, which force them to grow deep roots and conserve their energy by producing just a few bunches of high quality grapes. In fact, it is said that, in Bordeaux, God created grapes and roses because they are the only two things that can grow on such stony, unfertile ground. A rose bush is planted at the end of each row of grapevines in Bordeaux because the same conditions allow both to prosper.

Véraison ("vair-ay-zon") is the part of the ripening period when grapes change color, especially black or red grapes. All grapes start out as unripe, hard, dark green berries. It isn't until they ripen in the sun that white varieties will turn golden and red varieties will turn deep purple. Winemakers decide when to pick the grapes based on the ripeness or natural sugar content, which is measured right in the vineyards. What most wine books don't tell you is that the leaves of the grapevines also change color. At harvest time, the leaves of white grape varieties turn yellow and the leaves of red grape varieties turn red. This is how you can tell what is growing in any vineyard late in the season.

The finest wines are made from the first pressing of juice from the grapes called the *free run* wine, while less expensive wines are made from second or third pressings called the *press wine*. Press wine is harsher and accounts for the difference in smoothness between fine and inexpensive wines, although some fine red wines may have a small amount of press wine added for extra color, body, and structure. What is left over after all the juice has been pressed from the grapes is *pomace* (a dry mass of skins), *pips* (grape seeds), and yeast that can be used as a fertilizer for the soil of the vineyards.

Brandy by definition is distilled wine. It can be made anywhere grapes are grown. In Italy, grape brandy is called *grappa.* The finest examples are made in fine wine areas such as Barolo in the Piedmont or Tuscany. In France, there are three types of brandy, and *Cognac* is the most prestigious and costly of these. Cognac is made north of Bordeaux from white Ugni Blanc (French Colombard) grapes grown in the chalky soil of the finest vineyards or sandier soils. The dry white base wine made from these grapes is distilled in copper pot stills and then aged in oak barrels for many years, creating "libraries" of old Cognacs. The second type of French brandy is the darker, grapier *Armagnac* made south of Bordeaux and aged in black oak barrels. The third type of French brandy, called *Marc,* can be made in other wine areas, such as Bourgogne or Burgundy.

Brandy is also called an *eau de vie*, meaning "water of life," and can be the dry distilled spirit of any fruit. Kirschwasser, an eau de vie made from cherries, is used when making fondue. *Liqueurs* are always sweet, flavored spirits. Many liqueurs are based on brandy, or other spirits, that are then flavored with herbs, fruits such as raspberries, coffee beans, or orange peels—and then sweetened. They are not dry like brandy or eau de vie.

To do list

- ❏ Learn how tannins form in red wines
- ❏ Understand the benefits of aging red wine in oak barrels
- ❏ Look for concentrated fruit quality in bargain red wines

Making Dry Red Wines

Essentially, red wines are made from black grapes, which have been crushed and de-stemmed to get the black skins that contain all of the red color and flavor in contact with the clear juice inside the grapes. All grapes, no matter what color the skins—whether black, green, or pink—contain clear pulp or juice inside. Peel a grape to see for yourself!

Red wines must be fermented with their black grape skins for approximately 10–14 days, and sometimes much longer for the greatest reds. This prolonged maceration and fermentation allows for the maximum extraction of red color and flavor from the skins, and tannin comes along in the bargain. A winemaker is careful not to extract too much tannin from grape skins or stems (if the whole cluster is used and not de-stemmed), or the wine will taste very astringent and bitter from hard tannins. Soft tannins, however, add a desirable tactile dry complexity to the taste of the wine und contribute to its longevity, since tannin is a natural preservative.

Micro-oxygenation is the fairly new and controversial winemaking technique of introducing tiny amounts of oxygen into fermenting red wine, or red wine aging in the barrel, through a small tube. Advocated by famous Bordeaux enologist Michel Rolland, who recommends it to hundreds of his consulting clients worldwide, micro-oxygenation softens the tannins in red wines, making them jammy and the darling of wine critics, even when they are young. The wine movie "Mondovino" by Jonathan Nossiter carries a running joke about this technique.

The carbon dioxide that's produced during fermentation pushes the black skins up to the top of the fermenters, forming what is called the *cap* of skins on top of the juice. This cap of skins must be continually punched down or circulated back through the juice. There are several ways to do this, including some new techniques. (See the following note.)

Red wines also benefit from some of the heat that is released during fermentation, which is why many wineries not only age or mature their red wines in oak, but also ferment their reds in oak barrels as in the European tradition. Barrel fermentation and oak aging add a great deal of complexity and flavor to the red wine, as well as another dose of tannin from the wood tannin in oak. These two sources of tannin (black grape skins and oak barrels) give red wines greater aging potential than whites.

Many people confuse dryness (no sugar left after fermentation) with high tannin. When they say they don't like dry red wine, they really mean they don't like tannic or astringent wines. Acidity doesn't seem to bother them as much since they like white wines and whites are usually higher in total acidity than red wines.

note Brilliant food chemist Chaim Gur-Arieh, of the C.G. di Arie world-class winery in California's Shenandoah Valley of the Sierra Foothills, produces fabulous Zinfandel and Syrah because of his new invention: a fermenter with a rubber ring inside that keeps the cap of black skins constantly submerged in the juice so that the cap never hardens. Otherwise, the cap of skins can get as hard as concrete, which defeats the extraction process. As a result, C.G. di Arie red wines have more fruit concentration and softer tannins.

tip The best way to get used to the taste of dry red wines is to start with the grapiest (meaning fruitiest) and least tannic varieties, such as red Lambrusco, which is a slightly sweet, semi-sparkling red wine from Italy that is served chilled. The best-selling brand of Lambrusco in the U.S. is Riunite. Another fruity red from Italy is Dolcetto, which is similar to Gamay Beaujolais. Lemberger is another soft red grown in the U.S. that originates from Germany, as does the fruity Dornfelder red variety.

Even the more intense grapes such as Cabernet or Zinfandel can be made in a softer style, so ask your store's wine consultant for less tannic choices. Don't forget you can mix any red wine 50/50 with bottled water and get the health benefit without the tannin. This will acclimatize your palate to appreciate drier red wines.

Nouveau and Whole Cluster Reds

For less tannic wines, winemakers have developed other types of winemaking, such as *carbonic maceration* or whole berry fermentation, the process used to make *nouveau* or "new" wines, such as Beaujolais Nouveau in France. Though how or why it works is still a mystery, nouveau wines are made from grapes that ferment while they are still whole and attached to their stems. They sit on top of fermenting crushed grapes, releasing carbon dioxide in closed containers. Nouveau wines can be made from any red grape, even Zinfandel in California, but they are always much grapier, more deeply purple and very much yeastier than normally fermented red wines made from the same grape variety.

Nouveau wine is made in just a few days, and then rushed to market. We receive Beaujolais Nouveau before our traditional Thanksgiving turkey dinner in November every year, and the nouveau red is a perfect complement to the meal.

Other modern winemaking techniques for making less tannic, fruitier reds include *whole cluster fermentation* of Pinot Noir, once widely practiced in Burgundy, which is a popular technique today in Oregon. Instead of de-stemming the grapes and fermenting just the grape *must* of juice and skins, these fruitier Pinot Noirs are made using the entire cluster of grapes and stems during fermentation. Of course, most winemakers agree that using too many stems will make the wine taste too green or bitter and tannic. So a delicate balance is called for, like in any winemaking decision; for example, some of the wine in a batch may be whole cluster fermented, but the majority may not be for this reason.

Aging Red Wine in Oak Barrels

The alcohol that's produced during red wine fermentation also helps to extract the maximum amount of deep purple color, flavor, and tannin from the black skins. Red wines are then aged in wood, usually *oak barrels*, to soften their tannins and pick up more complexity. Each kind of oak—such as *limousin* oak used in Burgundy, France, for Pinot Noir and Chardonnay; or *nevers* oak used in Bordeaux, France, for Cabernet Sauvignon and Merlot; or even *American oak* barrels made in Missouri— adds its own flavor to the wine. Barrels made from new oak add a lovely vanilla aroma to the wine.

Fining, which clears the wine by removing tiny particles and floating in the wine, is done while red wines age in the barrels. Two of the most-often-used fining agents are egg whites, clay, and a type of earth. Fining also removes some of the tannin and may be done more than once. The final step may be *filtering* done with biological filters, which remove any yeast or other impurities left in the wine. This prevents the wine from re-fermenting once it's bottled, and it gives the wine a brilliant, crystal-clear appearance.

The wood tannins that the barrels add to the wine during aging further preserve the wine. Young red wines have the most tannin, but as red wine ages in the bottle, this tannin will precipitate as *sediment*. The wine will then taste smoother, but this means older reds will have to be *decanted* or poured off their sediment, strained through a funnel with built-in filter or coffee filter paper. Since wood barrels are porous, they also allow a very slow process of oxidation. After the wine throws its sediment in the barrel, the wine is *racked* (transferred) to a set of clean barrels, leaving the sediment behind. Racking is done every 6 months during the period of up to 24 months that the best red wines are aged in oak barrels.

Great oak-aged reds and some exceptional white wines can survive long enough in the bottle to reach a peak of perfection after several years of cellaring. That's why the finest older reds command such high prices and why they taste so much smoother after bottle aging. They have developed *secondary characteristics* of raisin or cooked fruit aromas, and their tannin has soft-ened. Older reds are more delicate, so they are usually served on their own or after dinner with the cheese course.

Please note that almost all red wines are fermented dry; that is, until there is no *residual sugar* left after fermentation. Yes, there are some famous sweet red wines—such as Porto from Portugal, Mavrodaphne from Greece, Maury or Banyuls from France, and Black Muscat from California—but the great major-ity of red wines made in the world today are dry, meaning close to zero residual sugar. This is why I like to call red wines "main course" wines. Nothing is finer with filet mignon, veal chop, pork tenderloin, venison, or crown roast of lamb.

note People who say they don't like dry red wines are drinking the inexpensive ones too warm. Red wines should be stored—and served—at 55 degrees F., which is cool "cellar" temperature. If you don't have a temperature-controlled cellar, place the red wine in ice and water (in an ice bucket, bowl, or sink) for at least 5 minutes before serving. Or chill in the refrigerator for about 20 minutes. Too much cold kills the beauti-ful aromas and flavors of great red wine, but a little chill is just right when serving out-doors or indoors on hot summer days.

Buying the Best Reds

The finest dry red wines have lots of concentrated fruit character—what I call the divine *extract* of the grape. Wine magazines call these wines "jammy," and the fruit concentration in these great reds balances their tannin, alcohol, and acidity. If we are lucky in our choices, we can sometimes find this concentrated fruit quality in bargain reds. But usually, you will have to pay a minimum of $20 to $35 a bottle for a better red that's a wonderful, deeply extracted example of that grape variety. If you spend $50 to $75 on a bottle of red, it had better be one of the very finest of its type. Collectors' items cost even more because demand far outstrips supply and because they have a greater pedigree. By pedigree I mean they usually come from a single vineyard or estate name—what we call *terroir*. (For more information about *terroir*, see "Vineyards Determine a Wine's Style and Price," in Chapter 2.)

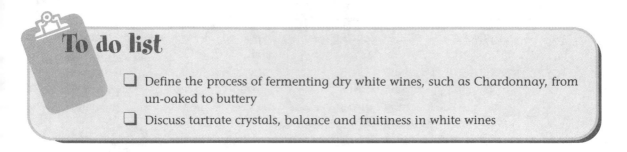

To do list

- ☐ Define the process of fermenting dry white wines, such as Chardonnay, from un-oaked to buttery
- ☐ Discuss tartrate crystals, balance and fruitiness in white wines

Making Dry White Wines—To Oak or Not to Oak

White wines are not fermented with their skins. The clear juice of the grapes (white or black) is pressed away from the skins after they are crushed and de-stemmed, and the juice is fermented on its own. The skins are not needed for color to make a white wine, though there may be some hours of *skin contact* for full-bodied whites (or *blanc de noir* wines, to be discussed later). White grape skins have little tannin, and temperature-controlled stainless steel fermenters keep the heat that is produced during fermentation from literally cooking the white wine. For less expensive dry white wines, fermenting the juice and bottling the wine without oak aging takes only a few months; so these wines are bottled as little as six months after harvest. Light, dry white wines age more quickly than any other type of wine and are for early drinking.

Fermenting White Wines

The best white wines—particularly Chardonnay—are *barrel fermented* in oak to give them added complexity; a toasty, yeasty flavor; and greater longevity. Some of these great Chardonnays will even be aged *sur lie*—on the "lees" or sediment of yeast that falls to the bottom of the barrels after fermentation, which gives the wine an added richness. Further *barrel aging* for the best whites is shorter than for red wines, however, taking only 6–18 months after the vintage or harvest. That is why white wines are released to the market much sooner than red wines, and why even the greatest whites do not live as long in the bottle as better reds.

Great white wines, especially Chardonnay (and some red wines too), undergo a second fermentation called *malolactic fermentation*. Malolactic fermentation is done in another set of barrels. It converts the tart green-apple-flavored malic acid in the wine to softer lactic acid, which has the flavor of butter or cream. This is the only process that can make a Chardonnay buttery. Malolactic fermentation gives a butterscotch complexity to the great white Burgundy wines of France, which were the original malolactic fermented Chardonnays. Finding these buttery Chardonnays is not easy, since many Chardonnays do not tell you on the front or back label whether the winemaker put the wine through malolactic fermentation. The price level is a good indication, however, because this second fermentation costs a lot more money and ties up inventory for several more months.

Wine is unique among beverages. Its enormous range of flavors and tastes belie the fact that it is composed of acids, tannins, and alcohol. Besides tartaric and malic acids, white grapes also tend to have a lot of citric acid. Citric acid makes these white wines smell and taste like the citrus fruits: lemons or limes. Now you can understand why buttery malolactic fermented Chardonnays are described as tasting like lemon butter, which makes them the perfect wine partner for lobster, crab, and fish.

No one wants his or her white wine to taste like wood, but oak-fermented creamy or buttery whites are very much appreciated with richer main courses. Oak barrel aging is a financial investment in any case, so winemakers decide on the basis of the variety and the greatness of their grapes in a certain vintage year or from a certain vineyard. Some white wines are not meant to be oak aged at all in order for them to retain their fresh, fruit flavors. So the question "to oak or not to oak" that a winemaker must answer before he begins white wine production is a very important one. Some American winemakers initiated the dubious practice of using heavily "toasted" (charred) oak barrels several years ago, but it made their Chardonnays smell and taste like burnt wood. Hopefully, you won't encounter them in the marketplace, but if you do, the aroma reveals all.

Chilling the Wine and Removing Tartrate Crystals

Finally, most stainless steel fermented white wines produced in the New World go through *cold stabilization*. In California wineries you can see the frost on the outside of the stainless steel fermenters as the wine is chilled until the *tartrate crystals* precipitate and can be removed. Tartaric acid is the main acid in grapes. Chilling white wine after fermentation causes the formation of *tartrate crystals*, which are like the *cream of tartar* used in making candy and meringues. Tartrate crystals can be the sign of a hand-crafted wine from a great vintage. I've seen tartrate crystals in some of the finest dry reds such as Zinfandel or Chianti from Italy, as well as in very sweet whites, and even inexpensive mass market wines. But when these crystals collect in the bottom of a wine bottle, some people think the crystals are

caution Serving temperature is crucial to your wine enjoyment. This is so true that *Mar de Frades* Spanish *Albariño* imported by William Grant & Sons (sells for $15 retail) comes with a thermo-sensitive label on the blue bottle that will show a blue ship above the waves if the wine has been chilled to its perfect serving temperature of 52–55 degrees F. It works because of special ink that only becomes visible at a certain temperature. Now aren't you glad you learned about the delicious, dry, seafood-friendly Albariño grape in Chapter 2? Most chilled whites are served in the U.S. after a couple hours in the fridge at our refrigerator temp of 42 degrees.

ground glass and don't want to drink the wine. Modern wineries preempt any consumer reaction by chilling the wine to remove the crystals, but even then some crystals may still form in extreme cold.

Adjusting the Wine's Fruitiness and Sweetness

This brings me to the definition of *fruity*. Fruity is often thought to mean sweet, but dry white and red wines also can be fruity. Fruity means the character of fresh fruits: red fruits, such as strawberries, raspberries, or cherries; black fruits, such as blackberries; blue fruits, such as blueberries or deep blue blackcurrants (cassis); tropical fruits, such as pineapple or mango; and citrus fruits, such as lemon or grapefruit.

For white wines in particular, this also may mean they have beautiful aromas of fresh flowers as well as the taste of fresh green grapes. So, in addition to deciding whether to age the wine in barrels, a winemaker also chooses how sweet to make the finished wine. Winemakers control sweetness by stopping fermentation before all the natural grape sugar has been turned into alcohol and carbon dioxide by the yeast.

White wines can vary tremendously in sweetness or the residual grape sugar left after fermentation. White wines can be made *bone-dry* with no residual sugar—the austere style of many French dry white wines from Bordeaux or Burgundy—or *medium-dry* with just the barest

> **note** One optional step in both red and white wine production is called *chaptalization*. Chaptalization is addition of cane sugar before or during fermentation to increase the alcohol content. This is only done in cold climates, such as Burgundy and Germany, where there may be vintage years when there is not enough sunshine to ripen the grapes. It does not make the wine sweeter, and it is not allowed in sunny climate countries such as Italy or Australia.

hint of natural sweetness like a German Riesling in the dry Kabinett style—or lusciously sweet like a Sauternes or Ice Wine. Real wine experts love all styles of white wine. They know that certain medium-dry white wines are actually better partners than dry white wines when foods have an orange juice marinade, a dried cherry sauce, or a fig or raisin stuffing. As you practice tasting a wide variety of white wines with different food partners, you can expect to gain an appreciation for the wide range of good white wines in many styles.

Making Rosé, Blush, and Blanc de Noir Wines

Rosé, blush, and *blanc de noir* wines are varying shades of pink. This pink color tells you that all three are made from black grape varieties that release or "bleed" their red color into the juice when they are pressed.

A *rosé* gets its characteristic deeper rose color from black grapes that have been crushed and fermented with their skins for 24–36 hours—just long enough to turn the clear juice a dark pink color. Then the juice is quickly pressed away from the skins. If the skins had been in contact with the juice for a few more hours, a red wine would have been produced, which is why some say rosé is halfway to being a red wine.

Rosés are much softer than a red wine and do not contain high levels of alcohol or tannin. And they can be made either dry or medium-dry. Most rosés are *still wines*, meaning non-sparkling, and have lovely berry aromas and flavors from the black grapes used to make them. Sparkling rosés range from expensive French Rosé Champagne to inexpensive Spanish Brut de Noirs CAVA or Italian Prosecco Rosé.

Blush wines are what the French call *blanc de noir*—white wines made from black grapes, which is how most French Champagne is made. Blush wines were first introduced to the U.S. by Sutter Home winery in California. Sutter Home grew a lot of black Zinfandel grapes (still do) but realized many Americans preferred white wines. So they made Zinfandel as a white wine by pressing the juice from the skins and fermenting it on its own. But just pressing the black Zinfandel grapes produced a blushing pink color in the juice. That's how White Zinfandel was born and why it's a blush (pink) wine instead of white. The French also call these blushing pink wines *vin gris* or gray wine because it's between white and black (red wine) as we explained in Chapter 2.

Unlike Rosé, which can be dry, blush wines are always slightly sweet, low alcohol, and fruity with blackberry flavors from the Zinfandel. Brunch is a perfect time to serve Rosé wines, especially Pinot Noir or Grenache Rosé, because they go so well with omelets, quiches, or ham and bacon. They are also best served chilled.

Rosés typically are very inexpensive. Sutter Home "Little Pink Box" White Zinfandel sells for $8 retail, which is equivalent to $2 per bottle since the 3 liter box holds as much as four regular-size 750 ml. bottles.

LET'S DO WINE AND CHOCOLATE

Chocolate and wine make great partners, and they have a lot in common. Chocolates are influenced and priced by *terroir* (where the chocolate beans were grown), just like wine. Some chocolates even have names that sound like wines, such as Côte d'Or (meaning hillside of gold), which in the wine world is the greatest district in Burgundy, France; or Weiss *Grande Noir* (or "great dark") semi-sweet chocolate. And, like great wine, great chocolate can be quite expensive. In New York City chocolate emporiums, the most elite chocolates cost hundreds of dollars per pound.

Different types of chocolate work best with different wines:

✳ **Milk chocolate** has a creamier texture, more dairy, and lower cacao content than other types of chocolate. *Cacao* is the name of the tree that produces the cocoa beans. The beans true chocolate component possesses the desirable antioxidants and mood lifting *theobromine* (the *theo* part of which means "from God"). Milk chocolate partners best with slightly sweet white or red sparkling wines, such as Asti Spumante or Brachetto (a very unusual sweet red sparkling wine) both from Italy. Also terrific with milk chocolate is bargain-priced *semi-secco* (slightly sweet) Cava sparkling wines from Spain. These three are divine with strawberries dipped in milk chocolate.

* If you prefer dry red wines, experiment with **semi-sweet chocolate** and any dessert such as brownies made with semi-sweet chocolate. Ask your wine store's wine expert for a red with concentrated fruit in the middle range of the taste, such as Zinfandel, Petite Sirah, Syrah or Shiraz, and Cabernet Sauvignon or Cabernet Franc. The sweetness and cacao content of semi-sweet chocolate is between those of milk chocolate and bittersweet or dark chocolate.

* **Bittersweet** or **dark chocolates**—the best are 60% to 70% cacao—are terrific with luscious, sweet red dessert wines, such as Zinfandel Port from California, or Ruby Porto from Portugal. If you are not sure you can take the sweetness of port, then choose a *blanc de noir* or rosé sparkling wine. Not all of these wines are expensive. I've had Prosecco rosé from Italy that was very reasonable. Even better was a Spanish Cava sparkling wine from the acclaimed Freixenet (pronounced "fresh-eh-net") company called *Brut de Noirs* (retail price about $8). This wine has deep rose-pink color, delicious strawberry aroma from the black grapes used to make it, and drier style.

CNN just reported the latest medical research says we get the most antioxidant benefit from eating *bittersweet* chocolate in moderation. Researchers discovered it actually had health benefits for your blood vessels if eaten in small amounts on a regular basis. That's one prescription I'll be happy to take! If you cannot afford expensive bittersweet chocolate, buy bittersweet *baking* chocolate from the grocery store. And while you are there, check out the wine department. Looking at the labels of the best wines gives you many clues as to why they are great.

To do list

- [ ] Learn the 10 steps used to produce Champagne or other sparkling wines in the classic *méthode champenoise*
- [ ] Learn how to buy, serve, and enjoy Champagne, and understand when (and if) it's wise to buy non-standard sized bottles

Putting the Bubbles in Champagne

Sparkling wines and Champagne are bubbly because they have carbon dioxide bubbles trapped in the bottle from a second fermentation. The most famous sparkling wine is *Champagne* from France made in the *méthode champenoise* or Champagne method that the French developed over many years to create the tiniest, longest-lasting bubbles.

> **note** The European Union prohibits anyone but France's Champagne district from using the word Champagne, but we dare to call even bulk process sparklers by this name in the U.S. Honoring the French tradition, however, I use the term "sparkling wines" for all bubbly that isn't real Champagne from France.

Wherever it is used, the *méthode champenoise*, or Champagne method, produces the world's finest sparkling wines. This method involves a second fermentation that takes place in the bottle—the same bottle that you eventually buy in the store. Many other countries, including Spain, Italy, and the United States, have successfully adopted this method for the production of their best sparkling wines. The following sections describe the *méthode champenoise* process for producing great sparkling wine.

Harvesting and Pressing the Grapes

Grapes are harvested 100 days after the grapevines flower in June. This places the time of harvest in the northern hemisphere in September or October. The CIVC (Comitè Interprofessionnel du Vin de Champagne), the official organization that represents the Champagne industry, declares great vintage years when the harvest is exceptionally good because of an excellent growing season. Prices for grapes from the best single vineyards in the Champagne region are always higher, with the 100%-rated vineyards getting 100% of the going rate, 95%-rated vineyards getting 95% of the going rate, and so on, based on their ranking. The finest Champagnes are *Vintage Champagne* from a single declared great vintage year, and those are from the best vineyards.

Experienced sorters cull out any green or rotten grapes in the vineyards before they get to the presses. This costs extra and is only done for top-of-the-line Champagnes. The grapes are pressed quickly in low, flat, wooden presses to extract the clear juice from the skins. Even with this quick pressing of the black grapes, the juice is tinted an "eye of the swan" blushing pink/gold color, which will be bleached out somewhat during the second fermentation.

Fermenting and Blending the Juice

The *first fermentation* in the méthode champenoise turns the grape juice into wine. But the juice from each vineyard and each grape variety is fermented separately, usually in stainless steel for temperature control (though some Champagne companies may ferment in traditional oak barrels). All these separate fermentations create a large number of individual wines that will later be blended in the *assemblage* of the cuvée.

The following spring, professional tasters blend the *assemblage* or *cuvée* (pronounced "koo-vay") from different vineyards and grape varieties so that the sum is better tasting than the parts. Most French Champagne is a blend or *cuvée* of 2/3 black grapes and 1/3 white grape. In French Champagne, the only black grapes allowed are Pinot Noir and their relative Pinot Meunier, and the only white grape allowed is Chardonnay. This means most French Champagne is actually *blanc de noir* though they do not label it as such. The exception to the rule of French Champagne being made mostly from black grapes is the more delicate, rare, and costly *blanc de blanc* Champagne. It must, by law, in France be made from 100% Chardonnay.

Each Champagne house or company has its own house blend or style, some using more Pinot Noir, some using more Chardonnay—although Chardonnay is expensive since it comes from one small hillside called the Côte des Blancs ("slope of white"). Most Champagne houses use very little Pinot Meunier in their top of the line cuvées.

Adjusting and Bottling for a Second Fermentation

After blending, a first *dosage* (pronounced "doh-saj")—technically called the "liqueur de tirage"—of sugar and yeast is added to the newly blended wine. Then the wine is bottled and closed with a cork or crown cap (looks like a soda cap) . The Champagne will remain in this bottle until it is purchased from a store's shelves by some lucky wine lover. The yeast finds the sugar and begins a *second fermentation* in the bottle. The second fermentation runs its course until the yeasts die from creating too much alcohol. The powdery sediment of dead yeast cells or "lees" in the bottle gives Champagne its characteristic yeasty, toasted bread or brioche flavor. The alcohol that is produced from the second fermentation bleaches the slightly pink/gold blanc de noir color somewhat. The bubbles of carbon dioxide produced during the second fermentation become an integral part of the wine, forming tiny, long-lasting bubbles that will rise in your glass for a long time.

Aging the Wine, Removing its Sediment, and Adjusting its Sweetness

Vintage Champagne is aged on its lees of yeast in the cellar for three years after harvest. Non-vintage (abbreviated NV and sometimes called multi-vintage) Champagne is a blend of juices made in years where the season did not produce grapes good enough to be declared and labeled with a single vintage year. NV champagne usually is aged on the yeast in the bottle for 15 months, though the most prestigious companies go over these minimum limits. Because French Vintage Champagne is made only from one vintage year, and a great one at that, it is more expensive than non-vintage Champagne.

Since no one wanted to drink the powdery sediment of yeast, the young Veuve (Widow) Cliquot developed the next two steps in the Champagne method to remove the yeast. Her name remains on one of the greatest French Champagnes whose top of the line Vintage Champagne is called "La Grande Dame" or the great lady. *Veuve Cliquot* Champagne is also available as a Rosé.

The first step in the process of removing the sediment takes place in triangular racks that hold the bottles upside down, and the lees of yeast are spiraled down onto the crown cap by hand *riddling* or rotating of the bottles. It takes almost two months of daily turning and shaking of the bottles until the yeast is in the neck. Imagine riddling thousands of bottles! No wonder some modern wineries use machine operated metal cages that automatically do the riddling.

The upside-down bottles with yeasty sediment in their necks are then aged in the ancient 60-foot-deep chalk tunnels dug by the Romans under the Champagne district. If you wish to visit one of the six remaining original Roman chalk tunnels still in use for Champagne making, we recommend a visit to Taittinger in Reims, France where a million bottles of Champagne are aging on their yeast.

The second step in the process to remove the yeast is called *disgorging*. After years of aging, the neck of the bottle is placed in a brine solution to freeze the yeast sediment. Then the cork or crown cap is popped. The frozen plug of sediment shoots out because of the pressure of the carbon dioxide bubbles trapped in this bottle. The wine is topped up with the same kind of Champagne, and a final *dosage* of sugar and older wine is added to achieve the various sweetness levels. Here are the descriptions of the levels of sweetness used to describe champagne:

- *Extra Brut* (also called Naturel in the U.S.) is the driest type, having no sugar added
- *Brut* is the most common style of dry Champagne having just the tiniest amount of sugar
- *Extra Dry* is actually medium-sweet and costs less because there is less of the original wine
- *Sec* and *Demi-Sec* are the next higher sweetness categories
- *Doux* dessert style Champagne is the sweetest of all

The wide range of sweetness found in these different types of champagne forms the truth behind the statement that "one can drink Champagne with every course of the meal."

Brut Champagne is perfect not only for a wedding toast to the bride and groom, but also for salty appetizers such as smoked salmon or sushi, light seafood dishes such as Dover sole or scallops, chicken or turkey, and veal or pork with cream or even mustard sauces.

Finally, the bottles are corked with a very thick *cork* made in sections to hold in the bubbles. The cork is wired down to make sure the cork remains firmly seated in the bottle so the Champagne doesn't go flat. Even so, experts know not to keep Champagne for too long because of the danger of it losing its bubbles and oxidizing. This danger is especially great for non-vintage champagnes, as you have no way of knowing how old they are. Now you know why the Champagne method is so great, and why it costs so much.

Buying and Enjoying Bargain Champagne, Big Bottles, and Splits

Champagne corks are large. When you remove them, they take on an hourglass shape, and you won't be able to get them back in the bottle. If you don't drink all of the champagne, you will have to use a screw down metal closure designed especially for re-capping sparkling wines. My husband and I never seem to have this problem.

If you think you'll drink less than a full regular-sized bottle of champagne in a single sitting, you can buy champagne in half-bottles or even splits. It should be mentioned that all wines age more quickly in smaller bottles and age more slowly in larger bottles. For example, the magnum or 1.5 liter (50.8 oz.) size is equivalent to two 750 ml. or 25.4 oz. regular-size bottles. Sometimes even larger bottles are available, such as the jeroboam, which holds four 750 ml. bottles or 3 liters of Champagne. In Bordeaux, a jeroboam holds six 750 ml. bottles or 4.5 liters. These larger bottles command a proportionally higher price because few are made and the wine ages more slowly. Since the Champagne method is done mostly with regular size bottles, the small half-bottles (375 ml. or 12.7 oz.) and even smaller quarter-bottle "splits" (187.5 ml. or 6.35 oz.) are filled from them, and can be disappointingly flat as a result.

> **caution** Please do *not* put any wine in the freezer! If it is Champagne or a sparkling wine under pressure, it may explode. And any wine will be "shocked" by such an extreme lowering of its temperature.

Though champagne is a luxury wine, you don't need to feel reluctant to enjoy it often. You will be very pleasantly surprised to learn that real French Brut non-vintage Champagne can be purchased for only $20 per bottle! Champagne is the wine of celebration—so always invite a lover or friends over to share when you pop the cork of a full-size bottle.

Fortified Wines: Porto, Sherry, and Madeira

Fortified wines are fortified by the addition of extra alcohol in the form of brandy or spirits to bring them up to an alcohol content of 18%–20%. Porto, Sherry, Madeira, Marsala, and Vermouth are all fortified wines. If the extra alcohol is added after fermentation, a dry fortified wine such as Sherry is the outcome. Adding the alcohol during fermentation results in a sweet wine such as Porto.

Marsala is made from white grapes grown on the volcanic soil of the island of Sicily, Italy. Marsala has a burnt caramel flavor and is 18%–20% alcohol like all fortified wines. The sweet *all'uovo* (egg) version is used in desserts such as Zabaglione. Dry *secco* Marsala is used when cooking veal. Marsala can also be flavored.

Vermouth made in the Piedmont area of northwest Italy is used worldwide as a cocktail or in cocktails. All vermouth is fortified wine with many herbal ingredients based on secret family recipes from long ago. Three types of Vermouth exist: rosso is a sweet red, bianco is a medium-sweet white, and secco is a dry white used in martinis. The main brands are Cinzano and Martini & Rossi.

Porto and sherry are two very popular fortified wines. The following sections discuss these wines in more detail.

Porto From Portugal

Port originated in Portugal, where it is called *Porto* to distinguish it from ports made elsewhere in the world. In Portugal, Port or Porto (the term I prefer to use for Portuguese Port) is defined as the sweet red, tawny, or white fortified wines bottled in Oporto (or its sister city), which is where the Douro River meets the Atlantic Ocean and the Porto companies are headquartered. White Porto is used as an *aperitif* or before-dinner wine, or mixed with tonic water to make a refreshing drink. But Portugal's most famous Portos are the higher priced, deep, black-red Vintage Porto; the more moderately priced and slightly less inky Late-Bottled Vintage Porto; the very affordable Ruby (red) Porto; and the fine 10- or 20-year-old Tawny Portos that are caramel or tawny brown around the edges.

The grapes for Porto are grown far inland from the sea in the *quintas* or vineyards located on steep, rocky cliffs above the Douro River. Many types of black grapes are planted, including the most important variety, *Touriga Nacional*.

All Porto starts out as sweet wine, because the fermentation is stopped at a midpoint by racking the wine into barrels containing brandy, which kills the yeast. (Please note that this is one of the eight ways to make sweet dessert wines; you will learn about the other techniques later in this chapter.) The brandy not only kills the yeast and stops it from fermenting any more grape sugar, but it also fortifies the Porto to 20% alcohol.

Porto is classified as *Vintage Porto* only in the declared great vintage years of exceptional quality. This means that Portuguese Porto and French Champagne are the only two wines in the world that do *not* put a vintage year every year on the bottle. So any Vintage Porto or Vintage French Champagne is from a great vintage year.

Vintage Porto is a collector's item because it can live and improve in the bottle for decades. The high alcohol, sugar, and tannin content of the Porto are what preserve it. That's why most Porto is bottled in opaque black bottles to keep light from the wine. Vintage Porto is aged in oak barrels for just two years, so it will throw a heavy sediment in the bottle as it ages. This must be decanted or separated from the Vintage Porto before serving. It is the most deep black-red color of any Porto, with lush aromas of licorice, chocolate, and black cherry.

Other classifications of Porto include the more moderately priced *Late-Bottled Vintage* (abbreviated LBV) that are from single vintage years but are aged longer in wood where it throws most of its sediment (LBV is not bottled until 4 to 6 years after harvest), which means it usually doesn't have to be decanted, especially if it's been filtered. *Ruby Porto* is a blend of vintages that is aged in casks for 2 to 3 years. It has a ruby red color and can be a real bargain. Finally, *Tawny Porto* is a lovely light tawny brown or caramel color around the edges. The Tawny Portos with indicated age, such as 10 or 20 years old and older are the best, tasting of lace cookies, candied orange, and spice. Australia makes a lot of award-winning Tawny Port.

The sugars in the wine have caramelized, making Tawny Porto a perfect partner for flan, shortbread cookies, pound cake, bread pudding, pumpkin pie, and spice or carrot cake. Tawny Porto also marries well with triple crème cheeses.

Besides chocolate, Zinfandel Port (from California), Ruby (not Tawny) Porto, Vintage, or LBV Porto (the latter three are from Portugal) are perfect matches with the English blue cheese called Stilton. At posh wine tastings, you may see a huge wheel of this exquisite blue-veined cheese on display next to the Porto, which is its classic partner on a continental menu. Sometimes they go one step further. They poke holes in the Stilton cheese and then pour the Porto into the holes so that it works its way down and turns the cheese red. Then they cut wedges of the Port-soaked Stilton for serving. Americans took this idea and made "port cheese balls" of cheddar with artificial pink color. Not the same thing, but any blue cheese is great with any ruby style port. Try it!

tip If you are in Napa or Sonoma, California, look for *Chocolate Port*, usually a Zinfandel Port, that is already mixed with chocolate. This port is thick and rich like the fudge topping on a sundae, but it sure has a kick! It's wonderful poured over ice cream or strawberries. Most gift shops there sell Chocolate Ports. But I have even been able to buy Deco "chocolate port" from Sonoma Port Works in the wine department of World Market stores in Atlanta. Remember, you can also "Google" to find any wine.

Sherry From Spain

Sherry is the fortified wine originally created in the area of Jerez de la Frontera (where we got the word Sherry) on the Atlantic Ocean in southwest Spain. The best Sherry vineyards have chalk soil, and the great white grape of Sherry is called Palomino. All Sherry starts out as a dry white wine and, therefore, is fermented to dryness. To make Cream Sherry and other sweeter styles, a sweeter white wine is added. In the case of Cream Sherry, the winemaker can add a golden wine made from naturally sweet Pedro Ximenes (abbreviated PX) grapes, or the lesser Moscatel grape. (This is one of the eight ways to make a sweet dessert wine, which you will learn about later in this chapter.)

Only the very rare *Añada* Spanish Sherry is ever vintage-dated, but there are new categories of Age-Dated Spanish Sherry: VOS (Very Old Sherry) and VORS (Very Old Rare Sherry), which are respectively certified a minimum of 20 and 30 years old. All other Spanish Sherries are made in a *solera system* that blends each new vintage into the year-old casks of wine below it in a "nursery" of barrels representing as many as 30 vintages. Wine is drawn from the oldest barrels for bottling, which makes space for younger wines to be added and integrated into the older wines. This produces a consistent taste year after year. It may take from 12 to 30 years to establish a *solera*.

The two major grape varieties used to make Sherry—Palomino and Pedro Ximenez— are kept in separate soleras until the final blending. While still in the barrels, the Sherry is classified according to whether natural *flor* (meaning flower) yeast is grow- ing on the surface of the wine in the barrels. The barrels are filled only 7/8 full to leave an air space for the fortunate but elusive *flor* to grow. The barrels that develop *flor* yeast are destined to produce the driest and finest types of Sherry, such as Fino, Manzanilla, and Amontillado. These and all of the other types of Spanish Sherry are explained below.

The types of Spanish Sherry are

- *Fino*, which is the lightest, most delicate and some say driest of the Spanish Sherries. Served chilled with Tapas appetizers
- *Manzanilla*, which is also very dry, has a salty taste because it is aged in barrels placed outdoors on the beach where the sea air penetrates the porous wood
- *Amontillado*, which tastes more medium-dry to me, has a pronounced nutty flavor that makes it perfect in and with soups
- *Oloroso*, which means beautiful aroma, is dry but a richer, fuller-bodied style of Sherry
- *Palo Cortado*, is a rare type of Fino that loses its flor yeast and acquires a char- acter between Amontillado and Oloroso
- *Cream*, which is the sweetest type of Sherry, is suitable on its own after din- ner, or with dessert

tip For dessert wine, I really prefer buying a *Pedro Ximenez (PX)* wine—it's labeled by this grape variety, not as Sherry—because it is absolutely fabulous, like liquid honey. Cigar smokers even dip the cut end of their cigars in Pedro Ximenez wines to put a sweet taste in their mouths.

Spanish Sherries have either *cork stoppers* or screw caps that allow you to easily remove and replace them so you can use as little or as much as you like at a time.

And since all but the Finos are fortified to a strength of 18% to 20% alcohol, you can keep them for a couple of months in your kitchen cabinet.

If you can only have one white wine on hand in the kitchen to use in cooking, your best bet is an Amontillado Sherry. It is perfect for cooking fish, soups, sauces, and beans because it makes them easier to digest. You could also use dry Vermouth as cooking wine, but an Amontillado Sherry has more flavor, color, and concentrated richness. Do *not* buy "cooking sherry"—it has additives and a lot of sodium. A real Spanish Sherry costs just $6 to $12 per bottle.

Madeira My Dear

Madeira is a fortified wine made on the island of Madeira, which sits in the Atlantic Ocean about 400 miles off the coast of Portugal. Madeira wine has been famous since the time of the 13 American colonies when the wine was sent in sailing ships, which took up to 2 years to reach our shores. During that time the thin, dry, acidic white Madeira wine was rocked and heated in its barrels until when it reached its destination it was a caramel-colored, sweet, concentrated wine. Since then Madeira wine has been baked to re-create this effect, and is the only wine in the world that is *madeirized* or oxidized on purpose to achieve a perfection of deep brown color and burnt sugar richness.

Madeira is usually a varietal wine named after the white grape variety used to make it. The five types of Madeira are

- *Sercial*, the driest type, used in Beef Wellington recipes and sauces for main courses and soups.
- *Verdelho*, called Verdejo in Spain, has slightly more body, color and richness, but is still very dry.
- *Bual*, which is very similar to Verdelho, is also considered a dry style of Madeira.
- *Rainwater*, which is a blend of varietals, is light and medium-dry in style and first became popular among America's founding fathers at the time of the 13 original colonies.
- *Malmsey*, the sweetest type, is made from the Malvasia grape and is used in the dessert called English Trifle, which consists of layers of cake, pudding, and fruit.

To make sweet Malmsey Madeira the fermentation is stopped in the middle to leave some of the natural grape sugar in the wine. All Madeira is baked in rooms as hot as ovens for several months. Then the wine is fortified to 20% alcohol and most of it is placed in a *solera* system for aging and blending. Like Sherry, Madeira is not usually vintage-dated. However, some Madeiras indicate age, such as a 5 or 10 year old Malmsey, and so forth.

Madeira is a little more expensive than Sherry, but is terrific in sauces and soups—especially bisques or cream soups because it keeps them from curdling and makes them taste richer. And all Madeira comes with a cork stopper so you can use a little at a time for cooking or drinking over a couple of months. Other countries also make Madeira, but it is not as good as the original from the island of Madeira.

To do list

- ☐ Learn the eight types of dessert wines
- ☐ Understand how winemaking techniques determine dessert wine types

Dessert Wines Made Eight Ways

As mentioned previously in this chapter, eight methods are used to make dessert wines. We've already discussed four methods—those used to make sweet Champagne, Porto, Sherry, and Madeira. To summarize, sweet Champagne has a dosage of sugar and older wine added to make it sweeter. This is how the rest of the world makes different sweetness levels of sparkling wine using the Champagne method. Porto was our example of a sweet dessert wine that is made by stopping fermentation with brandy to kill the yeast and leave the natural grape sugar in the wine. Cream Sherry is produced using a third method of making sweet dessert wine by adding a separate golden sweet wine made from a different grape variety. Finally, the technique for producing Madeira—baking the wine in ovens to carmelize the sugars and adding grape spirits to the barrels to stop fermentation before all the sugar is converted by the yeast—represents a fourth way to make dessert wine. The remaining four methods are discussed in the sections that follow.

Pressing Frozen Grapes: Eiswein or Ice Wine

The fifth of the eight types of dessert wine that we are discussing is *Eiswein* in German or Ice Wine in English. Since Germany has the northernmost vineyards in Europe, it must contend with very cold weather. In some growing seasons, it is so cold after normal harvest time that a hard frost (or snow) freezes the grapes. These frozen grapes are picked before dawn (when the grapes begin to thaw), and pressed to release a deliciously sweet juice that's fermented into Eiswein. In certain years, Eiswein grapes are harvested before Christmas and after New Year's so that two vintage years appear on the label.

Mother Nature alone makes this wine. As the frozen grapes are pressed, the water content of the grapes is held as ice crystals. The ice doesn't pass into the pressed juice, which makes the wine quite concentrated and sweet. In Germany, Riesling grapes are used to make Eiswein, but Ice Wines in other parts of the world can be made from other varieties, such as Gewürztraminer in New Zealand, Vidal in Niagara, Canada or New York state, and Muscat in California.

Some Niagara peninsula Ice Wines from Canada are in such demand that they can cost more than $90 per half bottle. German Eiswein, which is a world-class wonder of delight and delicacy, is a comparative bargain at less than half that price, and New Zealand Ice Wines are even less expensive. Like Canada, the U.S. does not allow the use of the German word Eiswein, so California wineries such as Bonnie Doon called their wine made from frozen grapes *"vin glaciere"* in French.

How Botrytis and Late Harvesting Produce Dessert Wines

The sixth way to make dessert wines is with raisin grapes that have been shriveled by Botrytis, the noble rot fungus. An example of a dessert wine produced this way is the prestigious Sauternes of Bordeaux, which is a Botrytis Semillon. The noble rot fungus is not a common occurrence. Only the right conditions of temperature and humidity in perfect vintage years set the stage for Botrytis to appear naturally. That is what is so amazing about any dessert wine labeled Botrytis. In addition, the grapes must be *late harvested*, which means that there must be extra weeks of sunshine to ripen the grapes long past the normal harvest time.

In Germany, the most expensive and sweetest wines made in great vintage years with plenty of sunshine are true *Trockenbeerenauslese*, which means they're made only from Botrytis-affected shriveled grapes. Only Botrytis can give a wine its distinctive honeycomb aroma—like the entire beehive of honey, royal jelly, and beeswax. That's why collectors are willing to pay the price for these golden sweet Botrytis wines. Another world-famous late harvest Botrytis desert wine is Hungary's Tokaji Aszú.

Other sweet dessert wines made from late harvest grapes do not necessarily have Botrytis. These wines are picked or harvested in stages in Germany with the *Spatlese*—meaning "late harvest" in German—coming in first. Workers are then sent back through the vineyards several times, a week or so apart, to pick the ripest grapes out of each bunch. So there are actually several grades of sweetness in the late harvest German wines. Winemakers in other parts of the world who want to emulate this late harvest style of dessert wine also have to pray for long weeks of sunshine so that they can harvest and produce these great dessert wines.

Making Vin Santo—Italy's Sweet Holy Wine

The seventh of our eight types of dessert wine is *Vin Santo*. Vin Santo was originally the name of the Greek dessert wine from the beautiful island of Santorini. When the Italians from Venice controlled Greece centuries ago, they became fans of Vin Santo. When they no longer controlled Greece, they decided to make their own supply of Vin Santo in Italy.

To this day, Vin Santo is one of Italy's most famous dessert wines. It is made in a special process where the white grapes are hung on hooks to dry on the upper level of the wineries where it is very hot under the roof, even with the shutters open. The drying process shrivels the grapes to raisins. These white raisins are crushed and then fermented in small oak barrels for a very long time. They create an amber color dessert wine that tastes and smells like fruitcake.

Each area of Italy uses its own homegrown white grape variety to make its version of Vin Santo. I've had wonderful examples of Vin Santo in Tuscany, particularly from the area of San Gimignano where the white Vernaccia grape is used. It was a highlight of our trip there to drink Vin Santo with excellent almond biscotti, and to do as the Italians do, dip and soften the biscotti in Vin Santo. Upscale Italian restaurants offer this as a dessert course.

Stopping Fermentation to Determine Sweetness

Our final and eighth type of dessert wine is made from very ripe grapes whose fermentation stops automatically when the alcohol level rises over 15 percent. At this level of alcohol, the wine yeasts die and no longer ferment any more grape sugar, leaving the wine sweet. At what point the fermentation stops is really determined by the winemaker, who controls the sweetness of the outcome by chilling the wine so low that fermentation stops, or by filtering out the yeast so there is no more yeast to continue fermentation. Of course, it all depends on how sweet the grapes were to begin with. Very ripe late harvest grapes can be twice as high in natural sugar as grapes that are used to make dry wines. That's why we must depend on Mother Nature to cooperate in the vineyard, or these great dessert wines simply cannot be made.

To do list

- ❑ Learn why winemakers use specific bottle colors for certain wine types
- ❑ Learn what a wine bottle's shape might reveal about its contents

"Reading" a Wine by its Bottle Color and Shape

Most bottles are made of transparent glass so that the clarity of the wine can be observed through it. Seeing sediment in a young red wine is a danger sign and usually means the wine was mishandled or heated in shipment. White wines are almost always bottled in clear glass. They do not need ultimate protection from light, since most are consumed while young. Ditto for rosé and blush wines. The deep *punt* or indentation in the bottom of the bottle is not to catch any sediment, but rather to make the bottle sturdy enough to withstand the pressure of the bubbles in Champagne, or the weight of bottles stacked on top of each other in a cellar.

Certain *bottle shapes* are reserved by tradition for certain types of wine. Experts can often make an educated guess as to what grape variety any particular bottle contains just by its shape. Here are the most common shapes and the type of wine they typically contain (see Figure 3.1):

FIGURE 3.1

How to "read" a wine by the shape of its bottle.

Alsace

Bordeaux

Burgundy

Champagne

Chianti

Côtes de Provence

Franken

German Wine Bottle

Porto

- High-shouldered Bordeaux bottles in dark green glass usually contain the red Bordeaux varieties such as Cabernet Sauvignon and Merlot, while clear glass Bordeaux bottles are traditionally used for the white Bordeaux grapes Sauvignon Blanc and Semillon. Also, brown Bordeaux-shaped bottles are used in Italy for fine red wines from Sangiovese in Tuscany.

- Sloping shouldered *Burgundy bottles* in mint or olive green glass are reserved for the Burgundy grapes Chardonnay and Pinot Noir. *Rhône bottles* are shaped similarly to Burgundy bottles but made of darker glass. These heavier Rhône bottles signal the Rhône grapes such as Syrah, or heavier wines such as Barolo from Italy.

- Tall, slim, green or brown *German bottles* foretell contents of German or Alsace grapes such as Riesling, Gewürztraminer, and Pinot Gris.

- Thick, heavy, dark green bottles with deep punts are necessary for *Champagne bottles* and sparkling wines to withstand the pressure of the bubbles.

- Finally, *Porto bottles* are opaque black glass to keep out the light and hide the sediment forming over many years of aging.

A REVEALING LOOK AT SOME WINE MYTHS

As you've been reading this chapter, some of your fondest notions about wine probably have been disproved. The most common misconception about wine is that more wine can be made anytime the winery needs product to sell. Wrong! Real wine (not the kind of homemade wine made from concentrate in a can) is made only once a year from freshly harvested grapes.

I once was asked by the assistant to a top CEO to get a prestigious single vineyard California Chardonnay that even he could not get. When I phoned the winery, they told me I should know better (I did, but I wanted to try for the bigwig). The winery said they simply did not have any more of that wine because the production from that vineyard is so small that only a few precious bottles are produced each year. And what they did have in the winery was still aging in the barrels. If I were speaking to the gentleman directly, I would have explained that he was lucky to have tasted such a "one of a kind" item from a great vintage because the wine can never be exactly repeated.

Other wine myths usually involve blaming wine for hangovers and problems whose caused by some other factor, such as water retention—how many of those salty peanuts and crackers did you eat? Wine is a natural diuretic because of its alcohol content. Since white wines are so high in acid as to resemble lemonade, and red wines can be so tannic as to be like iced tea, they have digestive properties. To avoid water retention, eat non-salty water crackers or wine crackers or good breads when you're drinking wine. Watch your indulgence of the saltier blue cheeses, and always drink plenty of water in all cases.

Summary

And now for the best news of all—you have already done your homework on wine vocabulary by reading this chapter. You have learned all of the important winemaking terms for whites, reds, Rosé, Champagne or sparkling wines, fortified wines, and dessert wines in this chapter. And don't worry if you need a brush-up on your wine vocabulary as you read through this book; our A to Z Dictionary of wine terms can be found in Appendix B.

In the next chapter, we will have a very easy time becoming conversant in vintage years and their influence on each type of wine. Until then, please keep in mind two of my favorite aphorisms (*aphorisms* are short pinpoint sayings that embody general truths):

Younger Tastes Better—This is especially true for moderately priced wines. And it really means that you do not know enough about wine—as yet—to buy older vintages with confidence and your hard-earned cash.

Please resist buying older wines if you do not know how they have been stored or transported. All wines age more quickly in general distribution.

Bland is Bad—As with food, you pay for, and want, more intensity of taste and flavor in better wines. As I've said before, if the wine has no concentrated fruit, it is not worth any price—no matter what is on the label.

Vintage Years/
Vintage Wines

Winemakers are fond of saying, "Wine is made in the vineyard." What they mean is that before a great wine can be made in the winery, great grapes are needed, and Mother Nature creates them. An estate can have the best grape varieties growing in the best vineyard conditions of soil and geography—but without the luck of a perfect growing season, it cannot bottle truly outstanding wine. Weather is the uncontrollable factor in the equation—and it is the reason why the same wine tastes slightly different each vintage year.

To build upon our wine knowledge from previous chapters, we now add practical definitions and lists of the best vintages for each type of wine. The wine crime most novices commit is *not* drinking wine too young, but rather buying it too old or keeping it long past its natural expiration date. This discussion of vintage years will reveal what you really need to be concerned with when choosing and buying great wines—and it will explain when you don't have to consider vintages at all. Our helpful vintage chart and advice will give you the tools you need to avoid the heartburn of oxidized wine (You learn more about how to detect oxidized wine in "How Old Is Too Old?" later in this chapter.)

4

In this chapter:

* Learn how weather and geography determine the quality of vintage years in each wine region, and how expert opinion determines their relative rankings and price tags.

* Understand how vintage years are charted and rated, and which vintages to purchase as gifts or for collecting and aging.

* Find great vintage red wines using our useful vintage chart that rates wine by region and type.

* Become a savvier wine buyer by comparing prices on the Internet, in stores, and from wineries for both recent and older vintages.

Shopping List

- ❑ Buy the same wine from two different vintage years and taste them side by side with the same food. Many times a store has a few bottles left of the previous year when they receive the newest vintage. You do not have to buy older vintages—just one year's difference in age represents two growing seasons with different climates. This makes a valid comparison tasting.

- ❑ Choose a wine "buddy" to share the wines and discussion. Talk through the tasting and ask each other about aromas, acidity, fruit intensity, tannin, oak, heat from the alcohol, and aftertaste. "Two tongues are better than one"—one of "Anita's Aphorisms."

- ❑ Engage the wine store's owner or consultant in conversation about vintage years. Ask for a printed vintage chart (wineries provide these for customers), or bring this book's vintage chart to the store. Find out what older vintages the store carries and how these vintages were rated. Ask the owner or consultant to describe the taste of the oldest wine he's ever had. But go during "off" hours when the store isn't busy and the staff has time to talk.

To do list

- ❑ Determine how weather impacts the greatness of a particular vintage year and how wines are rated by type for each vintage.
- ❑ Understand why a great vintage year for one wine may be a mediocre vintage for another.
- ❑ Learn how to determine the best time to drink any vintage and how to tell when a wine is past its prime.
- ❑ Use expert appraisals of vintages to choose good wines at a good price for everyday drinking, gifts, and collecting

Vintage Years—To Be or Not to Be

Autumn is a time of nature's bounty, when every culture gives thanks for the blessings of sweet apples, golden grains, and ripe grapes. Both animals and man depend on good harvests for food to get them through the winter and year ahead. Entire civilizations have disappeared; huge populations have moved as immigrants to foreign shores; and ferocious wars have been fought over precious fertile land, when famine rather than feast was the outcome.

Wine is agriculture, and grape growers are farmers who hope for good weather and fine crops. As in ancient times, many modern winemakers plant by the almanac and phases of the moon, recycle and replenish their soil, and perform ritual displays of respect for their vineyards with the understanding that the only things they can truly control are their own actions and philosophy. In the wine world, these nature-based vineyard practices are called *biodynamic agriculture.*

Agribusiness might laugh, but winemakers who literally "speak" to their vineyards have old country "green thumbs" that make grapevines grow abundant. Having been raised by a naturally talented grandmother gardener, I share the beliefs of traditional grape growers and say, *"I trust to luck but leave nothing to chance"*—another of "Anita's Aphorisms."

Weather cannot be controlled. I live in the southeastern United States, and the impact of several back-to-back hurricanes in early fall 2004 taught me the truth of that statement.

The effects of climate for a particular wine region include temperature (both winter lows and summer highs), hours of sunshine during the day, nighttime dips in temperature, fog, rainfall (too much or too little), frost (or hail or snow) at critical spring budding, and the impact of wind. No wonder grape growers keep journals of everything that happens during the growing season in order to assess the potential success or failure of the harvest.

WINE BELTS CIRCLE THE GLOBE

In North America we harvest grapes in September or October. But southern hemisphere countries are six months ahead of us. Our winter is their summer, and our spring is their autumn wine harvest. As a result, light, dry white or rosé wines from South Africa, South America (Chile, Argentina, and so forth), Australia, and New Zealand arrive in our wine stores with this year's vintage on the label even before we finish picking our grapes!

Winemakers may not be able to control the weather from year to year, but they can choose where to plant their vineyards. Like the Romans, they look for moderating influences on climate, such as proximity to an ocean, the protection of mountains and river valleys, and prime hillsides facing east (or slightly southeast) toward the rising sun. All of the world's greatest vineyard regions have some of these influences, but those with predominantly *maritime* or ocean-influenced climates have the most favorable conditions. Maritime climates create wonderful grape-growing conditions along the Pacific coastlines of California and Chile, parts of Australia, the two islands of New Zealand, and South Africa where the Atlantic and Indian oceans meet.

Since it is too hot at the equator and too cold at the poles to grow grapes, top wine-producing countries are located in corresponding northern and southern hemisphere *wine belts,* 30–50 degrees north latitude and 30–50 degrees south latitude, with both belts circling the world globe (see Figure 4.1). It is not a coincidence that Chile's prime wine regions are on the same latitude south as California's famous Napa Valley is north. But southern latitudes have a six-month head start on us (and Europe) regarding production and marketing.

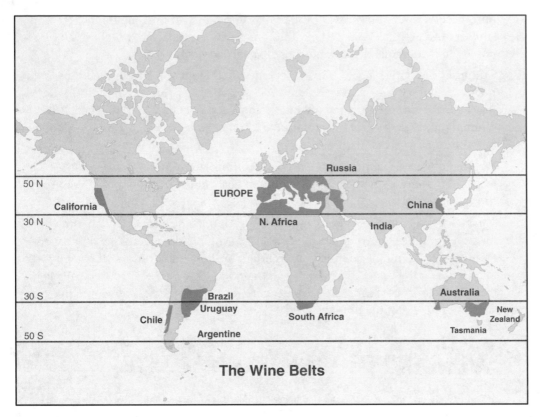

FIGURE 4.1

The wine belts of the world.

Defining "Vintage" Year

The word vintage comes from the French word *vendange* for harvest. Even if the geographical location is perfect, the quality of each *vintage year*— defined as the year of harvest—depends on the luck of excellent weather conditions during the growing season. A good vintage is a year in which the season's grape crop was superb. High quality grapes produce high quality wines. If the fruit isn't great, you can't make great wine. Areas with moderate climates experience more consistency in weather from year to year and in their ability to produce good wines. But even though they may win the weather sweepstakes most years, they may lose badly sometimes.

Except for Porto from Portugal and French Champagne, which are labeled "vintage" with a single year only in declared great years, every other bottle of wine may be labeled with a vintage year, even if it wasn't a good vintage. That's because each year there is a new crop of grapes (or new vintage), and vintners keep track of each season with this year of harvest. *Vintage charts* rate each of these vintage years for a particular type of wine so that wine buyers will know which years had ideal conditions and produced great wines with ideal levels of fruit concentration, acidity, and tannin that will keep them alive through years of cellaring. (A vintage chart for red wines bottled between 1985 and 2004 is located at the end of this chapter.)

Don't be impressed just by the fact that a wine is vintage-dated, however, as most wines come from a single vintage year unless they are non-vintage (multi-vintage) Champagne, Porto, Madeira, or Spanish Sherry. Be impressed only if you know a particular vintage year was rated highly for that type of wine.

> **caution** Be careful in your use of the term *vintage wines*. Wine experts refer to great vintage years, not vintage wines, as elite wines with a pedigree. Old wine books confused everyone by using the term vintage wines to mean the best estates or vineyards with top rankings or classifications. But we know that definition has no validity because of the simple fact that every year, (good or bad) grapes are harvested. So every wine has the potential to be labeled a "vintage" (year)—even low-end wines.

How Old Is Too Old?

Vintage dating is very useful because it tells you the exact age of the wine in the bottle. Inexpensive, dry whites, blush or rosé wines should be consumed within one to three years of the vintage year on the bottle. Inexpensive red wines (under $10) should also be consumed within the first year or two of release. But when you buy mid-priced reds averaging over $15 per bottle, you can choose to keep them 3–5 years after the vintage year on the bottle. Better reds in the $20+ price range last 5–8 years after the vintage. The best reds last 8–10 years.

Only ultra premium reds, great vintage Champagne, single-vineyard collectors' item whites, or sweet dessert wines last longer than 10 years and can be potentially cellared for 20 years or more. How long a wine will live in the bottle depends on the grape variety (amount of tannin), where the grapes were grown, the growing season of the vintage year, and how the wine has been stored and transported. Books that claim wines last decades are referring to wines that have spent most of their lifespan in very cool wine vaults untouched by human hands—not wines that have been in general distribution. If you don't know where that older vintage has been or how it's been handled, don't buy it. It could already be, as the French wine experts say, *mort* or dead.

How do you recognize wine that is oxidized or too old? That's easy. If it's white wine, the color *maderizes* or darkens to tawny brown, similar in color to apple cider vinegar. As white wines age, they also begin to taste rough, like really bad sherry—not good Sherry from Spain—and they give you instant heartburn, making them hard to swallow.

Now you know why we recommend drinking most light, dry white or blush wines within the first year of purchase or within three years of the label's vintage year. As red wines oxidize, they also turn brown; but they taste like vinegar (acetic acid). In fact, red wines have higher *volatile acidity* than whites. No matter how carefully you re-close your wines, very inexpensive red wines can become vinegary rather quickly, which is another good reason to keep them refrigerated.

You could make vinegar from leftover red (or white) wine, but you would need to use a "mother vinegar culture" to get it started. To order a jar (cost is about $10 plus S&H) of mother vinegar culture for white or red wines (specify the color), contact Ann Gordon at Wine Craft Atlanta, Tel: 404-252-5606, email: winecraftatl@usa.com.

Don't feel bad if you have been saving wine far too long. Open the bottle! It will be a learning experience for you to smell and taste the oxidation or *maderization* of wine past its prime. But always have some good wine handy to take the bad taste out of your mouth.

Even wine collectors make this fatal mistake of over-aging the wrong wines. Often I am shown a cellar list by the proud owner of many older vintages—only to discover that most of them the wines either were not suitable for aging, or were not good vintage years for the type of wine (and therefore, could not have been expected to last for decades). My expression for this sad situation is *"c'est la vie—vinegar,"* another one of my "Anita's Aphorisms." Of course, I am much too diplomatic to point this out to the defensive collector who'll say it's still an antique—albeit one that no one can drink and enjoy. You learn more about collecting and properly storing wine in Chapter 16, "Collecting and Storing Wine."

CASK-AGED BALSAMIC VINEGAR

Balsamic vinegar is the versatile, almost black Italian vinegar with a touch of sweetness that's made like a fine wine. It is splendid drizzled over chunks of Parmagiano Reggiano cheese, making a delicious, instant zebra-striped appetizer. Balsamic vinegar adds class to every course from salads to strawberries. Contrary to some old-fashioned wine books that condemn combining wine and vinegar, balsamic vinegar is a very wine-friendly ingredient because it is so mellow.

Genuine balsamic vinegar, called *Aceto Balsamico Tradizionale*, is made only in Modena, Italy, near the city of Bologna. Made in small batches from the juice of freshly pressed Trebbiano white grapes, it is boiled down by half to dark, naturally sweet syrup. The syrup is transferred to oak casks to ferment. Then it is aged for many years in smaller and smaller casks of various woods, ending with juniper. As the vinegar evaporates through the wood and concentrates, the best becomes as rare, precious, and pricey as a great Bordeaux. Balsamic vinegar can be sipped on its own after dinner, like divine Vintage Porto.

Luckily, you can purchase affordable everyday versions of real balsamic vinegar (always with the name Modena, Italy, on the label) from most groceries. If you have the funds and inclination, do a comparison tasting of modest-price versus high-end balsamic vinegars in order to train your palate to recognize smoothness and quality differences. This can be a great party game for your guests!

Who Says It's A Great Vintage?

Famous wine writers, such as Robert M. Parker, Jr., who writes and publishes *The Wine Advocate* (**www.erobertparker.com**), and whose nose is insured by Lloyds of London for $1 million, usually hail the greatness of a new vintage year after assessing the growing season, harvest, and tasting barrel samples of the newly fermented wine. When Mr. Parker appeared on a TV news program praising the 2000 vintage for red Bordeaux at New Year's Millennium celebrations, futures prices and demand for futures went sky high. The same happened early in 2004 when he raved about the 2003 vintage year for red Bordeaux wines.

In the October 2004 issue of *Food & Wine*, Mr. Parker had 12 dramatic predictions for the future of wine—including the ability to order any wine direct. He also predicted that Malbec from Argentina, Spanish wines, and wines from California's Central Coast would be big sellers; that we would see more unoaked wines, screwcaps, and diverse countries of origin; and that elite wines, of which there is a finite supply, would be priced out of everyone's reach. But as compensation, he predicteds there would be more wine values than ever before in low-priced, high-quality wines.

Mr. Parker is the author of many books on wine and is the topic of Elin McCoy's 2005 book, *The Emperor of Wine: The Rise of Robert M. Parker, Jr. and the Reign of American Taste*, HarperCollins Publishers, hardcover, $25.95.

Using Expert Appraisals of Vintage Wines

Expert wine appraisals offer helpful advance information about an upcoming vintage because they alert us to buy the more moderately priced red Bordeaux wines, California Cabernets, Australia Shiraz, and so forth that will be released much sooner than the elite estates. In fact, you might be able to just walk in a store and buy your reasonably priced, but great vintage year wine before the futures buyers even receive delivery of their much pricier collector's items! Vintages are important, but knowledge is power—and more fun.

This brings us to a very important point. Just because you hear wine experts rave about the 2000 or 2003 vintage does *not* mean that every kind of wine made in those vintage years is great. You can't make generalizations about vintage years. Vintage year ratings are specific to one type of wine from a specific growing region— which makes sense since every wine region (even each district, village, or vineyard in a region) has completely different weather and climate conditions in any given growing season. Also, vintage charts usually rate the red wines of an area rather than whites because reds are collectors' items.

The best winemakers are better able to make good wine even in a bad vintage year. That is why the name of the estate or winery is as important as the rating for a particular vintage year. These are the exceptions to the rule that make wine so interesting. If you can expect deep, dark, rich, layered, aromatic, concentrated, intensely grapey, long-lived reds in great vintage years, what can you expect from the in-between years? The answer is that wines from average vintage years will be lighter in color and body, lower in alcohol, less tannic, early maturing, and lacking in concentrated fruit. In other words, these are the kinds of everyday wines we can drink and enjoy now—and we don't have to break the budget to buy these bargains.

FUTURES ROULETTE

Buying wines on the futures market is a gamble that the wine you purchase while it is still in the barrel will go up in price once it is bottled and released by the winery. Experts want to lock in the pre-release price of highly rated new vintages and save some money on what they hope will be a very good investment. As investments go, ultra-premium wines may bring a good return, but wine dies after years in the bottle, whereas jewelry, art, or antiques never do.

Wine futures are usually for great new vintage years of French red Bordeaux wines, although some pricey California Cabernet Sauvignons are also handled this way. But wine futures come with risks. Since you sometimes pay your money in advance (in states where this is legal) to get a certificate of purchase, others earn interest on your money and you may not get delivery of the wine you paid for if the wine broker goes out of business. Great reds spend up to two years aging in barrels, so you are really paying for future wine and have to wait until it is released. There are wiser and more prudent things to do with your money.

The largest wine retailers—including Costco, which was named largest wine retailer in the U.S. in 2004—track what customers buy, and they have discovered that the trends are very seasonal. Whether the wine store is in the sweltering south or frigid north doesn't matter—Americans buy more white wines in summer.

Restaurants verify this seasonality in our drinking habits and attribute it to our craving for chilled wines when it's hot. Not a problem for me, since I serve my red wines ever so slightly chilled year round, not just in summer.

All stores report significant sales of real French Champagne from November to December each year, even when most of the top 25 wines by volume are inexpensive mass-market brands. This is proof that Americans do know quality, and wouldn't think of toasting Holiday celebrations with less than the best—especially if it's a French Brut NV bargain. This is why even warehouse retailers stock upscale wines along with the everyday values.

Sampling and Comparing Vintage Wines

By now, hopefully you're inspired to explore different grape varieties and wines from various countries—and vintages—with an assortment of foods. As always, your homework is to continue tasting! Your goal is to develop your ability to sniff varietal aromas, distinguish color shadings, and discern concentration of fruit. Most important, you are training your sense of taste and finding what pleases your particular palate. In this section, we talk a bit about tasting and comparing vintages. We also discuss avoiding some common mistakes such as choosing wines based on "special dates." (The year you were born or married is not a reliable indicator of great vintage years.) Chapter 14, "Being a Savvy Retail Shopper," offers more details about the process of choosing wines.

Things You'll Need

- ❏ Vintage chart
- ❏ Local newspapers, magazines, or online and other sources for wine tastings and vintage information
- ❏ Guide to wineries in your area
- ❏ Internet access

Vintage Tastings

The events calendars of major newspapers, wine magazines, and websites such as **www.localwineevents.com** list every kind of wine tasting. These events give you ample opportunity to compare different vintages from the same winery, or different wines from the same vintage year. Group tastings are also more economical, as it would cost you a lot of money to buy all those bottles yourself. Nothing builds companionship like shared experiences, and tasting wine is one experience that's much more rewarding when done in a group.

To further your learning process, I recommend the following:

1. Ask local wineries, wine importers, retailers, or wholesalers for an invitation to a *vertical tasting* where the same wine is tasted from several vintage years. A typical vertical tasting would be to taste Robert Mondavi Reserve Cabernet Sauvignons from 1984 to 2000.

2. Try to get an invitation to the other type of vintage year comparison tasting, which is a *horizontal tasting* of several wines from one vintage year. For example, I attended a wholesaler tasting that included both great red Bordeaux chateaux and great California Cabernets—all from the 2000 vintage. That was a revelation, as the Bordeaux were typically more oaky, and the

California Cabs varied considerably from mint and evergreen to lovelier soft black currant and cassis.

3. Search your local newspapers, city magazines, wine publications, and Internet sites for announcements about tastings of older vintages or articles about this year's wine harvest in different parts of the world. Even CNN scrolls vintage reports at the bottom of the TV screen. I recently learned that Champagne, France, had a fantastic 2004 harvest, in contrast to the 2003 growing season, which had devastating problems. Remember, you can "google" any wine.

4. Visit a winery in your state to observe actual winemaking or participate in a harvest. All 50 states now have some kind of winery—even if some of them make wines from fruits other than grapes. Your loyalty and support will be greatly appreciated by your state's wine pioneers. Do you doubt your state makes great wines? I've had good Ohio Chardonnay, great Long Island Cabernet, and incredible New Mexico sparkling wine. Forget what you might have read or heard in the past: the whole world of wine has changed for the better!

> **note** Please don't question the vintage year on a box wine or screw top bottle—except to demand that it be young and from the most recent vintage. We don't age box wine or screw caps.

Vintage Gifts

Suppose you want to find a wine from a vintage year that commemorates a birth year or anniversary? Good luck! Unfortunately, even the best people or happiest marriages may not share a great vintage year for wine. If a birth or marriage didn't occur during a great wine vintage year, then there is very little hope of finding these wines. Wines from not-so-good vintage years age more quickly, so collectors do not save them. And even if you do find wines from mediocre vintage years, they probably are not a pleasure to drink at this late date.

My advice is to buy current vintages of good wine you can afford and tell the recipient when to drink it and with what foods. Refer to Chapter 2 on grape varieties for food partners. Wine recommendations by country are in Part II, "Wine Countries and the Wines They Produce." And Chapter 16 has specific information on finding the cost of older vintages if you have unlimited financial resources.

What about the perfect wedding gift? Champagne is splendid, but please urge the newlyweds to plan on drinking a non-vintage at their next celebration. Don't pack Champagne for the honeymoon because that would mean carrying it in their luggage or on the plane—not a good idea. I foolishly did that on my return from

London, and the Champagne exploded in my suitcase, drenching my wine certificate. How prophetic!

A better wedding gift for the newlyweds to save until their fifth anniversary would be a top-of-the-line red wine. Any country or significant grape variety will be the right kind of red. If you spend $20–$50 on the wine, buy a current (or recent) vintage, with input from the store's wine consultant. When you explain to the bride and groom that the red wine is a perfect partner for veal chop or crown roast of lamb or filet mignon, you can persuade even white wine fanciers to crave red.

But if you know that red wine never crosses their lips, then I suggest a top of the line French white Burgundy, which is 100% Chardonnay and great with seafood. Another great choice is a rare dessert wine such as Vintage Porto, an Eiswein, late harvest Riesling, or Sauternes. Everyone loves having something sweet after dinner.

Charting Great Vintages

When I first began teaching wine school in Atlanta, the wine store where I worked had a wine vault full of older vintages that we were lucky enough to taste in class. I will never forget the taste of 1945 Château Latour, 1959 Château Mouton-Rothschild, 1966 Château Margaux, 1961 Beaulieu Vineyard Georges de Latour Cabernet Sauvignon from Napa, or 1959 Pierre Ponelles Nuits St. George Premier Cru. Although I understand why wine experts say they don't make them like that any longer, I don't agree with them completely. In recent years I have had reds from Italy, Spain, South America, Australia, and South Africa that were pure pleasure on the palate.

Since the experience of drinking very elite and expensive wines can seldom be exactly repeated, all we have left is our memory of how they tasted. That's why we spend so much time training our taste buds. Before offering you my chart of popular red wines, I'd like to advise you to follow a couple of my favorite "Anita's Aphorisms" when tasting and choosing wines:

- *"Wine is not a spectator sport; you have to taste to participate and learn."* To begin, you must buy, swirl, sniff, taste, swallow, and eat!
- *"Smoothest is best; bland is bad and younger is better for bargain wines."*

No matter how highly rated a vintage year or estate or vineyard may be, if an individual wine is not harmonious—with lots of fruit concentration to balance the acidity, alcohol, and tannin—it is not worth any price. That being said, I would like to present you with a vintage chart for popular types of red wine from 1985 to 2004 (see Table 4.1). I could have listed the greatest vintage years of the 20th century for red Bordeaux starting with 1945, but there would be so many. And I could have listed the greatest Vintage Porto years 1966 and 1977. Yes, 1977, which was a disaster vintage for every other kind of wine, was exceptional and exquisite for Vintage

Porto—and some of this rare 1977 Vintage Porto is not only still available, but it still tastes wonderful. But to be practical, I had to start my chart somewhere—and 1985 was a watershed year in Europe when modern winemaking techniques were universally adopted, thanks to the assistance of the European Union.

Vintage Chart for Red Wines 1985–2004

Year	Porto	Bordeaux	Burgundy	Rhone	California	Italy	Australia
1985	VG	X*	X*	X*	X*	X*	X*
1986	VG	X*	VG		X*	X*	X*
1987							
1988				X*		X*	
1989	X*	X*	X*	X*	VG	X*	
1990	VG	X*	X*	X*	X*	X*	
1991	X*	VG	VG		X*	VG	X*
1992	X*						
1993	VG						X*
1994	X*				VG		
1995	VG	X*	X*	X*	X*	VG	
1996	VG	X*	X*		VG	VG	X*
1997	X*				X*	X*	
1998		VG		X*	VG		VG
1999			VG	X*	X*	X*	VG
2000	X*	X*		X*	VG		
2001	VG	VG		VG	X*	X*	
2002	VG	VG	X*	VG	VG	VG	X*
2003	VG	X*		VG	VG	VG	VG
2004							VG

X* = EXCELLENT and VG = VERY GOOD

What's also missing from this chart are the following notes on recent vintage years for other very popular types of wines:

Champagne—Great vintage Champagnes were declared in 1985, 1989, 1990,1996, 1997, 2002, and 2004. Remember, any French Champagne with a vintage year on the label is from a great vintage.

German Whites—Great vintages in which the sweetest higher quality wines were produced include 1985, 1986, 1989, 1990, 1991, 1993, 1995, 1996, 1997,

1998, 2001, 2002, 2003, and 2004. Since sugar is a natural preservative, the sweeter the quality level and wine, the longer its lifespan.

South Africa—Great red wine vintages include 1995, 1998, 1999, 2000, 2001, 2003, and 2004. Well, it is a sunny climate, so there is more consistency. I'm never afraid of drinking their greatest reds too young since I've had recent vintages of typically heavy Syrah from South Africa that were *smokin'*, meaning zoom-out-of-this-world delicious.

Spain—Great red vintages in recent years include 2001, 2002, 2003, and 2004. Look for great reds from modern areas such as Priorat, Toro, Jumilla, Penedes, Ribera del Duero, and so on. Rioja is famous for more traditional oaky reds.

Chile and Argentina—Great recent vintages for reds were 2000, 2001, 2002, 2003, and 2004. In other words, every year so far in this millennium has had good grape ripening weather.

Greece—The greatest wine vintage in their modern winemaking history was 2003, for both white and red wines.

New Zealand—Their most famous wines are white, especially citrusy Sauvignon Blancs and unoaked Chardonnays. They are produced for early drinking, and many have screw caps. So vintage years are not as important, even for their terrific Pinot Noirs, many of which also have screw tops.

I hope these notes prove to you that great vintages can be produced worldwide. You learn even more about the great wine-producing areas of the world and specific wine recommendations in Part II.

Summary

Worrying about vintage years is only valid for expensive wines, when estimating longevity is important. Who cares what vintage year is on the label if you need to buy the wine to serve with tonight's dinner?

In this chapter, we allowed common sense and reality to prevail over wine snobbery. We defined "vintage" years; we discussed topics such as wine futures, vintage tastings, gifts, the influence of weather on the grapes, and how to recognize wine that's too old. We provided you with an easy-to-read red wine vintage chart. Now that you are armed with this insider information, you never have to feel on the defensive or the need to explain your wine choices.

In our next chapter, we begin decoding wine labels. We'll explain real labels of wines that are widely available, so that you can learn to read any label you might find in a wine store. You'll learn to unlock the secrets of each country's wine labeling, so you can join in the universal language of wine.

5

The Wine Label Decoder

O nce we understand how to decipher the information provided on wine labels, it's fun to find the hidden humor on some of the New World labels, which are often modern versions of European classics. We laugh along with the winemaker when we "get" the joke, especially when that wine with the funny name turns out to be surprisingly good. A case in point is the first of our wine labels, Goats do Roam, a South African red wine made from a blend of Rhône (and other red grapes) in the style of our second wine label, Côtes du Rhône from France. The names sound similar because there is a parallel between the wines in grape varieties used and style. Trying these two very popular $10 reds side by side makes a great comparison tasting.

It's almost as if wine labels have their own "code." In this chapter I give you the decoder to unlock their secrets. If you follow the step-by-step process I use to read any wine label, you will be able to figure out what type of wine is inside the bottle. And the 26 real wine labels, with my explanatory captions, at the end of this chapter provide ample opportunity for you to gain practice and confidence in reading just about any label you encounter, and in choosing wines to partner certain foods or menus. All of the wine labels I've chosen represent what's "hot" among current and widely available releases, and are some of the best of their category from the most reputable wineries and importers.

In this chapter:

✳ Learn to identify the three major types of wine labels, and understand how they relate to the wine laws of each country

✳ Learn to read varietal wine labels

✳ Decode appellation of origin labels

✳ Discover which labels are based on levels of sweetness

✳ Read detailed descriptions of 26 wine labels from around the world

Understanding What a Wine's Label Says About the Wine Inside

Every wine-producing country in the world's wine belts has its own set of government wine laws that regulate winemaking, grape growing, and labeling. That's a considerable number of countries and regulations. These wine laws protect you and guarantee that what is on the label is in the bottle. They govern permitted grape varieties; minimum percentages for labeling by grape variety; the location, size, and yield of the growing area; alcohol level; barrel aging; vintage designations; quality levels; sweetness; and so forth.

To make sense of this vast array of wine laws and labels in the shortest possible time, I'll explain what they all have in common. In some form or other, whether on the front label or back label, most wine labels emphasize one or more of five distinct categories of wine label information. This is how I learned to read a new wine label.

The five categories of wine label information you need to look for on any wine label, in this order, are

1. Grape variety (or varieties)
2. Where the grapes were grown (*appellation*, or name of origin)
3. Quality level based on sweetness or an official classification
4. Winery or producer
5. Vintage year

These five categories of wine label information are your indications of the quality of the wine in the bottle. Not all wine labels provide this valuable information. A French red Bordeaux label, for example, will not name the Bordeaux grapes used in the blend; instead, it will emphasize the official government appellation or name of origin for the district or village (and château or estate) in Bordeaux where the grapes were grown. Their wine laws assume you know the red Bordeaux grapes. (More about French wines in Chapter 9, "French Me! Choosing Wines from the Great Wine Regions of France") However, most of the world's wine labels fall into categories 1, 2, or 3 above; and these are the three types of wine labels.

Reading the Three Most Common Types of Wine Labels

The three major types of wine labels correspond to the first three of the five categories of wine label information:

- Varietal labels designate the grape variety (or varieties) used to make the wine
- Appellation (Name of Origin) wine labels emphasize the region, district, village, or vineyard where the grapes were grown for the wine

- Quality Level labels, based on sweetness or an official classification, either explain the natural sugar content of the harvested grapes and the wine's resulting ripeness or sweetness level, or they give a government ranking for the wine, such as "*cru classé*" or classified Bordeaux

Not all wine labels fall into these categories, of course. Many modern labels carry some combination of Varietal and Name of Origin information. In Germany and Austria, the labels can specify all three types of information listed above. You'll see an example of this type of label later, in the Selbach-Oster wine label, that lists Riesling (grape), Mosel (place name) and Spätlese (sweetness level). Be patient with yourself; you are being introduced to wine labels one step at a time. You won't want to give up when you see such intriguing, beautifully designed labels in the stores. Now you'll actually understand what's in the bottle and how it relates to similar wines from other countries.

Finding the Producer's Name

It is usually very easy to find the name of the producer on wine labels, as most wineries are proud to distinguish themselves from the competition. As you become more familiar with the well-known wineries, both through your reading in this book and your wine-tasting experience, you'll be able to use this label information as you choose good wines.

Notice, for example, the back label you see later in the section titled "Côtes du Rhône—Perrin Reserve—France." This label shows that the wine was made by the same Perrin family that owns Château de Beaucastel, one of the premier Châteauneuf du Pape estates (Châteauneuf du Pape is a more expensive and complex type of red Rhone wine). It is useful to know that the winery of a $10 wine is not a bulk producer, but rather an upscale operation.

Grapes are just the raw material. It takes winemaking artistry and skill to make great wine, even if the grapes are from great vineyards. That's why knowing the experience and reputation of the winery is so important. Some producers consistently create stunning wines, while others give us only a limited interpretation of the grapes.

Many great producers of fine wines also make less expensive wines, typically from younger vines in their vineyards. These wines are called *second labels*. In Bordeaux, it's not so easy to spot the second labels of great Chateaux, but they would be good values for your money. Look for references to other wine bargains from the same importers or producers in the tasting notes under each of the 26 wine labels in this chapter. We also provide the winery or importer websites to make it easy for you to find out if these wines are distributed in your city or if you can order them direct.

Reading the Wine's Vintage Year

Finally, the vintage year on the label is crucial to knowing how old the wine is, not just whether a particular vintage year is highly rated. In this chapter's examples, no label is older than 2000 (many of these labels are already onto the next vintage; and in fact, most of them are now 2003 and 2004). That's because the wines featured in this book are very moderately priced; and at this price point you should buy wines that are young, sassy and good drinking now. The better and pricier examples are capable of being cellared for a few years, but most of us are buying wine for dinner tonight or an approaching special occasion. We covered wine's life span in detail in our previous Chapter 4, "Vintage Years/Vintage Wines."

PUT AWAY YOUR CORKSCREWS!

Wineries are increasingly using *screwcaps* (also called *screwtops*). Finding that as many as 5% or 6% of wines closed with natural corks were affected by "cork taint," the awful musty, moldy corked smell in wine that's produced by trichloroanisole (TCA) in bad corks, wineries in New Zealand adopted a "screwcap initiative" and began using screwcaps for virtually all of their wines. Now Australian wines, and even some Bordeaux and Burgundy wines have screwcaps. According to a 2004 article in *Wine Business Monthly*, only 5 percent of U.S. wine makers they surveyed used screwcaps in 2003. But important California wineries, such as Beringer, Kendall Jackson, and R. H. Phillips, said they intend to use more screwcaps in the near future, though there is a long waiting list for the specialized bottling equipment (which may limit screwcap availability).

Also in 2004, Hogue Cellars of Washington—known for their Pinot Grigio and Reserve Cabernet—announced they would bottle the majority of their half-million cases of wine from the 2004 vintage in screwcap bottles. Hogue studied five types of wine closures on both red and white wines for three years. The bottles with synthetic (plastic) stoppers tended to oxidize after just two years. A significant number of the bottles finished with natural cork had cork taint. Wine in screwcap bottles retained its freshness the best. And Napa's Plumpjack Winery has been offering fabulous Chardonnay and Cabernet in a choice of cork finish or screwcap to collectors for several years.

Reading Other Descriptive Wine Label Information

We've talked about the three types of wine labels that emphasize the first three of the five categories of wine label information. Many additional descriptive terms could appear on that bottle of wine you're holding. Most of them are detailed in upcoming sections on American and other types of varietal labels, French and other types of appellation of origin labels, and German levels of quality based on sweetness.

The descriptive information on wine labels can be surprisingly varied and rich. But if you read the labels carefully, you'll often find additional clues to the type and quality of the wines they offer. Here are a few of the surprises I've found on labels.

Cline Cellars "Small Berry" Mourvèdre (Contra Costa, CA) caught my eye in the wine store—not because of the rare opportunity to buy this seldom-unblended Mourvèdre Rhône grape, but because of the notation "small berry." Smaller berries of red grapes indicate intense color and flavor because there is less clear juice to dilute the black skins. This wine was outstanding, and oh so smooth.

Other descriptive terms that you might spy on a wine label include unfiltered (non-filtre in French), which means the red wine will be more intense in color and fruit concentration. Also, be careful to note Nouveau on the label of French Beaujolais or Gamay Beaujolais from California. As we learned in Chapter 3, Nouveau or "new" wines are very grapey, yeasty, fruity reds that retain their freshness for only a few months, usually from release in November to the next spring.

To do list

- ❏ Learn about American and other New World varietal wine labels
- ❏ Contrast these New World varietal labeling laws with varietal label requirements in the European Union

Recognizing and Reading Varietal Wine Labels

Varietal wines are named for the type of grape from which they're made. This information on a wine label tells us what taste profile to expect, and enables us to find our favorites or an appropriate partner for our food menu. Varietal labels—whether European (Old World) or New World—are really the easiest to understand when you become familiar with the major grapes. But be aware that if the wine is a blend of grapes, no one grape may predominate or reach the minimum; so no grape name appears on the label.

American and New World Varietals

U.S. wine laws require that if a wine is named for one grape variety, a minimum of 75% of that grape must be used to make the wine. This protects consumers so that they get what they pay for. Since these regulations were passed in 1983, a whole lot of blending has been going on.

Blending is not bad. The French, for example, blend the five red Bordeaux grapes together to get a more complex wine. American winemakers want to do the same.

Here are examples of how American winery members of the trademark Meritage Association blend their wines:

- Their exceptional whites are blended from the three white Bordeaux grapes: Sauvignon Blanc, Sémillon, and Muscadelle.

- Their red Meritage wines are blended in the same way as great white and red Bordeaux. They use the same five red Bordeaux grapes, plus three more that were allowed to become extinct in Bordeaux but were resurrected elsewhere: Carmenèere, St. Macaire, and Gros Verdot.

However, the Bureau of Alcohol, Tobacco, and Firearms (ATF), which regulates wine production and sales in this country, doesn't allow American wineries to label their wines as Bordeaux—and rightly so. As a result, members of the Meritage Association label their Bordeaux-like blended wines as "Meritage" wines. To use the trademark name "Meritage" (pronounced like "heritage"), wineries must be members, and both their white and red wines must be blends of two or more of the eight red Bordeaux grapes or the three white Bordeaux grapes.

Most U.S. wine lovers have gotten used to reading varietal labels named after the predominant grape variety, understanding that up to 25% of the wine can be other grapes. The same is true of the varietal wines of other New World countries, including Chile (see the Carmenèere label by Morandé), Argentina (see the wine label later in this chapter for the Broquel Malbec by Trapiche), Australia (see the wine label for "Fifth Leg" red imported by Southcorp), New Zealand, and South Africa.

French Varietals

French varietal wines were always 100% of the grape variety named on the label because their highest quality wines were named by appellation of origin rather than grape variety. So if you see the name of one grape variety, such as Merlot, on a French wine label, that wine will be 100% Merlot. This is higher than the minimum 85% varietal labeling required by the European Union. (Please read explanation below.)

In France, most varietal wines are called Vin de Pays, or "country wines," and are very reasonably priced because their quality is below that of the Name of Origin wines, called Appellation d'Origine Contrôlée (AOC). (You learn more about Place Name of Origin labels in the next section of this chapter.)

Modern French labels, such as those by Chantovent, emphasize the grape name and then give "South of France" as the place of origin. Chantovent is imported by Star Industries, whose website can be found at **www.star-indust.com**.

The only exceptions to this Vin de Pays rule are the superb French 100% varietal Alsace wines (Vin d'Alsace) which are the only Appellation d'Origine Contrôlée wines named by grape variety. The finest grape in Alsace is considered to be

Riesling, followed by their world-famous very spicy Gewürztraminer, slightly spicy Tokay d'Alsace (which is really the Pinot Gris grape), and Pinot Blanc (which is a heavenly light white) .

European Union Varietals

When Old World countries such as France, Italy, Germany, Greece, and Spain joined forces in the modern European Union (EU), they were compelled to adopt consistent wine laws to make commerce easier to regulate. As a result, all European Union countries are required to use a minimum of 85% of the grape variety named on the label in their varietal wines. (Notice this is a higher percentage than for American labels.) However, even New World countries such as Chile, Australia, and New Zealand had to agree to this if they wanted to sell their wines as "varietal" in Europe; so they complied with Europe's minimum requirements. Technically, the EU is stricter with non-EU wines and requires them to be 100% of the varietal named on the label. But the aforementioned countries were given an exemption, and the U.S. was allowed to sell its 75% minimum varietal wines in the EU as well.

Many European Union countries have their own names for 85% varietal wines. In Italy, varietal wines are called IGT or *Indicazione Geografica Tipica*. When you pick up any Italian varietal wine, such as Pinot Grigio or Sangiovese, it is most likely an IGT and must be a minimum of 85% of the grape named on the label. In Germany, wines that have the grape name *Riesling* printed on the label are worth more money than other German wines (as long as the quality level of the wines being compared is the same) because Riesling is considered Germany's finest grape, grown only in their best vineyard areas.

To do list

❑ Understand how to translate the Appellation Contrôlée information on French wine labels

❑ Learn the importance of American Viticultural Area designations as the appellations of origin on American wine labels

Recognizing and Reading Appellation of Origin Labels

For students of wine, trying to remember the meaning of each Appellation Contrôlée is a most daunting task. These one-word names of geographic indication are so specific under the wine laws that seeing "AOC Margaux" on a French wine is supposed to immediately conjure its meaning: the red Bordeaux wine made predominantly from Cabernet Sauvignon grapes blended with the other approved grapes grown in the deep gravel soil of the village of Margaux on the left bank of the Gironde River in the district of the Haut-Médoc. Mastering a knowledge of these wines is quite an achievement, but we assist you in your quest with an entire chapter on French wines in Chapter 9, "French Me!"

The U.S. does not have a set of wine laws based on appellations of origin like the French do, but we do have dozens of American Viticultural Areas (AVAs), such as Napa Valley, California. A fine example of an American Appellation of Origin label is found on Beringer's "Private Reserve" Chardonnay (Napa Valley). If you read the front label of this very big, rich, buttery Chard, you'll see its pedigree: proprietor grown, fermented in French *Nevers oak* barrels, and aged *sur lie* for eight months.

tip And don't forget the "back story" on the back labels of most wines. I have included several of these back labels along with the front labels at the end of this chapter. The best back labels usually provide much more explanation of a wine's taste profile and producer. Refer to Wine Label #3, Bethel Heights Pinot Noir from Oregon, which is certified LIVE and Salmon Safe, and Wine Label #6, C.G.di Arie "Southern Exposure" Zinfandel, which was from a 130-year "old vines" vineyard and made in a revolutionary "submerged cap" fermentation tank.

You learn more about American and European Appellation of Origin wines in this section of the chapter. In future chapters we will discuss the grape growing areas of Australia and other New World countries.

Understanding French Geographic Indications on Wine Labels

If you recall from Chapter 1, the Greeks invented the idea of labeling wines with an appellation of origin or place name a thousand years before the French. But the Appellation d'Origine Contrôlée (AOC) wine laws enacted by the French government in 1935 started the difficult-to-memorize system of labeling wines with geographic indications of region, district, village, or vineyard. The entire French system was based on their fervent belief in *terroir* (vineyard geography, soil, and climate) as the foremost influence on the wine, rather than grape variety. Within a few decades, other European countries adopted wine laws that were translations in their own language of the French appellation of origin system. In fact, the French wine laws became the framework for those adopted by the European Union.

The actual AOC "controlled name of origin" is between (and sometimes also above) the words Appellation and Contrôlée on the wine label of European Appellation of Origin labels. To practice reading French AOC wine labels, go to the Côtes du Rhône, Moulin-à-Vent pronounced moo-law ah vahn), and Vouvray wine labels shown later in this chapter.

Italy's Denominazione di Origine Controllata

Italy initiated their government wine laws in 1963, translating AOC into Italian as *Denominazione di Origine Controllata* (abbreviated DOC, it means "name of origin is controlled"). The first official DOC wine, announced in 1966, was a lovely, dry white from Tuscany called *Vernaccia di San Gimignano* (Vernaccia is the grape, and San Gimignano is the famous Tuscan hill town that distinguishes this wine from any other).

Under the Italian wine laws, the 32 DOCG wines (the G stands for *garantita,* or guaranteed by the producers) are the highest rated of the more then 300 DOC wines available.

When I took a group of my wine school graduates on a tour of Tuscany, we visited the heart of the Chianti Classico area, where the producers in the "Gallo Nero" Black Rooster consortium (the black rooster appears on a small strip label around the neck of the bottles) have their vineyards. We were impressed at how strictly the DOCG wine laws were enforced. Wineries received only their allotment of pink DOCG labels, which are numbered consecutively so that they could not be used to boost production, and barrels of wine sat in the winery waiting for government inspection before they could be granted the DOCG. Please refer to the Banfi Chianti Classico "Riserva" DOCG label at the end of this chapter.

note Tommasi "Ripasso" Valpolicella has a back label spelling out the DOC, which verifies everything about this wine: origin, permitted grapes, winemaking. You see this wine label later in this chapter.

tip The word *Riserva* on Italian Chianti labels means the wine must be aged in a combination of oak and bottle for a minimum of three years before release.

Appellation of Origin Labels of Spain and Greece

Spain also has translated the same principles as the AOC and DOC wine laws into Spanish as their *Denominación de Origen* (abbreviated D.O. or DO) regulations. Presently 55 places of origin or DO areas exist, but only two regions—Rioja (reds are Tempranillo grape) and Priorato (reds are mostly Garnacha or Grenache grape)— have been granted the highest quality level of DOCa. The "Ca" stands for *calificada,* or classified.

Many red Rioja wines are very dry with noticeable wood tannin because they are made in traditional methods with lots of oak aging. The labels of these wines often indicate the length of time they were aged. The designation *Crianza* means a minimum of two years of aging before release, with at least 12 months of oak cask aging. *Reserva* means a minimum of three years of aging before release with at least 12 months aging in cask. *Gran Reserva* wines from great vintages are aged a minimum five years before release, with at least 24 months spent in cask. Most modern-style Spanish reds, such as the Viña Alarba "Old Vines" Grenache at the end of our chapter, are much more fruit forward. And check out the fabulous dry white Spanish label "Vionta" Albariño we've also included.

Greece also implemented a system of 20 Appellations of Superior Quality (liqueur wines, usually sweet), 8 Appellations of Controlled Origin (light wines 8–15% alcohol), and 100 Vin de Pays wines, as well as Table Wines and Traditional Appellation for Retsina. A good example of the Vin de Pays wines is Domaine Gerovassiliou's Malagousia "Regional White of Epanomi." It is delicious, and proof positive that the new breed of Greek wines from native and global grapes is outstanding.

note The importance of appellations or names of *geographic indication*, including Bordeaux, Champagne, Feta and Parmesan cheeses, and many more is so great that the European Union is fighting the U.S. and Australia over their use. The Europeans say that these are proper names and only the originals have the right to use them. The New World disagrees, saying it's impossible to undo decades of common usage: in their view, Parmesan cheese is still "Parmesan," whether it's made in Parma or in Wisconsin. Even developing countries are arguing over appellations such as Jamaica Blue Mountain coffee, Basmati rice, and Ceylon tea. I see the EU's point, and my palate can tell the difference.

American Viticultural Areas

Don't panic—the U.S. does not have a set of wine laws based on appellations of origin like the French do. America does, however, emulate the French by designating the specific AVA or American Viticultural Area (or even the single vineyard), on higher-priced wine labels. Beaulieu Vineyard's "Georges de Latour" Private Reserve Cabernet Sauvignon, for example, is designated as being created from grapes in the Rutherford AVA of Napa County in the state of California. You learn more about the California AVAs and wineries in Chapter 6, "Made in the USA: California and Beyond."

Pricey *cult wines* typically are produced in limited supply from low-production grapes in small vineyards. As a result, these wines are sold as collectors' items. The winemaker takes extra care with these low production grapes, giving them costly attention in the winery to make them very special in the bottle.

Understanding What the Label Tells Us About the Wine's Level of Sweetness

In Chapter 3, we looked closely at eight dessert wines and the winemaking techniques that produce their sweetness. We also explained how the name of Spanish Sherry or Madeira indicated whether it was dry or sweet. Please refer to the "La

Gitana" Manzanilla Sherry label and caption at the end of this chapter for more information. Now it's time to discuss wine labels where the name of the wine remains the same but the quality level changes depending on the sweetness of the wine.

Germany is the only country in the world to base its quality levels, under wine laws, on the natural sweetness or sugar content of the grapes and their condition at harvest time. There are six quality levels or Prädikat (special attributes) for German wines, which give stairstep sweetness levels from dry Kabinett, to medium-dry Spätlese, to medium-sweet Auslese and Eiswein, to raisin-sweet Beerenauslese (BA) and honey-rich Trockenbeerenauslese (TBA). By learning to recognize these code words or quality levels of sweetness, you can feel confident that you'll know the sweetness of the German wine you're considering, simply by reading its label.

The U.S., Canada, Australia, New Zealand, and other New World countries also use some of these sweetness levels on their late-harvest or dessert wines, but they translate them into English: For example, *Eiswein* becomes Ice Wine, *Spätlese* becomes Late-Harvest, *Auslese* becomes Select Late-Harvest, and BA and TBA wines become *Botrytis* (noble rot) varietals.

Austria uses a system similar to Germany's for the naming of their sweeter wines, even using the same German words, though Austria has its own measures for sugar content. The most popular Austrian wines are dry instead of sweet. We've included Austria's famous Grüner Veltliner in our collection of wine labels later in this chapter.

CHAMPAGNE AND SPARKLING WINES AND THEIR LABELS

When you see the word *Champagne* on a bottle of French wine, you know you're holding the real deal. This wine-label term tells you where the wine was made, how it was made, and what grapes were used in its production. The word Champagne is the Appellation Contrôlée or controlled name of origin. As you learned in Chapter 3, French wine laws prohibit the European Union from labeling any sparkling wine as Champagne unless it is from the French Champagne district, and is made in the *méthode champenoise* from the approved grapes. (However, this law does not apply to champagne made in the U.S.)

Since celebrities drink Louis Roederer Cristal Champagne, I must explain why it costs more than $175 at retail (for the currently available 1997 Vintage). First, it's real French Champagne, made in the French Champagne district, using both the approved method and grapes: Cristal is 55% Pinot Noir and 45% Chardonnay. Second, Cristal is always vintage Champagne from a single, declared great, vintage year. Third, Cristal is a *prestige cuvée*, which means it is made from grapes harvested from only the highest rated vineyards.

Roederer's other French Champagne, the Louis Roederer Brut Premier NV (non-vintage), is a blend of vintages for about $45, and Roederer Estate from Anderson Valley (Mendocino) California is $22. Roederer wines are imported by Maison Marques & Domaines USA www.mmdusa.net.

Sparkling wines made in the méthode champenoise or Champagne method are called "fermented in this bottle" in the U.S. Sparkling wines made in the U.S. or other areas of France or other countries are quite often great values for the money. We include the Mumm Napa "Blanc de Noirs" label at the end of this chapter as an example. And for a truly unique red sparkling wine, you'll find the Rumball Sparkling Shiraz is our last, but by no means least, label.

Decoding Some Sample Wine Labels

Without further delay, here are the 26 wine labels whose pictures are worth more than a thousand words. The actual labels were much more beautiful than these illustrations, with embossed lettering and golden graphics that we could not reproduce. Each label was chosen after tasting many wines from the hundreds of labels sent to me.

In general, the labels are ordered by country, then by grape variety. Fortified and sparkling wines are last. The labels represent the three types of wine labels: varietal, appellation of origin, and quality level based on sweetness. The first two sets of comparison labels contrast New World and France. All the U.S. reds are included as a group. That section finishes with reds from Italy and Spain. White wines come next, starting with South Africa, then the U.S., Spain, Italy, Greece, Austria, France, and Germany (the sweetest of these whites). The label series ends with a Sherry, Port, and two sparkling wines.

Each label is a lesson in itself, as are the captions. As my editor said when she first saw them, this is good stuff. May several of the labels prompt you to make a trip to the store. Enjoy!

One final myth about wine labels needs debunking. Uninformed people say "the fancier the label, the worse the wine." Wrong! What about the gorgeous "artist labels" that prestige wineries such as Château Mouton-Rothschild use to decorate the labels of each vintage year? Believe me, wineries do not waste beautiful (and costly) graphics and packaging on inferior wines.

note Some wineries may wonder how I could forget them. The truth is, some wineries did not respond when I asked for wine labels, and others could not give permission to send upscale labels for fear that they might be pasted for profit on rubbish bottles. So I did my best to cover all bases.

Goats do Roam, Charles Back—South Africa

FIGURE 5.1

Goats do Roam—The Wines of Charles Back—South Africa (red) 2003—$10. Neither the front nor back label gives the grape varieties, but this red wine is made from a blend of Rhône (and other grapes) in the style of French Côtes du Rhône wines— notice the similar sounding names.

wine name

vintage

winery

wine region

importer

Grapes: Blend of red Rhône varieties, such as Shiraz, Cinsault, Carignan, and other red grapes, including Pinotage

Food Partners: Meat stew or meatloaf, turkey chili, grilled vegetable pizza

Tasting Notes: Dark color, black cherry aroma, spicy character, grapey, some tannin and heat from the alcohol in the finish; serve slightly chilled.

note Goats do Roam's U.S. importer, Vineyard Brands, provided both of the first two wine label examples so that you can contrast the French and South African labels. Look for a terrific South African white, Boschendal Sauvignon Blanc, later in these label examples.

This $10 "spicy, fruit packed dry red wine" is owner Charles Back's best-selling New World answer to the French classic. Stores also sell Goats do Roam white and rosé wines as well. The same winery even produces an $18 Goat-Rotí red that resembles the upscale French red Rhône wine—Côtes Rôtie. Website: **www.goatsdoroam.com**.

Côtes du Rhône—Perrin Reserve—France

Grapes: 60% Grenache, 20% Syrah, 10% Mourvèdre, 10% Cinsault (see back label)

Quality Level: Appellation Contrôlée (abbreviated AOC) is this wine's AOC, in effect, the controlled or guaranteed place name—Côtes du Rhône, and highest quality level under the French wine laws

FIGURE 5.2

Côtes du Rhône—Perrin Reserve—Perrin & Fils Winery, France (red) 2003—$10. This wine is from the very sunny Rhône region in the south of France where Syrah/Shiraz originated.

special designation

grapes

wine region

winery   quality level

importer

Special Designation: *Réserve* designates a better wine for this winery

Food Partners: Roast chicken, grilled kebabs, Mediterranean or Indian cuisine

Tasting Notes: Charming; hints of black raspberries and black pepper; lively acidity and spicy tannins keep it dry, yet fresh. Website: **www.vineyardbrands.com**.

Bethel Heights Vineyard Pinot Noir—Willamette Valley, Oregon

FIGURE 5.3

Bethel Heights Vineyard—Pinot Noir—Willamette Valley, Oregon—Estate Grown—2002—$25. New plantings at this vineyard include Dijon clones.

vineyard

environmental certifications

vintage
grape

wine region

Grape: 100% Pinot Noir

Special Designations: Estate Grown (all grapes were grown in their own vineyards, and wine was made/bottled at their winery)

Certified LIVE (Low Impact Viticulture and Enology); "Salmon Safe" (certifies their farming protects the health of Oregon's rivers filled with wild salmon)

Food Partners: Salmon (yes, Pinot Noir red wine goes with fish!), portobello mushrooms, bacon quiche, Asian cuisine, and goat cheese

Tasting Notes: Elegant; silky; intense flavor of dried cherries; some anise or licorice; with tea in the finish. This good vintage year produced ideal ripeness; the wine was bottled unfiltered. For all these reasons, this wine is richer than most Pinot Noirs. Oregon Pinot Noir and Chardonnay are very Burgundian in style (in other words, they're much like the wines of Burgundy, France, where these grapes/clones originated). Website: **www.bethelheights.com**.

Moulin-à-Vent—Château des Jacques—Domaine Louis Jadot—Cru Beaujolais—France

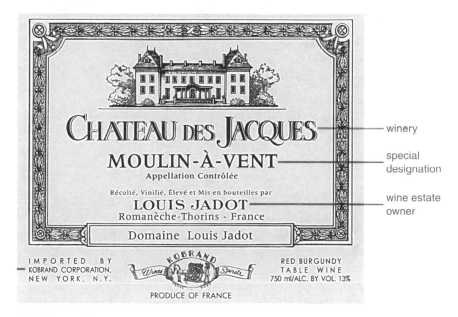

FIGURE 5.4

Moulin-à-Vent—Château des Jacques—Domaine Louis Jadot—Cru Beaujolais—France—2003—$20. Beaujolais is part of Burgundy, but their reds are made from Gamay, not Pinot Noir. Château des Jacques winery's vineyards have very rare crystalline granite soil with high manganese content that contributes to the greatness of this wine. The Louis Jadot company owns some of the best single vineyards in Burgundy, France.

Grape: 100% Gamay Noir (*noir* means "black" grape)

Wine Region: Burgundy

Quality Level: Appellation Contrôlée is Moulin-à-Vent (which means "windmill") and it's a Cru Beaujolais

Food Partners: Duck, tuna and olive salads, paté with grape tomatoes

Tasting Notes: Layers of red fruit; baked bread flavors; fruity but dry, with soft tannins that make it smooth and balanced. Moulin-à-Vent is one of the 10 best or "Cru" Beaujolais wines, and as such is more full-bodied and lives longer than regular Beaujolais—but it's much less expensive than most other red Burgundy wines. Website: **www.kobrand.com**.

Fifth Leg—Margaret River, Australia

grape blend

wine name
wine region
vintage

FIGURE 5.5

Fifth Leg—Margaret River, Australia—2001—$14. Current vintages of this wine are 2002 and 2003. Fifth Leg is Aussie for person who's a "free spirit," and Australia demonstrated this type of daring by being the first to blend Bordeaux and Rhône grapes to make Cabernet-Shiraz. This wine is barrel aged in American and French oak for 12 months.

Winery: Devil's Lair

Grapes: Cabernet Sauvignon, Shiraz, Merlot, and Cabernet Franc (blend varies year to year)

Food Partners: Lamb, gyros, pork chops, barbecue, including ribs, pasta

Tasting Notes: Dried cherry and mulberry aromas lead to hints of chocolate and spice and a luxurious finish for the price. Drink now or age up to three years. Website: **www.southcorpwines.com**.

note Southcorp also imports big name Australian wines, including Rosemount, Penfolds, and Lindeman. Rosemount's "Hill of Gold" Shiraz and Cabernet or Balmoral Syrah are excellent). Penfolds's Koonunga Hill Shiraz blends are a bargain at $9, considering Penfolds makes the most expensive Shiraz of all, called Grange. (Lindeman's upscale Chardonnays above Bin 65 are wonderful.)

C.G. di Arie—Zinfandel "Southern Exposure"—Shenandoah Valley, Sierra Foothills, California

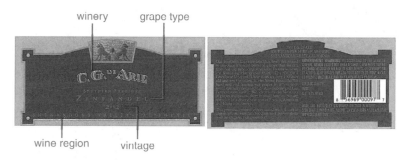

winery   grape type

wine region   vintage

FIGURE 5.6

C.G. di Arie—Zinfandel "Southern Exposure"—Shenandoah Valley, Sierra Foothills, California—2002—$30. If you're a member of the C. G. di Arie wine club (**www.cgdiarie.com**), you can buy this wine for $24 a bottle. The di Arie Winery has two art galleries and is as awesome as the talented co-owners, Chaim and Elisheva Gur-Arieh.

Grape: 100% Zinfandel

Food Partners: Risotto, roast turkey, lasagna, beef tenderloin

Tasting Notes: Layered aromas and tastes of blackberry, allspice, vanilla, and mocha, in a very rich, complex, yet very smooth blockbuster. "Old Vines" Zinfandel is more intensely flavored, and this is a superb example. The grapes are from the nearby *Grandpere* (Grandfather) vineyard with 130-year-old vines. This world-class winery uses natural gravity feed and its own Di Arie submerged cap fermentation tank that keeps the grape skins in the juice at all times, deepening color and flavor. Di Arie's regular Zinfandel is also terrific (and less expensive). Its Syrah is outstanding—look for Primitivo and other rare red varietals (the company doesn't make whites) in the near future. Website: **www.cgdiarie.com**.

Broquel—Malbec—Bodegas Trapiche—Mendoza, Argentina

wine name

FIGURE 5.7

Broquel—Malbec—Bodegas Trapiche—Mendoza, Argentina—2000—$15. The current vintage of this wine is 2002. Its importer, Frederick Wildman of New York City, also represents the great Alsace wine, Hugel, Chateau Fuissé Pouilly-Fuissé, Olivier Leflaive white Burgundy, Paul Jaboulet Rhône wines, Christian Moreau Chablis, and Pol Roger Champagne.

Winery: Trapiche

Grape: 100% Malbec

Wine Region: Mendoza

Importer: Frederick Wildman, NYC.

Food Partners: Steak, buffalo burgers, sausage calzone, black bean soup, bleu cheeses

Tasting Notes: Deep purple color; concentrated fruit; aromas of vanilla and oak; lots of raspberry and dark chocolate. Trapiche Winery, founded in 1883, introduced the first French grapevines to the area, including Malbec from Bordeaux. Today they use very modern winemaking techniques to maximize the fruit concentration in their wines rather than old-fashioned woodiness. Natural malolactic fermentation also softens the acidity of their reds. Broquel is my favorite label from Trapiche. I've never had a bad Malbec from Argentina—they are all good, even inexpensive ones. They are what I call "a tango for your tongue." And nothing goes better with beef.

Website: **www.frederickwildman.com**.

Morandé—Carmenère—Terrarum Reserve—Maipo Valley, Chile

FIGURE 5.8
Morandé—
Carmenère—
Terrarum
Reserve—Maipo
Valley, Chile—
2001—$11. The
current vintage of
this wine is 2002.

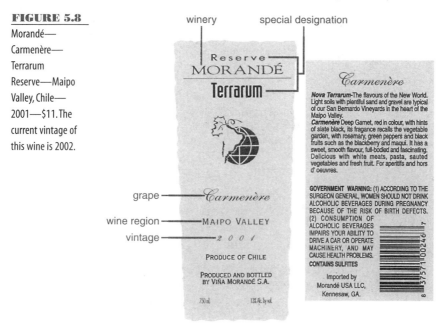

Special Designations: Terrarum Reserve

Food Partners: Chicken quesadillas, fried oysters, pork, skirt steak

Tasting Notes: Purple color; coffee bean; blueberry and herbal aromas with minty, green pepper finish. Owner Pablo Morandé pioneered the very cool Casablanca Valley, producing great Chardonnay, Pinot Noir, and Rosé of Pinot Noir starting at just $11 a bottle. But both his dry Sauvignon Blanc and Late Harvest dessert style SB are first class. And every one of his reds, especially the "Vitisterra" Syrah ($16) and Cabernet Franc ($21), are fabulous. My advice is to forget about buying cheap Chilean wines—you get much more taste for just a few more dollars. Website: **www.morandeusa.com**.

note Carmenère is Chile's signature red wine because this grape died out in Bordeaux after Phylloxera hit in the mid 1800s. Immigrants brought this grape to Chile before then, and because Chile never had Phylloxera, Carmenère and the other Bordeaux grapes thrived. At first, Carmenère was misidentified as Merlot in Chile, but now it's a very desirable varietal on its own.

Chateau Ste. Michelle—Merlot—Columbia Valley, Washington

FIGURE 5.9

Chateau Ste. Michelle—Merlot—Columbia Valley, Washington—2001—$16. Chateau Ste. Michelle (**www.chateau-ste-michelle.com**) was named "American Winery of the Year 2004" by *Wine Enthusiast* magazine. And the winery's "Eroica" Riesling ($20) made as a joint venture with the famous Dr. Loosen of Germany is superb, as are its sparkling wines, including new "Luxe."

Grapes: 90% Merlot, 5% Cabernet Franc, 5% Cabernet Sauvignon

Wine Region: Columbia (River) Valley, Washington;

Food Partners: Rosemary-grilled chicken, lamb chops, swordfish, caramel or butter pecan ice cream

Tasting Notes: Raspberry; cocoa aromas; velvety mouthfeel; toasty oak is balanced by berry fruit; hint of mint in aftertaste. Ideal weather during 2001 harvest allowed longer "hang time" for the grapes on the vines, giving them more intense flavor. Columbia Valley vineyards front the Cascade Mountains, and they have two more hours of sunlight daily than California, making Washington Merlots ripe and soft. Website: **www.chateau-ste-michelle.com**.

J. Lohr Estates—Cabernet Sauvignon "Seven Oaks"—Paso Robles, California

Grapes: 78% Cabernet Sauvignon with Petite Sirah, Merlot, Petit Verdot, Syrah, Zinfandel, and Alicante Bouchet (an old California red varietal from Spain)

Wine Region: Paso Robles, San Luis Obispo County, California

Special Designation: Seven Oaks Vineyard

Food Partners: Ravioli with marinara sauce, prime rib, vintage cheddar, chocolate cake

FIGURE 5.10
J. Lohr Estates—
Cabernet Sauvignon
"Seven Oaks"—
Paso Robles,
California—2002—
$15. J. Lohr Winery
(**www.jlohr.com**) is
named after owner
Jerry Lohr, and he
rightfully takes pride
in his very smooth,
jammy wines.

special designation

wine region   winery

Tasting Notes: Black currant aromas; deep color; no sharp edges; balanced; good fruit; pleasant finish. Paso Robles wines are very much in demand these days. The soils in this vineyard are gravelly clay loam to limestone, which are ideal for Cabernet Sauvignon. I also highly recommend J. Lohr's "Los Osos" Merlot from Paso Robles, "Riverstone" Chardonnay from Monterey, and upscale single vineyard wines. Website: **www.jlohr.com**.

Banfi—Chianti Classico DOCG "Riserva"—Tuscany, Italy

FIGURE 5.11
Banfi—Chianti
Classico DOCG
"Riserva"—Tuscany,
Italy—2001—$17.
Banfi Winery
(**www.banfi.com**)
is American owned,
but voted best win-
ery in Italy for their
glorious estate
outside Montalcino
in Italy.

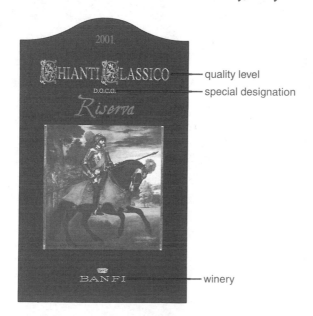

quality level
special designation

winery

Grapes: Mostly Sangiovese, with some Cabernet Sauvignon and Canaiolo Nero

Wine Region: Tuscany

Special Designations: DOCG name of origin is guaranteed by the producers, which is the highest quality level for Italian wines.

Quality level: Chianti Classico must be from the "classic" or finest Chianti district between Siena and Florence; and Riserva from best vintages, aged two years in oak

Food Partners: Linguine with red clam sauce, lasagna, eggplant Parmigiana, Pecorino cheese, veal chop

Tasting Notes: Lovely ruby color; aromas of gourmet cherries and violets; refreshing acidity; harmony of licorice and spice in the taste; elegant finish.

Website: **www.banfi.com**.

Banfi creates great olive oil, modern dry whites, and a yummy red sparkling dessert wine called Brachetto Rosa Regale. Banfi also produces the finest red wines, including top-of-the-line Brunello di Montalcino, as well as "Super Tuscans" such as SummuS, which is a blend of Tuscany's great red grape Sangiovese and Cabernet Sauvignon, with added Syrah.

Tommasi—Valpolicella Classico Superiore DOC—"Ripasso"—Veneto, Italy

FIGURE 5.12
Tommasi—
Valpolicella Classico
Superiore DOC—
"Ripasso"—Veneto,
Italy—2000—$20.
Tommasi Winery
(**www.
tommasiwine.it**)
also makes excellent
"Super Venetian" red
with Cabernet Franc
called Crearo, and
terrific Pinot Grigio.

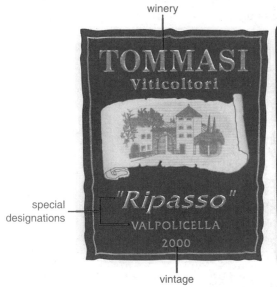

winery

special designations

vintage

Grapes: Blend of red grapes, primarily Corvina

Wine Region: Veneto (includes Verona vineyard area to west of Venice)

Special Designations: DOC is Valpolicella; Classico from the heart of the district; Superiore from better vintages that produced more alcohol; and ripasso, meaning the wine was refermented on the "lees" of leftover grape skins and yeast from the Amarone, making it richer than regular Valpolicella, which is a very light red.

Food Partners: Seafood in marinara sauce, chicken cacciatore, bean soup, stuffed red peppers

Tasting Notes: Aromas of flowers and dried berries; pretty plum flavors; medium body; very smooth; leaving fresh palate. Tommasi is well known for upscale Amarone (1998, $50) which is the big, bold, most special type of dry "Recioto" Valpolicella made from the ripest bunches of grapes at the top of the vines. The grapes are dried to raisins, concentrating their grape sugars and raising the alcohol content. One glass is said to give you the gift of intuition. Website: **www.tommasiwine.it**.

Viña Alarba—Old Vines Grenache (Garnacha)—DO Calatayud, Spain— Bodegas del Jalón—Jorge Ordoñez

FIGURE 5.13
Viña Alarba—Old Vines Grenache (Garnacha)—DO Calatayud, Spain— Bodegas del Jalón—Jorge Ordoñez—2003— $7. This wine's DO or Denominación de Origen (name of origin) Calatayud is located southeast of Rioja and is one of the new breed of Spanish wines with global appeal from unusual wine regions.

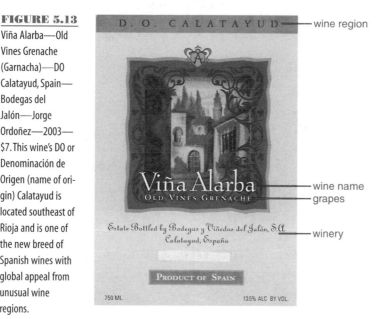

Grapes: Old Vines Grenache with 15% Syrah

Wine Region: Calatayud

Representative: Jorge Ordoñez, USA offices in Dedham, MA—Tel: 781-461-5767

Food Partners: Paella, Serrano ham, Manchego cheese, lamb empanadas, pork or beef ribs

Tasting Notes: Lots of jammy fruit for the money; quite balanced, with pepper and spice to give it zing. Fifty-year-old Grenache vines—one of the red Rhône grapes called *Garnacha* in Spain that makes some of their best reds—provide enormous depth and finesse in this bargain wine. The name Jorge Ordoñez on the back label of a Spanish wine is a good indication of quality because he represents some of the greatest estates in Spain, including the limited supply Numanthia and Termes reds from DO Toro (made from Tinta de Toro, which is another name for Spain's smooth Tempranillo red grape) .

Boschendal—Sauvignon Blanc—South Africa

FIGURE 5.14

Boschendal—Sauvignon Blanc—South Africa—57 Main Street Imports—2002—$13. This wine's current vintage is 2004. Boschendal Winery was founded in 1685 in the French corner of Paarl on the cape of South Africa where the Indian and Atlantic Oceans meet. This lovely winery sits in front of the Groot Drakenstein mountain range and its un-irrigated hillside vineyards produce powerful wine for the price.

Grape: Sauvignon Blanc

Wine Region: Franschhoek, Paarl

Food Partners: Grouper, oysters, lemon chicken, Arina Goat Gouda (Holland), Thai cuisine

Tasting Notes: Delicate, citrusy, ruby red grapefruit and gooseberry flavors with herbal undertones—very refreshing on its own, or with food. Delicious from first sip to last; no oak is used to keep the wine crisp and dry. Website: **www. 57mainstreet.com**.

St. Supéry—Meritage (White) "Virtú"—Napa Valley, California

winery

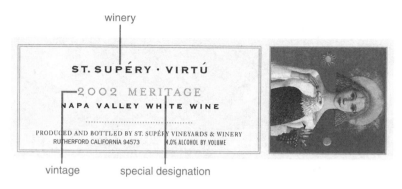

ST. SUPÉRY · VIRTÚ

2002 MERITAGE

NAPA VALLEY WHITE WINE

PRODUCED AND BOTTLED BY ST. SUPÉRY VINEYARDS & WINERY
RUTHERFORD CALIFORNIA 94573   4.0% ALCOHOL BY VOLUME

vintage   special designation

FIGURE 5.15

St. Supéry—Meritage (White) "Virtú"—Napa Valley, California—2002—$25. This beautiful "artist" label depicts an angel holding grapes (Virtú) with a bald eagle in the foreground. Meritage (pronounced like heritage) wines are collectors' items, hence the higher price—but they are powerhouse wines in taste and make very special gifts.

Grapes: 47% Sauvignon Blanc, 53% Sémillon

Wine Region: Napa Valley, CA

Special Designation: To use the trademark name *Meritage*, U.S. wineries must be members, and both their white and red wines must be blends of two or more of the genuine Bordeaux grapes.

Food Partners: Turkey tenderloin, sea bass, Proscuitto and melon, lemon meringue pie

Tasting Notes: Pear and peach aromas from Sauvignon Blanc, then luscious fig flavors from Sémillon, mouth-filling richness, and a dry finish. Wow, adding Sémillon to the Sauvignon Blanc as they do in Bordeaux for the greatest white Graves wines kicks it up a notch in complexity and flavor. Website: **www.stsupery.com**.

note St. Supéry CEO, Michaela Rodeno, was president of the Meritage Association (**www.meritagewine.com**). St. Supéry's Meritage Red ($50) is a powerful wine; the winery's regular Sauvignon Blanc and Cabernet also are delicious and very reasonably priced.

Beringer—Chardonnay "Private Reserve"—Napa Valley, California

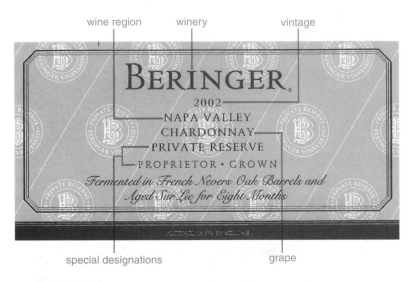

wine region   winery   vintage

special designations   grape

FIGURE 5.16

Beringer—Chardonnay "Private Reserve"—Napa Valley, California—2002—$35. This label explains that the wine is "Proprietor Grown," fermented in French Nevers oak (from forests near Bordeaux), and aged for 8 months "sur lie" (on the lees of yeast that fall to the bottom of the barrel), giving the wine toasty notes and creamy richness. The wine also goes through malolactic fermentation to make it buttery. This is done for only the finest Chardonnays destined to be cellared for up to 10 years.

Special Designation: Private Reserve (grapes are from their best single vineyards)

Food Partners: Lobster, crab cakes, scallops, clam chowder, swordfish

Tasting Notes: Tropical fruit aromas such as pineapple, vanilla from new oak, and butterscotch fill every corner of your mouth with silk and acidity, and then explode in the most memorable fashion. Website: **www.beringer.com**.

note Beringer is part of the family of fine wines that include Australia's Wolf Blass and Greg Norman. Beringer's "Wine & Cheese Pairing Wheel & Guide" $10 Item #BK285-001 is available from IWA catalog. Tel: 800-527-4072.

Vionta—Albariño—DO Rías Baixas, Spain

FIGURE 5.17
Vionta—
Albariño—DO Rías
Baixas, Spain—
2003—$18.
Albariño is the
queen of white
grapes in Galicia, in
northern Spain on
the Atlantic where
seafood is king. This
is one of the
Heredad Collection
of ultra-premium
Spanish wines pre-
sented by Freixenet,
the leading CAVA
sparkling wine pro-
ducer in Spain.

winery

ALBARIÑO — grape
RÍAS BAIXAS — wine region
DENOMINACION DE ORIXE

2 0 0 3 — vintage

Estate Bottled
•
Single Vineyard
•
Limited Release
— special designations

Produced by
Comercial Oula, s.a.
Vilanova de Arousa
Galicia - Spain

R.E. 5607- PO.

750 ml. ◆ Alc. 12 % By Vol.

PRODUCT OF SPAIN

Winery: Vionta

Grape: Albariño

Wine Region: DO Rías Baixas, Galicia

Special Designations: Single Vineyard, Limited Release

Food Partners: Crab legs or cocktail, avocado soup, grilled shrimp, fish tacos

Tasting Notes: Lively aromas and flavors of green apple, lemon, and apricot followed by ginger in a dry, full-bodied extraordinary white. Cold fermented in stainless steel to preserve its tart acidity, this wine is the perfect partner for any
contemporary menu, including Chinese. Website: **www.heredadcollection.com**.

Settesoli "MandraRossa"—Fiano—IGT Sicilia (Sicily) Italy

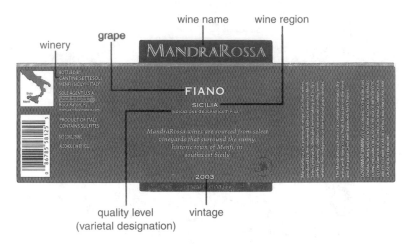

winery · grape · wine name · wine region

quality level (varietal designation) · vintage

FIGURE 5.18

Settesoli "MandraRossa"—Fiano—IGT Sicilia (Sicily) Italy—2003—$9. You will love this Fiano because unlike other dry, tropical flavored whites, it never becomes bitter after exposure to the air. Sicily has the sunny, Mediterranean climate perfect for very modern-style citrusy dry white wines such as Fiano, which is similar to but silkier than Viognier.

Winery: Settesoli

Grape: 100% Fiano

Quality Level: IGT—Indicazione Geografica Tipica (Italian wines named after grape variety with minimum 85%)

Food Partners: Proscuitto with melon, calamari, linguine with white clam sauce, pesto pasta, Asiago cheese, almond biscotti

Tasting Notes: Aromas of mango, Mandarin oranges, and tropical flowers lead to a dry white with lots of character that stayed fresh for days after it was opened. Website: **www.palmbayimports.com**.

Domaine Gerovassiliou—Malagousia—Epanomi, Greece

Grape: Malagousia

Wine Region: Epanomi, Thessaloniki

US representative: Sofia Perpera

Food Partners: Prawns with Ouzo and feta, Greek grilled fish, eggplant, Thai basil rolls

FIGURE 5.19
Domaine
Gerovassiliou—
Malagousia—
Epanomi,
Greece—2003—
$16. This winery's
owner, Mr.
Gerovassiliou, is a
pioneer of modern
winemaking in
Greece, including for
international vari-
eties such as Syrah.
The Gerovassiliou
Winery's peninsula
vineyards benefit
from three sides of
ocean influence.

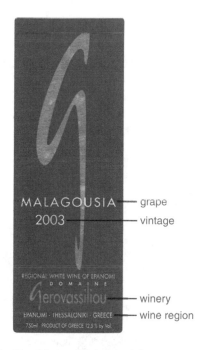

— grape
— vintage
— winery
— wine region

Tasting Notes: Spritzy, with aromas of peaches, jasmine, and citrus. Bursting with flavor, yet light and delightful. Malagousia is one of the three best native white grapes grown in Greece for making dry wines—the other two being Moschofilero (by *Tselepos*), which is a pink-skinned grape like Pinot Grigio and Gewürztraminer, and Assyrtiko (by *Sigalas*) from the island of Santorini. These contemporary Greek white wines, including their famous white dessert wine Muscat from the island of *Samos*, rival any of the of the world's best. Website: **www.allaboutgreekwines.com**.

Pfaffl "Goldjoch"—Grüner Veltliner—Austria

Grape: Grüner Veltliner

Wine Region: Weinviertel

Importer: Austrian Specialty Wine Company, Franklin, TN.

Food Partners: Trout, veal cutlets, chicken or turkey sausages, pork chops with apple-sauce

Tasting Notes: White pepper and vanilla aromas with powerful layers of exotic fruit and a very clean, dry, crisp finish.

Grüner Veltliner is the most widely planted white grape in Austria, and it makes wonderful dry—not sweet—wine. Website: **www.austrianwine.net**.

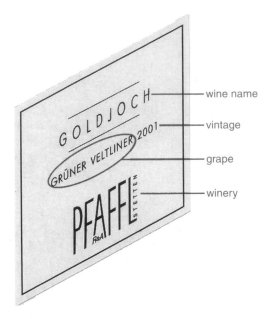

wine name

vintage

grape

winery

FIGURE 5.20

Pfaffl "Goldjoch"—Grüner Veltliner—Austria—2001—$22. The respected Pfaffl winery grows the grapes for this wine in the most northern part of Austria—Weinviertel—where the black soil is rich with desirable limestone. Pfaffl makes several versions of this grape, but this "Goldjoch" was rated 93 points out of 100 by *Wine Enthusiast* magazine at the end of 2002.

B&G (Barton & Guestier)—Vouvray—Loire, France

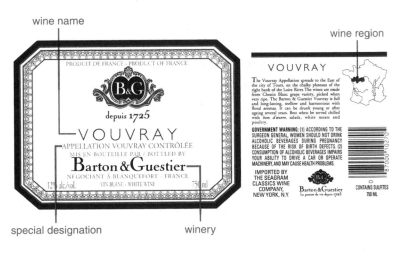

wine name

wine region

special designation

winery

FIGURE 5.21

B&G—Barton & Guestier—Vouvray—Loire, France—2002—$9. When you taste this charming medium-dry white from the village of Vouvray in the Loire River Valley of northwest France, you will think you are having a summer picnic by the river—even if it's snowing outside!

Winery: B&G (Barton & Guestier)

Grape: Chenin Blanc

Wine Region: Loire

Special Designation: Appellation Contrôlée (AOC) name of origin is Vouvray Importer: Diageo-Chateau & Estate Wines.

Food Partners: Hors d'oeuvres, corn chowder, chicken and papaya salad, potatoes au gratin, halibut with lemon ginger sauce, pound cake

Tasting Notes: Crystal clear with nougat candy and floral aromas, flavors of ripe green grapes, and pleasing but short finish. Website: **www.aboutwines.com**.

note Remember that French AOC wines do not give the grape variety—you are expected to know that Vouvray is made from Chenin Blanc grapes, which also do well in California and South Africa.

Selbach Oster—Riesling–Spätlese—Mosel-Saar-Ruwer, Germany

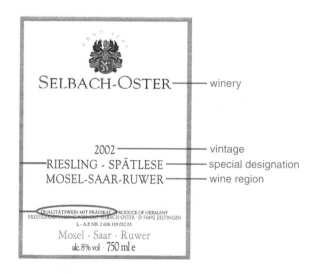

FIGURE 5.22

Selbach Oster—Riesling-Spätlese—Mosel-Saar-Ruwer, Germany—2002—$18. The Selbach–Oster Winery's owner, Johannes Selbach, produces some of the most famous single vineyards, such as Bernkasteler Badstube, but this modern type of label emphasizes the grape variety and quality or sweetness level, rather than the vineyard.

Grape: Riesling

Wine Region: Mosel-Saar-Ruwer

Special Designations: *Spätlese* meaning means "late harvest"

Quality level: *Qualitätswein Mit Prädikat* are highest quality-level wines made from naturally sweet grapes only

Food Partners: Ham, fried chicken, shrimp salad with fruit, Asian cuisine, pumpkin pie, spice or carrot cake

Tasting Notes: Green apple; apple blossom aromas with a touch of white peach and just a kiss of slight sweetness; it is elegant, refreshing, and tastes like fresh green grapes. This wine family has a 300-year history in the elite Mosel River area, where Riesling grapes are grown on steep cliffs in rare Blue Devonian Slate soil, giving the wines crispness and a drier finish. Never too sweet, the Spätlese is made from grapes "late harvested" or picked several weeks past normal harvest time, which is possible only in great sunny vintage years. Spätlese is the second highest Prädikat wine, so their are three levels of sweeter wines above it under the German wine laws. Website: **www.selbach-oster.de**.

Bodegas Hidalgo—"La Gitana"—Manzanilla Sherry—Sanlúcar de Barrameda, Spain

FIGURE 5.23

Bodegas Hidalgo—"La Gitana"—Manzanilla Sherry—Sanlúcar de Barrameda, Spain—Non-vintage—$10. "La Gitana" means "the Gypsy," and it is the most popular brand of Manzanilla Sherry in the world. Six generations of the Hidalgo family have upheld a tradition of bottling the finest Sherries. The Hidalgo winery uses soleras that were first established in the early 19th century. (A solera is a nursery of old wines that are blended with new wine every year to create a consistent taste).

Grape: Palomino

Wine Region: Sanlúcar de Barrameda

Special Designation: DO (*Denominación de Origen* or name of origin) *Manzanilla*, which is the lightest and driest type of Sherry, and the only wine in the world with a unique salty flavor

Food Partners: Tapas, appetizers, grilled seafood, ham, green/black olives, stuffed mushrooms, sushi, nuts, cheese

Tasting Notes: Yeast and almonds in the aroma; whisper of salt from the sea and tart acidity; very flavorful, dry but light and an aftertaste of green olives. Manzanilla is unique among Sherries because it is made on the seashore where the *flor* yeast can grow year-round on top of the wine in the barrels, giving this type of Sherry its salty tang. Website: **www.classicalwines.com**.

Ramos-Pinto—Porto Ruby—Portugal—Maison Marques & Domaines, USA

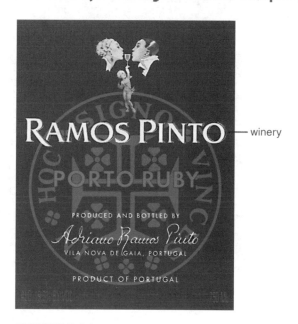 — winery

FIGURE 5.24

Ramos-Pinto—Porto Ruby—Portugal—Maison Marques & Domaines USA—Non-vintage—$15. Ruby Porto is a wooded Porto that is a blend of different vintages and this powerhouse example is aged three years in large chestnut casks. The Ramos-Pinto winery owns its own vineyards in the Douro River Valley, and then ages and bottles their Portos in the city of Vila Nova de Gaia on the Atlantic Ocean.

Grapes: Touriga and Tinta Barroca

Wine Region: Porto

Special Designation: Ruby

Food Partners: Stilton (blue) cheese, semi-sweet or dark chocolates (and chocolate layer cake, chocolate cherries, or mousse), Port wine sauce for meat or pheasant, Black Forest cake and walnuts

Tasting Notes: Deep ruby color; abundant aromas of plum, black cherry, and anise or licorice, with rich, chocolate aftertaste. Like all Porto, it is a fortified wine with 20% alcohol and is served in small port glasses after dinner.

note Importer Maison Marques & Domaines represents very fine labels, such as French Champagnes Louis Roederer "Cristal" ($175), Roederer Brut Premier NV ($45), and Roederer Estate sparkling from California ($22)—as well as prestige reds such as Dominus (Napa, CA).

It is ready to enjoy now, doesn't have to be decanted (no sediment), and is a great value for money considering most vintage Portos are three times the price. Website: **www.mmdusa.net**.

Mumm Napa—Blanc de Noirs—Napa Valley, California

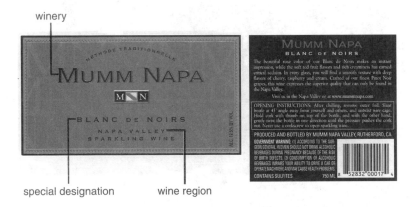

FIGURE 5.25

Mumm Napa—Blanc de Noirs—Napa Valley, California—Non-vintage—$18. Winner of three gold medals plus a double gold medal at 2004 wine competitions, this is my favorite California "blanc de noirs," or pink sparkling wine. Notice that the back label has proper and safe directions for opening the bottle, which has natural carbon dioxide bubbles from fermentation under pressure.

Grapes: 85% Pinot Noir and 15% Chardonnay

Special Designation: *Blanc de Noirs,* meaning "white wine from black grapes" or pink sparkling wine

U.S. Representatives: Allied Domecq

Food Partners: Caviar, avocado and crab salad, smoked salmon, filet mignon, baked brie, chocolate mousse

Tasting Notes: Brilliant pink coral color; bouquet of strawberries; fine pinpoint bubbles that cleanse the palate and long, yeasty, dry finish. Made in the true Champagne method by the Mumm Napa winery, this beautiful Napa wine is the American sister to the renowned G.H. Mumm Champagnes of France, who are famous for Cordon Rouge (red ribbon) Brut V. and N.V., as well as sweet dessert style "Joyesse" Demi-sec ($26). Website: **www.mummnapa.com**.

> **tip** For an additional treat try Mumm Napa's top of the line elegant, dry sparkler DVX—it's wow! You can order a very useful book, *Sparkling Recipes for Every Occasion*, for $9.95 from Mumm Napa by phoning 707-967-7700.

Rumball—Sparkling Shiraz—Coonawarra, Australia

FIGURE 5.26

Rumball—Sparkling Shiraz—Coonawarra, Australia   Non vintage—$25. Coonawarra in South Australia is well known for great red wines such as Shiraz, but this Shiraz was made into a distinctive red sparkling wine using the true Champagne method. The Rumball Winery's owner, Peter Rumball, revived Sparkling Shiraz in the 1980s, and it is distinctively Australian.

Grape: Shiraz (Syrah)

Wine Region: Coonawarra, Australia

Special Designation: Sparkling (Red)

Food Partners: Roast duck, pork tenderloin, turkey, aged cheddar, blue cheese or Parmigiano-Reggiano, chocolate truffles

Tasting Notes: Gorgeous deep black red color; lovely crown of red bubbles; aromas of black raspberry and spices; fabulous dry finish. Serve well chilled. Ready to drink now. What a very pleasant surprise this will be for your guests! The color alone will attract them, but the surprising concentrated fruit character and dry taste will make them cry for more. Websites: **www.rumball.com.au** and **www. scottstreetportfolio.com**.

Summary

My intent was to make this chapter interesting enough for you to keep reading, without overwhelming you with information. Certainly the wine labels will give you confidence in your new abilities. Remember, you do not have to memorize all of these wine laws or labels. If you only end up retaining a small percent of this wine education, you will still know more than most people—including some people working in the wine business!

We will have ample opportunity to highlight more wines that deserve your dollars, both in upcoming chapters on individual countries and in our "tear out" shopping card that you can take to the store.

Part II

Wine Countries

Made in the USA—
California and Beyond

The Wine Institute in California (**www.
wineinstitute.org**) confirms that there
are approximately 3,000 wineries in the
United States—847 of which are in California. The
U.S. also has more than 140 AVAs or American
Viticultural (grape growing) Areas, each with its
own unique *terroir* (soil, climate, and geography).

American wineries are also powerhouses of production. In 2003, California shipped a record 627
million gallons of wine, with a retail value of
more than $21 billion dollars. That's a lot of fer-
mented grape juice!

The abundance of great American wines seems
limitless when you consider that wineries in previously unheard of places, such as Shelton
Vineyards in North Carolina's new AVA Yadkin
Valley, win international wine competitions. And
what a surprise to find sparkling wines made in
the true Champagne method from Gruet winery
in New Mexico, or fine wines from Ste. Chapelle
in Idaho! Any of these could satisfy a wine connoisseur's taste buds.

Since 7 out of 10 bottles of wine sold in the U.S.
are produced in California, this chapter focuses on
that state's dream wines and fun new wine areas.
In addition, we will highlight the best of the rest
of North America's wine country, from Long
Island Cabernets to Oregon Pinot Noir.

To do list

☐ Understand how California's geography and climate produces great wines
☐ Learn about California AVAs and their wineries
☐ Find out what makes a "cult" wine, and how wines become collectible
☐ Learn what's currently "hot" in California wines

Mother Lode—California's Wine Gold

The modern history of California viticulture began in 1861 when Agoston Haraszthy, now recognized as the "Father of California Viticulture," was commissioned by the governor to bring the "noble" European grape varieties to California. Haraszthy also founded the Buena Vista Winery in the town of Sonoma and was probably also responsible for bringing the black Zinfandel grape to California.

As a result of these superior grapes, California wines won international medals in the late 1800s. By 1920, there were 700 wineries in California. Prohibition put most of these wineries out of business, except for those owned by long-established wine families, such as Beringer and Beaulieu Vineyard in Napa, and Sebastiani in Sonoma, which survived. In 1933, after Prohibition ended, E & J Gallo began operations. This winery now produces the fine Gallo of Sonoma wines from its 6,000 acres of organically farmed vineyards in the Dry Creek AVA.

A dormant period in California winemaking followed until 1966, when pioneers such as Robert Mondavi (recognized by the California legislature for a lifetime of achievement in the promotion of California wines) began the prestigious Napa Valley vineyards. It wasn't until the famous Paris Tasting of 1976, when Warren and Barbara Winiarski of Napa Valley's Stag's Leap Wine Cellars won first place with their Cabernet Sauvignon against the greatest Bordeaux, that upstart California was permanently printed on the world's wine map.

Though premium wines account for just 15% of California's production (in France, Appellation Contrôlée wines account for about 47% of wine production), California's fine wines outsell its bulk wines dollar for dollar in the U.S., as well as in wine-savvy England and label-conscious Japan. Sir Peter Michael and wife Maggie, owners of one of England's most elite restaurants—the Vineyard at Stockcross outside London—are such California wine boosters that they not only feature them prominently in their restaurant; but they also opened the highly rated Peter Michael Winery in Sonoma, CA.

Prestigious Italian, Spanish, and French wine families also participate in California wineries. This includes Antinori of Tuscany, co-founder of Atlas Peak winery in Napa; Spain's #1 sparkling wine producer Freixenet, who owns Gloria Ferrer sparkling wines in Sonoma; Baroness de Rothschild of Château Mouton-Rothschild, who created the joint venture Opus Winery in Napa with Robert Mondavi; and the Moueix family of Château Pétrus, who established Dominus winery in Napa. In addition the great Champagne houses of France—Taittinger, Moët & Chandon, Deutz, Roederer, Mumm, and Piper-Heidsieck—all have California wineries making great sparkling wines.

How California's Great Grapes Climate Produces Great Grapes

Called the "golden state" sunny California can "mine" wine gold just about anywhere within its borders. But it is California's long Pacific Ocean coastline that provides cooling temperatures, rain, and fog to some of the best vineyards, lengthening their growing season and producing superior grapes and wines.

From north to south along the Pacific coastline, the important coastal counties are

- The four north coast counties north of San Francisco: Napa, Sonoma, Lake and Mendocino

- Livermore County, across San Francisco Bay

- Santa Clara, Santa Cruz, Monterey, San Benito, San Luis Obispo, Santa Barbara, Temecula, and San Pasqual Valley (San Diego)

Figure 6.1 shows where these counties are.

The coastal mountains effectively block California's advantageous ocean influence, except where there is a break in the range. Such a break occurs at San Francisco Bay, which leads to the Livermore and Lodi AVAs further east, and at higher mountain elevations the Sierra Foothills AVA in the old gold mining area of the Sierra Nevada Mountains.

The very hot, large San Joaquin Valley (400 miles long and 100 miles wide) lies further inland, and it is planted with Thompson Seedless white grapes used to mass produce generic (non-varietal) wine, such as California Chablis. A lot of red blending grapes such as Carignan are also planted here for California burgundy.

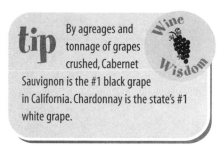

tip By agreages and tonnage of grapes crushed, Cabernet Sauvignon is the #1 black grape in California. Chardonnay is the state's #1 white grape.

Wine Wisdom

The University of California at Davis, which trains most of California's winemakers, developed a system of five climate zones based on the total number of degrees—called *degree days*—the temperature rises above 50°F each day of the growing season from April 1st thru October 30th, the ripening season for wine grapes. The larger the number of these degree days, the hotter the climate. These climate regions explain why and where California's best grape varieties are planted.

Map of California.

- **Region I**: The very cool Carneros AVA that overlaps the bottom of both Napa and Sonoma Counties is Region I. Carneros is perfect for growing the cool-weather grapes of Burgundy, including Chardonnay grapes with a lovely lime character and Pinot Noirs with beautiful cherry and spice flavors.

- **Region II**: Comparable to the climate of Bordeaux, Region II is exceptional for both red and white Bordeaux varietals: Cabernet Sauvignon, Merlot, Cabernet Franc, Sauvignon Blanc and Sémillon, and Meritage wines originate in Region II areas. Cabernets from Rutherford in Napa, for example, are said to have yummy chocolate/cherry profiles with a characteristic allspice finish.

- **Region III**: Found in the warmer areas of all the coastal counties, including Lake, Livermore, and Monterey. Region III climate is suitable for Bordeaux varietals, other French grapes such as Chenin Blanc, Syrah and the other Rhône grapes, Sangiovese and other Italian grapes, and Zinfandel.

- **Region IV**: Areas of Lodi and the Sierra Foothills in Amador County have a moderately hot, dry, sunny climate in summer and make some of the best Zinfandels, Syrah, Primitivo (from Italy), and Touriga (from Portugal) in California.

note To learn more about wineries from each of California's five climate zones, see "California AVAs and Wineries" later in this chapter.

- **Region V**: The inland San Joaquin Valley has a hot climate and short growing season suitable for raisin or eating grapes and generic wine.

California AVAs and Wineries

Now that you've been introduced to California's most popular wines, wineries, and wine-growing regions, here's a condensed guide to some of California's important AVAs and major wineries in those AVAs. This highly selective list will help you plan a trip through California wine country and choose wines for purchase. But be advised: wineries may be located in one AVA but have vineyards in other AVAs. Those areas will appear on their wine labels. It all depends on the *source of the grapes*.

Napa Valley

The Napa Valley is one of California's most productive wine-growing areas. It has 15 AVAs, starting with the Napa Valley AVA itself. For more information about Napa AVAs and wineries go to their website: **www.napavintners.com**.

The following list names the remaining Napa AVAs and includes representative samples of some of Napa's finest wineries:

- **Napa Valley North**—Sterling, Chateau Montelena, Cuvaison, Clos Pegase
- **Spring Mountain**—Cain Vineyards, Newton, Paloma
- **Howell Mountain**—Dunn, Burgess, La Jota, Chateau Woltner
- **St. Helena**—Beringer, Rombauer, Freemark Abbey, Colgin, Spottswoode, Turley, Viader, Grace Family, Merryvale, Duckhorn, Louis Martini, Heitz, Joseph Phelps
- **Rutherford**—St. Supéry, Staglin, Niebaum-Coppola, Beaulieu Vineyard, ZD, Mumm Napa, Caymus, Rutherford Hill, Sequoia Grove, Peju Province, Cakebread
- **Oakville**—Robert Mondavi, Opus, Turnbull, Silver Oak, Franciscan, Far Niente, Cosentino, Lewis Cellars, Screaming Eagle, Dalla Valle, Plumpjack
- **Mount Veeder**—Mount Veeder, Mayacamas, Hess Collection, Harlan, Chateau Potelle

- **Yountville**—Domaine Chandon, Dominus
- **Stags Leap District**—Stag's Leap Wine Cellars, Stags' Leap Winery, Shafer, Steltzner, Robert Sinskey, Pine Ridge, Silverado, Clos du Val
- **Napa (town) and east**—Pahlmeyer, Jarvis, Trefethen, William Hill
- **Atlas Peak**—Atlas Peak Vineyards
- **Carneros**—Saintsbury, Acacia, Truchard
- **Chiles Valley** and **Wild Horse** AVAs

Sonoma County

Sonoma County has 14 AVAs, including newly approved ones such as Rockpile. For a complete list of wineries by AVA, go to **www.sonomawine.com**. There are the important Sonoma AVAs and some of my favorite Sonoma wineries:

- **Alexander Valley**—Simi, Jordan, Clos du Bois, Chateau Souverain, Geyser Peak
- **Dry Creek Valley**—Dry Creek Vineyard, Gallo of Sonoma, Ferrari-Carano
- **Chalk Hill**—Chalk Hill Winery
- **Green Valley**—Iron Horse, Miramar Torres Estate
- **Russian River Valley**—Kistler, Rodney Strong, Piper-Sonoma, Korbel
- **Knights Valley**—Peter Michael
- **Sonoma Mountain**—Benziger
- **Sonoma Coast**—Sonoma–Cutrer
- **Sonoma Valley**—Chateau St. Jean, Kenwood, Arrowood, Sebastiani, Buena Vista, Matanzas Creek, Ravenswood
- **Carneros-Sonoma**—Gloria Ferrer, MacCrostie, Cline, Schug, Viansa, Domaine Carneros (Taittinger)
- **Rockpile**, **Bennett Valley** and **Northern Sonoma** AVAs

Mendocino and Lake Counties

Mendocino County AVAs include Mendocino, Anderson Valley, McDowell Valley, Potter Valley, Cole Ranch, Redwood Valley, Yorkville Highlands, and Mendocino Ridge.

Mendocino wineries include Fetzer (organic label is Bonterra), McDowell Valley Vineyards, Lolonis, Jepson, Roederer Estate, and Scharffenberger.

Lake County AVAs include Lake, Guenoc Valley, Clear Lake and Benmore Valley.

Lake County wineries include Guenoc, Steele, Konocti and Kendall-Jackson.

Sierra Foothills and San Francisco Bay Area

The Sierra Foothills wine region between Sacramento and Lake Tahoe includes these AVAs: Sierra Foothills, Amador County, Shenandoah Valley, Fiddletown, El Dorado County, and Calaveras County.

Sierra Foothills wineries are concentrated south and east of Placerville, and include C.G. di Arie, Karly, Renwood, Sutter Home, Montevina, Boeger, Stevenot, and Ironstone.

In the San Francisco Bay area, you'll find the AVAs of Livermore Valley, Marin County, San Mateo, Santa Clara, Alameda County, and Central Coast.

Wente is the most famous and extensive Livermore Valley winery. Marin county wineries include the elite Sean H. Thackrey winery.

Central Coast, South-Central Coast, and Southern California

Monterey County AVAs include Arroyo Seco, Carmel Valley, Chalone, Homes Valley, San Lucas, Santa Lucia Highlands, San bernabe, Santa Cruz, San Benito, and Monterey.

Monterey wineries include J. Lohr, Chalone, Bernardus, Blackstone, Morgan, Jekel, Mer Soleil, Smith & Hook, Ventana, Chateau Julien, Kendall-Jackson, and Hahn. In San Benito, Calera is my favorite. In Santa Cruz, I recommend Bonny Doon, David Bruce, Ridge, and Pedrizzetti. For more information about Monterey wines go to their website: **www.montereywines.org**.

In the South-Central Coastal region, San Luis Obispo County encompasses the AVAs of Arroyo Grande, Edna Valley, Paso Robles, and York Mountain. San Luis Obispo wineries include Laetitia and Talley in Arroyo Grande; Edna Valley Vineyards in Edna Valley; Eberle, J. Lohr, Justin, Rosenblum, Meridian, Wild Horse, Tablas Creek, L'Aventure, Pretty-Smith, EOS, Dark Star, Claiborne & Churchill, and Peachy Canyon; and York Creek Vineyards in York Mountain.

The other important area of the south-Central Coast is Santa Barbara County, where the movie *Sideways* was filmed (see sidebar). Santa Barbara County is divided into the two AVAs of Santa Ynez Valley and Santa Maria Valley. Santa Barbara's popular wineries include Fess Parker, Au Bon Climat, Lane Tanner, Byron, Cambria, and Gainey.

Southern California AVAs include Temecula (on the border of San Diego and Riverside counties) and San Pasqual Valley in San Diego County. Most people are familiar with the long-established Callaway winery in Temecula, but are unaware that there are other fine Temecula wineries, including Mount Palomar, Stuart Cellars, Hart Winery, Churon, and Bella Vista Cilurzo. San Diego's San Pasqual Valley is home to the respected Orfila winery.

A "ROAD TRIP" FILM FOR WINE-LOVERS

The hilarious movie *Sideways* is the saga of two guys who tour the wineries of the Santa Ynez Valley in Santa Barbara County, California, 130 miles north of Los Angeles. The character played by Paul Giamatti in the movie is a real "wine geek" who loves Pinot Noir because it's so difficult to grow, but is extremely critical of wines that do not meet his lofty standards. Though he doesn't have the money to indulge his expensive wine habit, he orders bottle after bottle of the best French Burgundy and Bordeaux at dinner, as well as several of California's rare cult wines. (You learn more about cult wines later in this chapter.)

But he blows his cool when personal problems stress him to the brink of craziness. At one winery, he slaps down money and demands a "full" glass of wine to take with his tranquilizers. (Drinking and popping pills is definitely unwise.) The server tells him they are only permitted to pour little samples. That's when the desperate wine snob grabs the "dump" bucket, filled with everyone's discarded wine and guzzles it.

The best line in the movie came from the movie's heroine, who explained the reason for her great love of fine wine: "because it tastes so good." Exactly.

For more information about touring Santa Barbara, CA, wineries, call 1-800-676-1266 or go to the website **www.santabarbaraca.com.**

Cult Wines and Collectibles: *Wine Spectator*'s Top 100

Most of the new wine collectors I meet fill their cellars with pricey California Chardonnays and Cabernet blends with a "name." There's always a waiting list for wines that have gained recognition from the *Wine Spectator*. Other wine magazines also list desirable "cult wines" that are very hard to obtain because of limited supply and distribution, and "collectibles" that are coveted by collectors because they are rated among the best of their type in a particular vintage.

Who gives these California wines their "name recognition?" For years it's been Marvin R. Shanken's twice-monthly magazine, *Wine Spectator*. Every year, a *Wine Spectator* panel ranks the world's "top 100" wines and chooses a "wine of the year." Of the magazine's "top 100" winners for 2004 (announced in the Dec. 31–Jan. 15, 2005 issue), 22 were from

note One winery with very highly sought after "name" wines is Silver Oak. This winery makes two different Cabernet Sauvignons —one from Alexander Valley in Sonoma County, and the better of the two (to my taste) from Napa Valley. Aficionados of Silver Oak also pay thousands of dollars and wait years for original oil paintings of these wine bottles by Georgia artist Thomas Arvid (**www.thomasarvid.com**).

California. These wines ranged in price from $11 to $250 with an average cost of $40, which is not really much money to pay for the best. A number of these wines were discussed in Chapter 5, "The Wine Label Decoder."

Of the California wines in the "top 100," most have extreme name recognition, including Lewis Cellars, Araujo, Peter Michael, Williams Selyem, Pride, Beringer, Worthy, Truchard, Paloma, and Sea Smoke. But the list also includes real California bargains, such as Acacia (Pinot Noir), Seghesio and Rosenblum (Zinfandel), Sebastiani and Villa Mt. Eden (Chardonnay), Chalone (Syrah), Buehler (Cabernet Sauvignon,) and Gloria Ferrer sparkling wine.

> **note** With bureaus from New York to Napa and Italy, *Wine Spectator's* articles have the most up-to-date winery news, such as the story about Constellation Brands (the largest wine company in the world) buying all of the Robert Mondavi wineries for $1.3 billion. The magazine's website has online wine classes, and a list of U.S. wine courses (**www.winespectator.com**).

Several other U.S.-based wine magazines are also important sources of information for new wine enthusiasts. One of the best is even called *Wine Enthusiast*. (They also have a comprehensive catalog of wine gifts and accessories.)

Current California Favorites

What am I currently drinking from California? I confess to being enamored of rich yet smooth Cabernet Franc from Lang & Reed, Andrew Geoffrey, and Trinitas—starting at $24 per bottle. I also love "Super Tuscan" Sangiovese/Cabernet blends made in California such as Ferrari-Carano "Siena" and Shafer "Firebreak." I like big Zinfandels, such as the highly respected Turley and Cline, and Syrahs, such as upscale Lane Tanner and even $10 Rock Rabbit.

But my great love is "special occasion" Cabernet blends such as Quintessa, Groth, Shafer, Duckhorn, Turnbull, and Viader. Priced from $45 to $75 per bottle, they are ultimate taste experiences with steak, lamb, or chocolate cake. And if you want your Port already mixed with chocolate, then try "Deco" natural Chocolate Port from Sonoma Valley Port Works at www.portworks.com.

> **tip** Remember, *single vineyard* wines are invariably the finest available, and *reserve* wines are also usually among the best in California (even though the U.S. has no legal definition for them).

WAREHOUSE AND WINE CLUB BARGAINS

Who has the lowest overall prices on the best wines? One answer has to be Los Angeles Wine Co., which buys in lots at a locked-in price, and offers these rock-bottom deals directly to customers at their warehouse in LA, by phone from their newsletter, or online at their website: www. lawineco.com. I am greatly impressed by this company's president, Steve Bialek. It's obvious he knows his wines and is a talented buyer. He has great Porto, Bordeaux, Spanish, Italian, German, and California wines, with the added advantage of no middle-man markup in the state of California.

One of the least expensive online wine-of-the-month clubs is www.**fruitforward.com**. For just $20, members of Tricia and Charles Smith's wine club receive two bottles of wine each month: two reds or whites, or one of each. Tasting notes and ideas for food pairings come with the wines' histories. Remember that *fruit forward* refers to wines with lots of up-front berry aromas and fruit concentration. This is not a derogatory term for California- and other new-style wines. Only old-style wine experts who prefer their wines oxidized and devoid of fruit think it is.

California Cuisine

Many California chefs and restaurants use the state's bounty of olive oils, nuts, farmstead cheeses, duck, lamb, fish, venison, organic fruits, vegetables, and herbs to their advantage. Among them is Alice Water's iconic Chez Panisse restaurant in Berkeley, and Thomas Keller's re-opened and already-booked-ahead French Laundry restaurant in Yountville (in Napa Valley). Napa also has two major wine centers that emphasize food and wine classes: COPIA American Center for Food, Wine & the Arts, founded with help from Robert Mondavi and Julia Child in the town of Napa; and the Culinary Institute of America's Greystone campus and restaurant in St. Helena (**www.ciaprochef.com**). And if you want to make dishes with California grapes, the California Table Grape Commission provides great recipes for everything from chocolate grape tartlets to pizza and burritos at **www.tablegrape.com**.

Crystal Ball—California's Future

In the March 2004 *Southern Beverage Journal*, Jean K. Reilly wrote an insightful article about California wine's recent troubled past and improving future. Having overcome Phylloxera's return in the '90s, winery bankruptcies, low grape prices, and the snooze factor of over-familiarity, California is poised for a rebirth.

Americans are drinking more wine. But with our annual per capita consumption rate of just 8.8 liters compared to 35–60 liters in Europe, our domestic wine market is just beginning to climb. And California varietal wines taste so good, even in the lowest price categories.

Oregon Wines

Oregon's wine country is concentrated in the Willamette River Valley, which stretches for 100 miles from Portland south to Eugene. It is as cool and rainy as Burgundy, France. In Oregon counties such as Yamhill, the soil is reddish and very similar to Burgundy's Côte de Nuits. As a result, Oregon Pinot Noir is recognized the world over for its excellence, thanks to pioneering Oregon wineries who brought the first Dijon clones of Pinot Noir and Chardonnay grapes to America.

Oregon winemakers also have a well-deserved reputation for being able to grow and produce excellent examples of unusual European grape varieties, including Pinot Blanc, Pinot Gris, Melon de Bourgogne (the grape of Muscadet in Loire, France), and even Pinot Meunier from Champagne. And most Oregon winemakers use organic agriculture to protect the environment and wildlife.

Oregon wineries are to be commended for succeeding with difficult-to-grow Pinot Noir. Such wineries include Bethel Heights, Sokol Blosser (one of the best bargains), King Estate (gorgeous chateau-style winery), Erath, Eyrie, Ken Wright, Rex Hill, Chehalem, Adelsheim and Ponzi, Beau Frères, Argyle, and Van Duzer. All of these wineries appeared in *Wine Spectator*'s 2004 top 100 list.

Washington Wines

Washington state is at the same 46° north latitude as Bordeaux, France. Washington's wine country covers the entire Columbia River Valley in the dry, sagebrush-covered hills of the eastern part of the state. The Columbia Valley includes the Yakima Valley wine area, as well as Walla Walla Valley and Red Mountain AVAs, which are quite a driving distance apart. (Plan on overnight stays when you visit.) Cooler areas of Washington state produce fine dry Rieslings, Gewürztraminer, and sparkling wines.

The growing season in the Columbia basin is extra long and the grapevines get two more hours of sunshine during the day than Napa Valley. This ideal weather pattern means that almost every vintage year is a good one. Even the deep, nutrient-poor, sandy loam soils are comparable to St. Emilion in Bordeaux, which is why the red Bordeaux varietals do so well in Washington. As evidenced by their huge popularity in the marketplace, Washington Merlots are nearly always premier examples of the grape, especially those from Kiona, L'Ecole No. 41, Woodward Canyon, Andrew Will, Glen Fiona, Seven Hills—and Columbia Crest, Waterbrook, Cougar Crest, and Chateau Ste. Michelle—all wineries that had wines in the *Wine Spectator*'s "top 100" of 2004.

New York State Wines

When I began my wine career in 1977, I became a huge fan of New York wines when I drank Dr. Konstantin Frank Chardonnay. This exceptional Finger Lakes winery continues Dr. Frank's wine heritage with wonderful Rieslings and the very rare Rkatsiteli varietal from Russia, which is a white grape with a crisp, limestone character.

In addition to the Finger Lakes, the Hudson River Valley and Long Island are two other productive wine regions in New York. The Hudson River Valley is known for Pinot Noir and the white hybrid grapes Seyval and Vidal. Long Island's acclaimed North Fork and Hamptons areas produce incredibly fine Cabernet Sauvignon, Cabernet Franc, and Merlot. The Long Island Bordeaux blends from wineries such as Lenz, Palmer, and Millbrook are world class.

From Our Founding Fathers—Wines of Virginia

Thomas Jefferson was such an avid wine grower that he worked mightily—though unsuccessfully—to establish European varieties here, including the first Italian Sangiovese grapes.

Now Virginia boasts an impressive number of wineries spread across six AVAs, including Jefferson's Monticello and George Washington's Birthplace, Northern Neck. When I spoke at the Ritz-Carlton Hotel's annual wine weekend in McLean, Virginia, a few years ago, Virginia wines proved popular among all the participants—not just politicians.

And with good reason. I tasted excellent Chardonnays and incredible Virginia reds including Cabernet Franc, Bordeaux (Cabernet Sauvignon/Merlot) blends, and Norton. Norton is called America's best native red wine grape, and it was discovered in Virginia. Other states also make this very light, dry red that tastes of tart plums.

The Wines of Canada and Baja California, Mexico

Canada's Niagara Peninsula in Ontario is said to produce some of the best Ice Wines outside of Germany. These superb, sweet white dessert wines are made from grapes frozen by winter snows. Collectors' items, such as Inniskillin, sell for $92 per half bottle— twice as much as German Eiswein. But other Niagara brands are more reasonable. Canada Ice Wines also differ from German Eiswein in taste because they are made with more robust American hybrid grapes such as Vidal instead of more delicate German grapes. (See the wines of New Zealand in Chapter 7, "Down Under Wines Up in Quality—Australia, Tasmania, New Zealand, and South Africa," to learn about the lowest-price natural Ice Wine.)

From the uppermost corner of North America's vineyards to the most southwestern corner in Mexico's Baja California, we have covered the cornucopia of our continent's wines.

Summary

We have much to be proud of regarding wine in the U.S.: California's winemaking expertise, Oregon's foresight in bringing Dijon clones from Burgundy, and every state's striving to bring out the best in their *terroir* and grape varieties. American wines lead the world in providing consistent quality and are the pure pleasures to drink. Our wines have also inspired many American chefs and food artisans to produce the world's most varied, healthy, and delicious cuisine. Take a bow, and carry on!

In our next chapter, we travel "down under" to Australia, Tasmania, New Zealand, and South Africa for more New World wine treasure.

7

Down Under Wines Up in Quality—Australia, Tasmania, New Zealand, and South Africa

On October 22, 2004, *USA Today* carried a front page "Money" section article about Australian wine. For the first time in history, it had replaced French wine as America's #2 import wine. Now Australia is looking to surpass our #1 wine exporter, Italy. Great Britain is still Australia's largest export market. A London wine friend told me that fully 45% of England's import wines are now from Australia. (Another 40% come from California.)

Australian wines are wonderful. They use varietal labels like California; and their best whites and reds also include Chardonnay and Cabernet Sauvignon, such as Penfolds "Bin 707." Inexpensive "lifestyle" wines, including Australia's "Yellow Tail" (produced by Casella Estate Winery) are among the most popular red wines (Shiraz and Merlot) in America. And Southcorp's "Little Penguin" line (a better example of these red grape varieties at $6 per bottle) sold 1 million cases its first year in the U.S. Considering that Australia began with wine sales of fewer than 1 million cases to the U.S. in 1990, it is a significant achievement for them to sell almost 20 million cases by 2004.

This chapter explains Australia's finest wine growing regions and their specialties. We will also cover the exciting wines of New Zealand and South Africa, which are on everyone's list of "best buys."

To do list

- ☐ Learn about Australia's geography, winemaking history, and fabulous Shiraz wines
- ☐ Understand how Australian winemakers create top blends
- ☐ Learn about Australian sparkling and dessert wines
- ☐ Identify the top wineries in South Australia
- ☐ Learn about the wines of New South Wales, Victoria, Western Australia, and the island of Tasmania

Winemakers and Winemaking in Australia

Australia's wine country is divided into states, zones, regions, and sub-regions. The six largest wine producing zones are Lower Murray, Big Rivers, North West Victoria, Fleurieu, Barossa, and Limestone Coast, with most of Australia's premium wines coming from these last three zones. Other important zones, based on the high quality of their wines, include the Mount Lofty Ranges zone of South Australia (with its famous regions of Adelaide Hills and Clare Valley), the Hunter Valley zone of New South Wales state around Sydney, the Western Australia zone near Perth with its respected Margaret River region, and the Island of Tasmania. You learn more about each of these wine-producing zones and some top wineries later in this chapter.

Australia is geologically an ancient land, but the timeline of its wine industry closely parallels that of California. Many of the founding wine families of Australia—Penfold, Lindeman, Reynell, Hardy, Seppelt, and Brown—pioneered wineries in the 1860s that continue today. And several of the original South Australia "old vines" Shiraz vineyards they planted more than 100 years ago still produce Australia's finest single-vineyard wines, including Henschke "Hill of Grace."

Now there are more than 1,600 wineries in Australia. Most of the wine production is concentrated in Southeast Australia: from Sydney in New South Wales to Melbourne in Victoria, to Adelaide in South Australia, as well as Western Australia, Queensland, and the island of Tasmania. The variety of Australian wines is as vast as the continent itself.

One out of every 10 wineries in the *Wine Spectator*'s Top 100 for 2004 was Australian, which is an accolade in itself. These 10 outstanding Australian wineries were Greg Norman Estates (yes, owned by the famous golfer), Leeuwin, Elderton, Green Point,

Torbreck, Penfolds, Two Hands, Wolf Blass, Rosemount, and Peter Lehmann. Rosemount (voted "winery and winemaker of the year" in Australia) and Wolf Blass make the most incredible range of wines, including, respectively, top-of-the-line "Balmoral," or "Show Reserves," and "Platinum" or "Black Label" wines. These wineries make some of the finest Chardonnay, dry Sémillion, Cabernet, Merlot, Shiraz, and blends in Australia.

> **tip** Missing from *Wine Spectator*'s top 100 list, but with my vote for most innovative blending and wine names, is the d'Arenberg Winery. It produces the very popular "Stump Jump" Grenache/Shiraz red, "Money Spider" Rousanne (another white Rhône grape similar to Viognier and Marsanne), "Laughing Magpie" Shiraz-Viognier (a blend of red and white Rhône grapes), "Sticks and Stones" Tempranillo blend (Spain's red grape), and "Dead Arm" Shiraz (my favorite).

Australian Shiraz and Blended Wines

Shiraz (pronounced sheer azz', which reminds me of the word pizzazz) is Australia's name for the Syrah grape of France's Rhône region; and, as Australia's universal black grape, it is used to make good to exceptional quality red wines. Australia grows the Shiraz grape in more acres than any other varietal.

Before the Australian government disallowed it, Shiraz was often called "Hermitage" because it is the same Syrah grape used in the famous Hermitage red wine of the Rhône in France. But this was too confusing, so Shiraz and Syrah are the preferred names for this grape. Even the ultimate Australian cult wine and collectible, Penfolds "Grange" 100% Shiraz, is no longer called Grange Hermitage.

Since Australian Shiraz became the U.S.'s most popular red wine, some California wineries have begun labeling their Syrah wines as Shiraz. So don't assume that every Shiraz you encounter will always be from Australia. By the way, it is believed that the Syrah grape first grew thousands of years ago in Ancient Persia, where it was called Shiraz.

Daring Australian winemakers blend Shiraz with Cabernet Sauvignon—something French growers never considered because the grapes come from two very different wine regions in France. The same is true for the unusual Aussie blending of Sémillon and Chardonnay grapes to make their unique Sem-Chard wines. This light, dry, yet fruity style is a better match for Australia's Asian-influenced Pacific Rim cuisine. The same can be said for other interesting white blends from down under, such as Traminer-Riesling.

Perhaps the most intriguing Australian blended red is 3-way GSM, meaning Grenache-Syrah-Mourvèdre. This is the classic blend of red Rhône grapes used in Côtes du Rhône or Château Neuf du Pape. The white Rhône grape Marsanne is also a winner in Australia, where it can be dry or medium-dry and have even more intense tangerine/mandarin orange aromas and flavors than Viognier, while sharing some of its power and full body.

Wine laws require that the first grape named on the label of these blends—as in Cabernet-Shiraz or Shiraz-Cabernet—must have the higher percentage content (though there is no minimum). The actual percentages of each grape used must be specified. It is clear that Australian winemakers make their own rules of blending.

Australian wine laws follow those of the European Union. For an Australian wine to indicate one grape variety or vintage year or region on the label, 85% of the wine must be from that grape or vintage or AGI (Australian Geographic Indication) area.

Down under winemakers not only have that Crocodile Dundee sense of humor; but they also have his fearlessness when it comes to tackling any of the world's grapes, including dark, spicy, luscious red Bordeaux grape Petit Verdot as a separate varietal. My favorite Australian Petit Verdot wines are from Piramimma and Ellens Landing wines.

Australia's Sparkling and Dessert Wines

Aussies also make fruity, red Sparkling Shiraz (remember our Rumball wine label #26 in Chapter 5?), which is my favorite because it is drier than the other sparkling Shiraz, and is fantastic with Asian dishes such as chicken satay in Thai or Indonesian peanut sauce. Terrific *méthode champenoise* sparkling wines are also made in Australia's cool Victoria area where the cool weather grapes Pinot Noir and Chardonnay do so well. Another cool area, Clare Valley in South Australia, produces some of Australia's best Riesling.

Of the dessert wines that have won acclaim for Australia, the three most praiseworthy are Tawny Port (such as Chateau Reynella "Old Cave" Tawny), Botrytis Sémillon (such as DeBortolli "Noble One," Australia's answer to Sauternes), and Reserve Muscat wines—all of which get even better with some cellaring (aging).

Try making an English dessert called "trifle" with alternating layers of pudding and cake soaked with Australian Tawny Port, Reserve Muscat, or Tokay (similar to sweet Muscat, but really the Muscadelle grape). Yum.

South Australia's Wine-Producing Zones and Wineries

The state of South Australia—which is part of the huge land area of Southeast Australia—is Australia's largest wine area in terms of production. It includes the important zones of Barossa, Mount Lofty Ranges, Fleurieu, and Limestone Coast.

note Jan Stuebing of the Australian Wine Bureau in New York City provided statistics and wine zones information for this chapter. I recommend their website if planning a trip to Australia: **www.wineaustralia-usa.com**. Other very helpful Australia wine websites are **www.awbc.com.au**, **www.winestate.com.au** (an Australian wine magazine), **www.australianwines.com** (Southcorp wine importers), **www.pacwine.com** (Pacific Wine Partners, formerly BRL Hardy the largest wine producer), and **www.beringerblass.com.au** (Beringer Blass owns Beringer in California and Wolf Blass in Australia).

Barossa

The Barossa zone north of Adelaide encompasses the Barossa Valley region, one of the oldest wine areas in Australia. Because it's moderately warm and comparable to Bordeaux, it is known for great red wines. The name Barossa refers to its "red soil," which is iron rich and perfect for growing Shiraz, Cabernet, and Merlot. The weather has a broad temperature range but low humidity and rainfall, and plenty of sunshine. This also makes it ideal for producing full-bodied white dry wines and dessert wines. Pioneering wineries located in Barossa Valley include Wolf Blass, Penfolds, Peter Lehman, Seppelt, Dorrien, Yalumba, and Torbreck.

Within the Barossa zone, the region of Eden Valley is located at higher elevations. It has cooler weather, which produces great Chardonnays, elegant Rieslings, rich Shiraz, delicious Reserve Muscat, and world-class Cabernet.

Wineries include Mountadam, Henschke, and Hill-Smith.

YOU *CAN* TAKE IT WITH YOU

Australia's Yalumba Winery, located in the Barossa Valley of South Australia north of Adelaide, is home to a notable innovation in wine labeling. In 2004, Yalumba began distributing wines with easily removable, perforated tear-off tags on the back label. The tags bear the name of the wine. You can keep the tags in your wallet and use them as a reminder when shopping in your local store. These detachable tags are available on Yalumba's "Y Series," which retails for $11/bottle, and the $9 Oxford Landing wines. Thankfully, both brands are widely available.

This is so much easier than trying to do the impossible in soaking off wine labels, which are stuck on with industrial-strength glue (to prevent the labels from falling off in buckets of ice or refrigerators).

Mount Lofty Ranges

The Mount Lofty Ranges zone includes three regions: Adelaide Hills, Adelaide Plains, and Clare Valley. Adelaide Hills, as its name implies, is at higher elevations and has a cool climate with many valleys. This provides diverse microclimates, making it ideal for Pinot Noir and other red and white wines.

Remember, a winery can be located in one region and yet have vineyards or contracts with growers in other regions. That is the case with Wolf Blass, which is located in Barossa but also accurately identifies its wines by the appellation where the grapes were grown, such as Adelaide Hills. Wineries located in Adelaide Hills include Bridgewater Mill, Petaluma, Chain of Ponds, and Shaw & Smith.

Clare Valley, as explained earlier, has some of the coolest weather in Australia. But at its southern end, a significant amount of limestone, some reddish soils, a warmer climate, and many crisscrossing creeks and valleys help create excellent Riesling—even late-harvest or Botrytis Riesling—as well as Chardonnay, Cabernet, and Shiraz. Wineries include Leasingham (gosh, they make wonderful Cabernets), Mount Horrocks, Knappstein, and Mitchell.

Fleurieu

The Fleurieu zone of South Australia has five regions: Currency Creek, Kangaroo Island, Southern Fleurieu, and the two most important, Langhorne Creek (whose most famous winery is Temple Bruer) and McLaren Vale.

The McLaren Vale area descends from the foothills of the Adelaide Hills and Mount Lofty Ranges to the cooling and protective influence of the nearby ocean. As a result of this varied terrain and climate, it produces a considerable variety of grapes including Petit Verdot from Piramimma Winery and Chenin Blanc from Coriole. Other wineries include Hardys, d'Arenberg, Chateau Reynella, and Rosemount Estate.

Limestone Coast

Limestone Coast is a new zone in South Australia with limestone cliffs that overlook the ocean southeast of Adelaide. It is home to excellent Shiraz producers such as the "shark" himself, Greg Norman Estates.

The Limestone Coast zone includes the famous regions of Coonawarra and Padthaway. The Coonawarra region is considered by many wine experts to be Australia's best area for Cabernet. Having "Coonawarra" on the label of a Cabernet or Shiraz makes it more valuable. The reasons these reds are top quality are Coonawarra's unique red *terra rossa* soil, which lies in a thin layer over soft limestone, and its cool, windy, rainy weather except during the sunny summers. Rumball makes their terrific Sparkling Shiraz from Coonawarra grapes. Coonawarra wineries include Wynns Coonawarra, Mildara, and Katnook.

Padthaway lies very near Coonawarra and has similar growing conditions. The patches of reddish soil are great for Pinot Noir (as in Burgundy, France), and its enviable limestone soil vineyards produce some of the greatest Chardonnays in Australia. One of the best-known wineries, Lindemans, prizes its "Padthaway" Chardonnay, and it is a revelation when compared with their inexpensive "Bin 65" Chardonnay. Bin numbers in Australia have no meaning except to an individual winery. They are arbitrary numbers given to certain wines. The idea came from England, which gave arbitrary bin numbers to Sherry and Port.

New South Wales and Its Hunter Valley Zone

New South Wales, abbreviated NSW, is also part of huge land area of Southeast Australia. It is the state that includes the famous Hunter (River) Valley zone north of Sydney.

The volcanic soil in the foothills of the Brokenback Mountains of the Hunter Valley is responsible for many of its excellent Chardonnays. And although Hunter Valley has diverse soils from red to black to white, and wide climate ranges from hot to cool, their world-class Chardonnays have brought them the most prestige. In fact, a special category of wines called "Benchmark" was established for 100% Hunter Valley wines. Wineries include Rosemount Estate, Tyrrell's, Evans Family, McGuigan, Wyndham Estate, and Rothbury. (Rothbury is also the name of the sub-region.)

Victoria's Wine-Producing Zones

The state of Victoria, which includes the city of Melbourne, has several zones and many regions. Victoria has a well-deserved reputation for fine sparkling wines made in the true Champagne method (or *méthode champenoise*), particularly from the cool Region of Yarra Valley. Even French Champagne houses or their California winery partners make sparkling wines in Yarra Valley.

Another Victoria region, Bendigo, is the home of the prized Water Wheel Vineyards and Winery. Its Goulburn Valley region is the home of famous Chateau Tahbilk Winery. Both of these wineries produce award-winning Shiraz. Also, Victoria's Rutherglen and Glenrowan Regions north of Melbourne produce spectacular dessert wines such as Tawny Port, Muscat, and Tokay.

Western Australia and the Margaret River Zone

The city of Perth in the state of Western Australia is located far to the west on the continent of Australia. Perhaps their best wine region, just south of Perth, is Margaret River. Margaret River has the most maritime or ocean-influenced climate in all of Australia. Renowned for great Cabernets and Merlots, Margaret River has the same moderately warm growing conditions, dry climate, and even some of the same gravelly soil as in Bordeaux. Wineries include Evans & Tate, Cullen, Leeuwin Estate, Devil's Lair (producers of "Fifth Leg;" see wine label #5 in Chapter 5), and Cape Mentelle.

Wine-Producing Regions of the Island of Tasmania

Tasmania is the island to the south of mainland Australia. Contrary to the long-standing but erroneous belief that Tasmania was too far south and too cold for growing grapes, this ecologically pristine island has an enviably long growing season with reliably steady weather for ripening grapes before harvest.

As a result, Tasmania produces some of the best Pinot Noir I've ever tasted. Even their "second labels" are wonderful, such as "Ninth Island," made by Pipers Brook winery in northern part of the island. Pipers Brook also produces one of Tasmania's many great *méthode champenoise* sparkling wines from Chardonnay and Pinot Noir

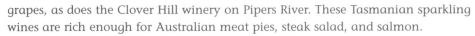

grapes, as does the Clover Hill winery on Pipers River. These Tasmanian sparkling wines are rich enough for Australian meat pies, steak salad, and salmon.

Gewürztraminer and Riesling from Tasmania, especially from Morilla Estate are also fantastic and filled with floral aromas and flavors. (Morilla Estate also includes deluxe accommodations, a restaurant, museum, and tasting room.) Pinot Gris also does well here.

Tasmania's southern coast offers plentiful fishing and great lobster beds from the Tasman Sea. One winery here, Apsley Gorge, is not only run by a former lobsterman, but is also located in what used to be a fish factory. Their specialty is gold medal Pinot Noir and Chardonnay blend—perfect for a steamed lobster dinner.

STEAMED LOBSTER AND AUSTRALIAN WINES

In tribute to my dear friend Anita Schnupp, her husband Steve, and my husband Michael, who's from Boston and Cape Cod, we're going to give you some tips on doing your own fabulous lobster dinner. Anita and Steve treated us to perfectly steamed 3-pound lobsters on their outdoor deck one beautiful summer evening. Anita had ordered ahead, and the Maine lobsters were flown in from New England.

Maine lobster can actually come from anywhere along the north Atlantic coast, from Newfoundland to North Carolina, although one of the best areas is the pristine (less polluted) area of Portland, Maine. Maximum size limit is 4 pounds to protect the breeding stock. Larger lobsters, such as those served at The Palm restaurants, are not from Maine, but probably are from Nova Scotia or Canada.

Female lobsters have wider tails to hold the thousands of eggs (*roe*) they bear. Male lobsters are built for fighting and have bigger claws. Size is not a predictor of quality; in fact, the bigger lobsters are just as sweet as the small ones. It all depends on how you cook them.

Steaming lobsters rather than boiling them is the best method of cooking because it's a slower process with less chance of overcooking. For each pound of lobster, steam approximately 10 minutes or less. Lobsters must be elevated above the level of the water in the pot. Use a rack, colander, or heatproof bowl in the pot to hold the lobsters above the water. Or put some large potatoes in the water at the bottom of the pot and balance a heatproof dish on top of the potatoes to hold the lobsters. The potatoes will cook and provide you with a ready-made side dish.

Steam up to four lobsters per large pot. Add salt, herbs, and lemon to the water. Cover tightly and bring to a boil. Test for doneness by breaking open one of the lobsters where the body meets the tail, but don't break it completely. The tail meat should be white, not translucent. Roe should be bright red when cooked.

Enjoy steamed lobster with a rich, buttery Chardonnay or sparkling wine from Australia or its island of Tasmania.

Enjoying the Wines of New Zealand

New Zealand's location at the far south latitudes of the Southern Hemisphere gives the country a cool, wet climate that produces some of the world's most citrusy, crisp white wines. New Zealand Sauvignon Blancs are known for their gooseberry and ruby red grapefruit flavor profile. They have become a New World standard for that grape variety, in contrast to the old-style weedy or groan-inducing vegetal character of some Sauvignon Blancs.

Consumer Reports magazine regularly reviews wine. In their November 2004 issue, they rated the best Cabernet Sauvignon, Shiraz/Syrah, and Sauvignon Blanc. The only wines that were rated "excellent" were two New Zealand Sauvignon Blancs: Babich 2003 ($13), and Villa Maria Private Bin 2003 ($11), which rated Best Buy. The latter is a screwcap wine from Vineyard Brands (**www.vineyardbrands.com**).

New Zealand is a two-island nation (North Island and South Island). The most pure-fruit Sauvignon Blancs and Chardonnays are made at the northern end of the South Island around Marlborough. The Marlborough appellation on a bottle of New Zealand Sauvignon Blanc, Chardonnay, or Pinot Noir has a certain cachet that brings more money in the marketplace. Some of the best wineries from Marlborough on the South Island include Cloudy Bay, Omaka Springs, Geisen, and Nautilus. Even the native Maori make excellent Pinot Noir under their Tohu label.

> **note** Most New Zealand whites (and reds such as Pinot Noir) are so fresh that they are bottled with screwcaps—even the pricier versions—and receive no barrel fermentation or oak aging. In fact, New Zealand wineries adopted their own "Screwcap Initiative" because they didn't want any possibility of cork taint ruining the bracing, clean taste of their wines.

The North Island is not as uniformly cool and rainy as the South Island. The Bordeaux grapes including Sauvignon Blanc, Cabernet, and Merlot do well here, along with Riesling, Pinot Noir, and Chardonnay in the cooler areas. The four best wine areas on the North Island are Auckland, Hawke's Bay, Gisborne, and Wairarapa. The best wineries in Auckland include Babich, Kumeu River, Matua Valley, Villa Maria, and Nobilo. Te Mata in Hawke's Bay is one of New Zealand's prestige wineries, and Ata Rangi and Martinborough are considered the finest wineries in Wairarapa.

One of the best bargains in New Zealand sparkling wine is the dry, but fruity $10 Lindauer Brut NV. It's not only great for salads, oysters, and Asian cuisine; but it is also perfect for making the popular brunch beverage, Mimosas, made of adding orange juice to sparkling wine.

To do list

- [ ] Learn about coastal South Africa's great wine-growing districts of Paarl and Stellenbosch
- [ ] Choose a fine Pinotage wine from the Overberg or Swartland wine-producing regions

Choosing Great Wines from South Africa— Where Two Oceans Meet

The Dutch grew wine grapes in South Africa as early as 1655. By the 1700s, South Africa's Muscat of Constantia became a world famous dessert wine. French Huguenot settlers brought their winemaking skills with them to the Cape, Africa's southernmost peninsula. A hundred years later, the British developed a need for Cape wine because they were at war with neighboring wine-producer France.

Then Phylloxera and the Anglo-Boer War (1899–1902) negated all previous gains in the fledgling wine industry of South Africa. Only the creation of the KWV (Co-operative Winegrower's Association of South Africa) in 1918 saved the country's wine industry. Today KWV has 4,300 growers and supplies 70% of South Africa's exports. The best of the KWV wines is Rooderberg red; but the organization also sells tons of light, white, medium-dry Chenin Blanc, called *Steen* in South Africa because it is planted in more acres than any other grape.

As a result of sanctions associated with apartheid, South African wines were absent from the American market for almost 20 years. Today, South African wines are back and better than ever. With more than 4,000 producers, the list of wineries has really grown. By the year 2000, South Africa had become the world's 8th largest wine producer.

Wines and Wineries of the Paarl and Stellenbosch Wine Districts

The Cape we refer to as the home of South Africa's vineyards is the country's cool coastal southern peninsula where the Atlantic and Indian Oceans meet. This maritime influence gives its main city, Cape Town, and surrounding river valley vineyards a Mediterranean climate with the Cape Range Mountains as background. Ideal climate and soils, great grapes, and improved viticulture lead to bountiful harvests. And since their location is southern hemisphere, harvests are in February, not September (like Europe or the U.S.).

Among the best viticultural areas, the most important are nearest the coast in the Coastal region or Western Cape. One such prime coastal or cape area is Paarl (meaning "pearl"), named for the lovely town of Paarl, a half-hour drive from Cape Town. Paarl is famous for Rhône grapes such as Shiraz, and wonderful Cabernet, Merlot, Sauvignon Blanc, and Chardonnay. My favorite Paarl wineries include Fairview (the makers of the acclaimed "Primo" Pinotage as well as Goats do Roam; see wine label #1 in Chapter 5), Backsberg (very good Chardonnay), Glen Carlou (very good Merlot), and KWV. Paarl includes the French Huguenot area of Franschhoek, where Boschendal (Sauvignon Blanc wine label in Chapter 5) has a showcase winery.

South of Paarl is the acclaimed Stellenbosch area, closer to and just to the east of Cape Town. It is considered one of South Africa's premier red wine districts. It includes top wineries such as Clos Malverne and Rust en Vrede. Stellenbosch is also the university that trains South Africa's most successful winemakers in enology and viticulture.

South Africa's Overberg and Swartland Regions, and Their Pinotage Grapes

In addition to historic Constantia, the other coastal wine districts are Overberg, home of the new, very cool Walker Bay area of weathered shale soils ideal for excellent Chardonnay and Pinot Noir; Robertson, with its lime rich soil that creates great mineral character in their Chardonnays; and Swartland, which makes great Ports and prize-winning examples of the noble grapes because of improved clonal selections.

This brings me to Pinotage, South Africa's unique red grape. It is a cross between Pinot Noir and the more robust red grape Cinsault (pronounced san soe), which is a red Rhône grape from France similar to Syrah.

Since its birth in 1925, Pinotage has become a symbol of South Africa and is one of its most exciting dry red wines. Imagine a Pinot Noir pumped up on vitamins. That's what Pinotage tastes like. It is also very drinkable when young, ages well, and has a distinctive wild, spicy, earthy, and exotic flavor like Africa itself. Try it with South Africa's meat stew *bobotie* or spicy Latin American dishes or Fusion (Asian/Mediterranean/American) cuisine.

As for ultimate cult wines, South Africa's Bordeaux style reds are their Cadillacs of wine, including the incomparable collectible, Meerlust.

BUYING DOWN UNDER WINES ONLINE

If you would like a detailed price list of wines available for purchase over the Internet from Australia, New Zealand, and South Africa, be sure to order the "Southern Hemisphere Wine Center News" from website www.southerwines.com, or call 1-800-504-9463. You must be 21 years old to order and sign for deliveries. Title passes to the buyer in California.

When you buy six bottles or more of the featured items in their color brochure, you will receive a 10% discount. Members of their Wine Club also receive special pricing for reorders featured in the Wine Club Packs. I love the fact that they arrange their price list by grape variety and type so that you can study all the different Sauvignon Blancs, and so on, before you decide. They also sell quite a number of interesting blends, dessert, and sparkling wines.

KWV wines of South Africa also publishes John Platter's *South African Wines 2004: The Guide to Cellars, Vineyards, Winemakers, Restaurants, and Accommodations*. It is extremely comprehensive. For more information go to www.platterwineguide.com.

Summary

We've shared quite a journey through the intriguing wine countries at the bottom of the world. You are beginning to get the picture—there are so many good wines to try from the most far-flung places. Choosing any one of these bottles from down under is almost as good as traveling to Australia, Tasmania, New Zealand, or South Africa. And maybe these wines will inspire you to pack your bags one day.

In our next chapter, we travel to another part of the Southern Hemisphere—South America—where Chilean and Argentinean wines rule. And in keeping with this Latin wine theme, we will include the spectacular wines of Spain.

Latin Lovers—Chile, Argentina, and Spain

In this chapter:

* Examine narrow Chile's diverse geography, river valley vineyards, and fabulous wineries

* Understand Argentina's signature Malbec wines and its prestigious Mendoza wine region, which benefits from proximity to the Andes Mountains

* Learn the secrets of Spain's organic wines, unique grape varieties, and best winemakers

8

What better valentine to give your sweetie than romantic wines from Chile, Argentina, or Spain? As fiery as their flavorful cuisine, and as passionate as their dances, the Tango and Flamenco, these warm Latin wines turn up the heat without sacrificing softness.

The seductive wines of Chile, Argentina, and Spain have made the wine world swoon for their intensity of flavor, fruit concentration, and sensuality. Their greatest wines are such recent arrivals that they are sold for a song. Allow me to sing their praises by naming the best wine buys from this trinity of countries. Try any of them and you'll get "a tango for your tongue."

To do list

- ❑ Learn how Chile's long Pacific coastline creates an ideal maritime climate
- ❑ Identify Chile's 13 river valley wine regions
- ❑ Learn how to read Chilean wine labels

Chile's Magnificent Climate, Wine, and Cuisine

Chile (pronounced *chee' lay*) is a major wine-producing country in South America. Chile's mouth-watering foods and wines come from a diverse and impressive geography that covers four major climate zones from the hot, dry deserts in the north to the cold Antarctic influences in the south; and from the magnificent snow-capped Andes Mountains in the east to the fish-filled, cool Pacific Ocean in the west.

Spanish settlers coming from Peru first planted grapevines in Chile in 1551c. That's 200 years before the Spanish missions brought grapes to California. Beyond the introduction of viticulture by the Spanish, Chile and California share other similarities associated with the production of fine wines. Chile is only about 110 miles wide, but its Pacific coastline is more than 2,600 miles long. This incredibly long coastline along its western border isn't Chile's only wine-related similarity to California. The

midpoint of Chile's wine country is at the same latitude south (36 degrees) as Napa Valley is north. Chile's topography is also similar to California's; Chile's coastal range of mountains separates the Pacific from the Central Valley and Andes Mountains plateau, as well as the highlands further east. All of Chile's wine regions have ideal Mediterranean climates, and three-fourths of their 44,000 acres are planted in red grapes (the remainder in white grapes). Chile is now the fifth-largest exporter of wine to the world, enjoying yearly increases in sales of 20%.

> **tip** Chile makes incredibly good olive oil, particularly the Olave brand. Chile is also a top exporter of paprika, farmed salmon and scallops, frozen strawberries, tomato paste, raisins, and almonds. And Chile grows huge amounts of nectarines, apricots, and eating grapes that and arrive ripe and fresh in the U.S. during our winter months. Their culinary success is a direct result of their good agricultural practices and work ethic.

Chile's Wine Regions

Thirteen Chilean valleys benefit from rivers fed by snow-melt water from the Andes. The *terroir* in these valleys provides consistently excellent conditions for growing superior wine grapes. These 13 river valleys were first adopted as Chile's wine regions, each with its own DO, or *Denominaciones de Origen*, in 1994. All of them benefit from the Pacific's mild Humboldt Current, which closely brushes Chile's coastline. The following is a discussion of Chile's 13 wine regions and their finest wineries. These river valley DOs have replaced the generic Central Valley appellation on most Chilean wine labels.

The semi-desert Coquimbo Region is Chile's northernmost wine region. It encompasses the Elqui and Limarí River valleys. The Elqui area is known for Syrah grapes, and the Limarí valley is famous for its organic vineyards.

Further south is the Aconcagua Valley wine region, home of one of Chile's finest and oldest wineries—Errázuriz. This winery was founded in the mid-1800s at the same time as Carmen, Concha y Toro, and Cousiño Macul wineries, and is located in the middle of this dry, bright, transverse valley. Boxed in by the Coastal Range, the valley's midsection is perfect for red grapes. Both the Errázuriz "Don Maximiano" and the Seña Winery's highly prized Cab blends are testaments to that. (The Seña Winery is a joint venture of the Chadwick family of Errázuriz and Robert Mondavi.)

The cool Casablanca Valley wine region, similar in climate to California's Carneros region, is very near the coast northwest of Santiago. The Morandé Winery in this area makes sublime Chardonnay, Sauvignon Blanc, and Pinot Noir from Casablanca grapes—all are worth twice their price.

The Veramonte Winery is also located in the Casablanca wine region. I've mentioned their top-of-the-line red blend "Primus" before as a partner for upscale Mexican dark chocolate mole sauce. And Casa Lapostolle, directed by Alexandra Marnier-Lapostolle of the Grand Marnier (liqueur) family of France, makes their excellent "Alexandre Cuvée" Chardonnay (and Merlot and Syrah) from Casablanca Valley vineyards. Just south of this wine region is the San Antonio Valley region, another good Chardonnay and Pinot Noir area. The Leyda winery is in this region.

Chile's largest wine region (in number of wineries) is Maipo Valley, home to reasonably priced Santa Rita, Yelcho and Santa Carolina Wineries. Maipo surrounds Chile's capital city of Santiago, making it the world's largest urban wine region. Visitors have a choice of dozens of top wineries, including Viñedo Chadwick (the family that owns Errázuriz), which makes Chile's most expensive red. Maipo is also home to Concha y Toro (whose premium Cabernet "Don Melchor" 2000 [$41] is outstanding and a *Wine Spectator*'s Top 100 wine of 2004) and top-of-the-line Viña Almaviva Winery, which is co-owned by Château Mouton-Rothschild of Bordeaux. Also in Maipo is another French Bordeaux venture, the Aquitania Winery, owned by Bruno Prats of Château Cos d'Estournel and Paul Pontallier of Château Margaux. Chile impressed the French!

note Morandé also has one of the top-rated restaurants in Chile: House of Morandé.

Traveling a little further south, nestled in the Andes, we reach the Cachapoal Valley a top red wine area. Morandé is headquartered here and has contracts with vineyards that are the source of their divine "limited edition" Cabernet Franc, Carmenère, and Syrah.

The well-known Colchagua Valley around Santa Cruz is another prime Cabernet area, as evidenced by the excellent reds from Casa Silva, Montes, La Playa, Casa Lapostolle

tip The Cachapoal and Colchagua regions formerly were considered a single wine region, known as the Rapel Valley. These two wine regions have achieved their own individual identities, so their names (as the source of the grapes) have replaced "Rapel" on many wine labels.

(whose "Clos Apalta" red Bordeaux blend was a *Wine Spectator* "top 100" wine), and Viu Manent, which is one of Chile's best producers of Carmenère. The Los Vascos winery in this region also is owned by the Bordeaux company, Domaines Rothschild of Chateau Lafite-Rothschild.

note   For more information on the wines of Chile, go to www.winesofchile.org.

The Curicó Valley wine region is home to Valdivieso and the Miguel Torres winery owned by the famous Torres family of Spain. The Miguel Torres winery is recognized for Cab, Merlot, and Cab Franc.

Further south is Chile's largest wine region in size, the Maule Valley. This region grows Cab, Carmenère, and a large amount of the non-noble, very light País red grape, which is the same variety as California's original Mission grape. Maule is the home of the Calina Winery, owned by California's Kendall-Jackson.

Chile's southernmost wine regions are the Itata, Bío Bío, and Malleco Valleys. These regions also grow the País and Moscatel de Alexandria (sweet white) grapes, but the very cool areas in these three valleys show increased plantings of Riesling, Pinot Noir, and Chardonnay.

Chilean Wine Labeling and Vintages

As we've already mentioned, Chile uses a system of "names of origin" called *Denominaciones de Origen* (DO), just like Spain. However, unlike French wines, Chile names most of its wines by grape variety. Chile also abides by European Union wine laws that require varietal wines be a minimum of 85% of the grape variety named on the label.

The term *Reserve* on a Chilean wine label has no legal meaning. But, in my experience, all of the Chilean Reserve Merlot, Cabernet Sauvignon, Carmenère, Cabernet Franc, or Syrah I've tasted have been much better than the non-reserve versions and cost just a couple of dollars more. If your taste buds have been burned by low-end, bulk-processed, large-bottle wines, I strongly recommend you upgrade your Chilean wine pleasure. You won't have to bust your budget to do it. Remember, most Chilean wines are sold for a song.

Chile's very temperate wine country climate also means that most vintage years are good ones. In fact, every vintage year from 1998 to 2002 was rated very good to excellent (2001), with 2003 rated outstanding. These are the vintages that collectors will collect.

CHILE'S LINK TO FRANCE: THE CARMENÈRE GRAPE

Though Merlot is Chile's most popular wine, the most sought-after red wine from Chile is Carmenère. Like Merlot, this red grape originated from Bordeaux, France. Carmenère is actually considered to be the *antecedent* (ancestor) of Cabernet Sauvignon, but it was allowed to die out in the vineyards of Bordeaux. French immigrants brought Carmenère (without Phylloxera) to Chile in the nineteenth century. Often mislabeled as Merlot in Chile, Carmenère ripens later than Merlot and makes an intensely purple wine with plum, coffee bean, mint, and bell pepper flavors. Chile is the only country in the world that grows as much Carmenère for its own separate varietal wine. It is also fabulous when blended with Cabernet Sauvignon and Cabernet Franc in Chile's top reds.

Chile never had Phylloxera during the European plague because of the country's formidable geographic barriers. As a result, Chile's grapevines remained ungrafted and were provided back to France so they could recover from Phylloxera. The vines that Chile grows now are descendants of these nineteenth-century ungrafted vines, which, for the most part remain ungrafted. Some wine experts believe this accounts for the high quality of Chile's wine grapes.

Argentine Wines Tango For Your Tongue

Spanish missionaries first planted grapes in Argentina in 1562, though the noble varieties arrived with the Italian, French, and Spanish immigrants of the mid-nineteenth century. Today, Argentina's 500-mile-long wine country has hundreds of wineries. In fact, Argentina makes as much wine as the U.S. Chile may have the limelight in exports, but Argentina's potential is as vast as the Andes.

Argentina is a huge country, with equally large vineyard areas. Argentina has a system of controlled *appellations* (names of origin), the first of which was Lujan de Cuyo in the Upper Mendoza River Valley.

Argentina's most important wine region is the Mendoza, which is really an arid, desert area fed by river water from the snow-packed Andes Mountains that separate Argentina from Chile. The Mendoza wine region contains five distinct sub-regions, and these geographic indications are used on Argentinean wine labels. One of Mendoza's subregions, Maipu (not to be confused with Chile's Maipo Valley) is also one of Argentina's greatest wine areas. Another of these sub-regions, Valle de Uco, produces two delicious Malbecs: B Crux (imported by Jorge Ordoñez), and the Malbec wines of JF Lurton (a French winemaker with wineries in both Chile and Argentina).

Mendoza is where 75% of Argentina's wine is produced—40% of which is made from the red Bordeaux grape Malbec. Argentine Malbec has a coveted deep, black/red color, aromas of chocolate and raspberry with a satin mouth feel, cherry cordial aftertaste, and elegant finish with some heat and a lick of wood.

Bodegas Salentin (sometimes spelled Salentein) in the Mendoza area of Argentina makes some of the yummiest Malbec and Cabernet Sauvignon for the incredible price of $12 to $14 a bottle. I was surprised by the quality of these reds (and their Chardonnay, too). But I was flabbergasted when I tasted their "second label" El Portillo, which was only $6 to $7 a bottle. The El Portillo reds, especially the Merlot, blew me away with their richness—so much so that I just had to put both the Salentin Malbec and the El Portillo Merlot on the next wine list I did for a restaurant client—and customers loved them.

Other major Mendoza wineries include Bodegas Salentin, Navarro-Correas, Norton, Don Rodolfo, Ben Marco, Susana Balbo, and Vallentín Bianchi. The latter winery's Cabernet Sauvignon San Rafael Famiglia 2002 ($18) was a *Wine Spectator*'s Top 100 wine.

Since 1990, Argentina's viticultural standards have risen because of the work of top enologists such as Michel Rolland from Bordeaux, who consulted for Argentina's well-known Trapiche winery. And progressive winery owners such as Nicolas Catena created a quality revolution that attracted many French and California wineries to invest in Argentina. His Bodega (winery) Catena Zapata 2002 Mendoza Malbec ($22) was a *Wine Spectator*'s Top 100 wine in 2004, and his "Agrelo Vineyard" Chardonnay is a hit with consumers.

The rest of the wine trade has praised Argentina *terroir* and also climbed aboard, including California wineries, French Champagne companies, and the great Château Cheval-Blanc of St. Emilion in Bordeaux, which makes Cheval de los Andes in Argentina (a joint venture with well-known Argentinean winery Terrazas de los Andes, owned by Domaine Chandon of California).

To do list

- ☐ Learn Spain's wine regions and wine labeling standards
- ☐ Identify the grapes varieties and wineries behind some of Spain's best wines

Wonderful Wines of Spain

Spain has more grapevines planted than any other country in the world, but its arid climate limits production. This is turning out to be a very good thing for the quality of its wines. The excitement is in finding those new bargain reds from previously untapped areas. Spain's new winemakers deserve a prominent place on the world stage.

Spain's Wine Regions and Wine Label Designations

As in France and Italy, Spain has government wine laws that control the names of origin and quality levels of wines from more than 50 *Denominaciones de Origen* (DO) viticultural areas. Two of these wine areas are given the highest ranking of DOCa or *calificada* (classified)—Rioja and Priorato (often called Priorat).

Spain's most important wine regions and DOs are

- Cataluña (around Barcelona), which includes the prestige DOs of Penedés and Priorato as well as Tarragona, Terra Alta, Costers del Segre, and CAVA for sparkling wines
- Aragón (on the Ebro River), whose most important DOs are Rioja, Campo de Borja, and Navarra
- Castilla y Leon (on the Duero River), which includes the important DO Ribera del Duero and the increasingly popular DOs of Rueda, Toro, Bierzo, Cigales, and Calatayud (at far eastern end of the Duero)
- Alicante, which includes one of my favorite DOs Jumilla
- Valencia
- La Mancha
- Jerez (the DO for Sherry and Brandy)
- Galicia (on the Atlantic Ocean in the upper northwest), whose best area, Rías Baixas, is the home of Albariño, Spain's great dry white for seafood (See Chapter 5 Wine Label).

Spanish wine laws strictly limit growing area, permitted grapes, wine types, alcohol content, and aging levels for the great reds. Under Spain's DO wine laws the highest classification is *DOCa*, the *Ca* meaning *Calificada*, or qualified wine region. So far, Rioja and Priorato are the only two DOCa wines and areas. Varietal wines named by grape rather than place of origin are under the categories of *Vino de la Tierra*, which is equivalent to French *Vins de Pays* (or Italian IGT wines). Spanish wine laws specify three other levels, with Vino de Mesa being the lowest.

Newer grape growing areas in Spain, such as Extremadura and Calatayud, shorten the wood aging of their Crianza wines to keep them fresher and grapier. The youngest wines are *Joven* or *Sin Crianza* wines, made without any oak aging.

Spain's Great Grapes, Wines, and Wineries

In the last few years, we have thrilled to the taste of Tempranillo, wine made from Spain's silky smooth native red grape. Tempranillo makes an elegant, yet rich, warm, and inviting red in several of Spain's famous wine regions, including Rioja. Spain also grows several of the Bordeaux grape varieties. The Torres family of

Spain's Penedés wine region north of Barcelona even makes a 100% Cabernet Sauvignon wine called "Mas La Plana" that's world famous.

Spain's other exciting red grape is *Garnacha*, Spanish for the Grenache grape, which is one of several Rhône grapes planted in Spain, including Syrah, Carignane, and Mourvèdre (called *Monastrell* in Spain). Like Tempranillo, Garnacha can be blended with Cabernet Sauvignon and/or Merlot. On its own, Garnacha makes a velvety, concentrated, dark, spicy/berry red wine. Some of today's finest examples come from the tiny but prestigious region of Priorat, sixty miles southwest of Barcelona. Many of Priorato's wines are collectors' items. The Scala Dei Priorato Cartoixa 2000 $26 was a *Wine Spectator*'s Top 100 of 2004. Several 100% Monastrell wines from Jumilla DO are fabulous and reasonably priced.

Ribera del Duero is one of the most popular types of red wine from Spain. Ribera del Duero vineyards are grown on lime-rich soils, perfect for red Bordeaux grape varieties, and Tempranillo and Garnacha. Two of Spain's legendary reds, Vega Sicilia and Pesquera, are Ribera del Duero wines. Most Ribera del Duero reds are great values. (My favorite is Capellanes.) These varietal wines carry the grape name Tempranillo on the label and must be a minimum of 85% Tempranillo under EU wine laws. The local names for Tempranillo in Ribero de Duero are Tinto Fino or Tinto del Paris.

I also must rave about the reds of Toro, which are also made from Tempranillo (called Tinta de Toro). Many of the Toro winery estate vines are ungrafted and very old, which is the secret of their licorice or chocolate cherry richness. Their Termes 2002 ($24) was a *Wine Spectator*'s Top 100 wine. If you can ever afford their $50 Numanthia, you'll say it's one of the best wines you've ever tasted.

Spanish reds are best with *paella* (saffron rice with chicken, sausage, and seafood), Serrano ham, and *tapas* (Spanish appetizers) of olives or shrimp. Spanish reds also are divine accompaniments to fabulous Spanish cheeses: Manchego (sheep's milk cheese); Murcia al Vino (a tangy cow's milk cheese with a purple rind from being washed in wine); soft, buttery Tetilla; and the natural blue cheese, Cabrales.

Spain's modern white wines are made in a crisp, citrusy pineapple style. Try the lovely, clean Verdejo grape variety, which is the same *Verdelho* grape used to make Madeira. Try the Martinsancho brand from major importer Classical Wines of Spain. Spain also grows the unusual Torrontes white grape, but I prefer Argentina's Susana Balbo version of this grape. And Spain's delicious, dry Rosés, such as Marqués de Caceres Rosado, are perfect partners for quiche or omelets and brunch.

Spain's best sparkling wines are called CAVA, which means they are made in the true *méthode champenoise* or *méthode traditionelle*. Spanish white grapes such as Parellada and Xarello, as well as Macabeo (also known as Viura), are used to make their sparkling wines, although Chardonnay is also allowed. Spanish sparkling wines from Freixenet (especially their Rosé sparkler Brut de Noirs) or Codorniu are incredible values. Segura Viudas Winery's Brut Heredad Reserva is wonderful as well and is another excellent value. CAVAs make great Mimosas for brunch (sparkling wine with orange juice), and are a perfect aperitif (before-dinner wine). They are terrific with *tapas*.

Summary

The splendid wines of Spain, Chile, and Argentina are as exciting as their Latin culture. Critics hail each new release, and the public rejoices at the prices. And what better reds to wash down slice after slice of fire-roasted meats served in those very popular Brazilian steak houses? Without Chilean Carmenère, Argentina Malbec, or Spanish Tempranillo, we wouldn't be able to digest the meat well enough to romance our dinner partners.

In our next chapter, we cover the French classics.

French Me! Choosing Wines from the Great Wine Regions of France

It's taken me 26 years to perfect my technique for teaching French wines, which includes a lot of humor and cajoling students to do their homework. I even created a T-shirt called "French Me!" that summarized French wines and the grapes used to make them: "The French Originals," Bordeaux = Cabernet and Merlot; Rhône = Syrah and Viognier; Burgundy = Chardonnay and Pinot Noir; Beaujolais = Gamay; Loire = Sauvignon and Chenin Blanc; Alsace = Riesling, Gewürztraminer, Pinot Gris and Pinot Blanc; Real Champagne = French! *Compris?*

In this chapter, you learn about all of these wonderful wines and the French regions in which they're produced.

In this chapter:

* Learn about the Bordeaux region of France and its incomparable wines

* Understand why true Champagne is only made in France

* Learn about the wines of the Burgundy region, from Chablis to Beaujolais

* Learn how to choose great wines from the Loire Valley, Alsace, Rhône, Languedoc, and Provence

To do list

- [ ] Learn the districts and villages of Bordeaux and how these translate to "controlled names of origin"
- [ ] Understand how Bordeaux wines are blended
- [ ] Discover the difference between Bordeaux and Burgundy vineyard classifications

Great Wines of Bordeaux

The Bordeaux region in southwestern France on the Atlantic Ocean has been famous for red wines since the twelfth century, when Henry II's marriage to Eleanor of Aquitaine gave the English control of this region. The English developed a special relationship with the red wines of Bordeaux, calling them *claret*, which, by definition, is any red Bordeaux wine. Bordeaux red wines are blends of Cabernet Sauvignon, Merlot, Cabernet Franc, Malbec, and Petit Verdot in any combination. The great white wines of Bordeaux can be blends of any combination of Sauvignon Blanc, Sémillon, and Muscadelle. Though the area also produces some Rosé, the Bordeaux estate reds command the attention.

Bordeaux Wine Districts and Their Blends

The Romans planted the first vineyards in Bordeaux. They appreciated its special geographic features—gentle hillsides facing due east into the sun with forest and ocean at the back for protection and moderate climate. They also admired the deep gravel soil and the native black Cabernet Sauvignon grape. Figure 9.1 whos where the bordeaux wine region is located. You also can refer to this figure for the locations of the other regions discussed in this chapter.

FIGURE 9.1
The great wine
regions of France.

Bordeaux includes five major wine districts:

- *Haut-Médoc*—located along the left bank of the Gironde River, produces great, predominantly Cabernet Sauvignon red wines

- *Graves*—named for the gravel soil, produces dry red wines made from Cabernet and Merlot blends, and dry white wines made from Sauvignon Blanc and Sémillon

- *Sauternes*—a district renowned for sweet white dessert wines made predominantly from Botrytis Sémillon

- *St. Emilion*—a district of sand and limestone soils, well-known for dry reds made mostly with Cabernet Franc and Merlot grapes

- *Pomerol*—whose reds are the original Merlots.

All Bordeaux reds are blends of two or more of the five Bordeaux grapes: Cabernet Sauvignon, Merlot, Cabernet Franc, Malbec, and Petit Verdot. The proportion of each variety planted differs from one *château* (or estate) to the next. These grape varieties have layers of berry, mint, plum, or cedar; when blended, they create a smoother and more elegant, complex wine than any of them alone could produce. Blending also makes Bordeaux winemakers less dependent on one varietal and allows them to increase the percentage of the grapes that do better in each vintage.

White Bordeaux wines are usually blends of the three main white Bordeaux grapes: Sauvignon Blanc, Sémillon, and Muscadelle (not to be confused with the French Loire wine Muscadet). To make dry white Graves wines, winemakers use more of the lighter, herbal, and citrusy Sauvignon Blanc, adding small amounts of Sémillon grapes with its fig-like flavor for richness.

To make the luscious white dessert wine Sauternes, sweet, late-harvest, and Botrytis-covered Sémillon grapes are used with maybe a tiny bit of the other two white grapes. Sauternes is fantastic with apple or pumpkin cake or pie.

Bordeaux Châteaux and Their Classifications

For the Paris Exposition of 1855, Bordeaux wine brokers sorted through thousands of châteaux to come up with the 1855 Classification of the Médoc, which is a ranking of great reds (no whites) from the Haut-Médoc (the brokers also included one red wine from Graves). Only 61 châteaux are listed in the 1855 Classification, categorized into five levels of quality called *Five Growths,* or *Crus*. Within each of the five levels of quality, the estates are considered equal.

This official classification is valid today because its ranking still determines price. Because there have been changes in land holdings since 1855, the current list of châteaux and their *cru*, or level of quality, is provided in Appendix E, "Bordeaux Classifications and Burgundy Vineyards," at the back of this book. The 1855 Classification of the red wines of the Haut-Médoc is referred to often by every wine importer, distributor, or retailer that sells the listed châteaux, and by wine writers who rate their current vintages. Separate classifications were done for other types of Bordeaux wines, including Graves and St. Emilion. Condensed versions of these are also provided in Appendix E.

Most people have heard the names of the five châteaux (abbreviated "Ch.") in the *First Growth*: Ch. Lafite-Rothschild, Ch. Latour, Ch. Margaux, Ch. Mouton-Rothschild, and Ch. Haut-Brion (the only Graves in the list). Except for Haut-Brion, every château in the 1855 Classification is from the Haut-Médoc. Wines of the Haute-Médoc often are further classified by the names of the region's important wine *communes* or villages. These four commune names and Haut-Médoc are the AOCs of these classified châteaux:

- *Margaux,* which produces the smoothest, most berry-like reds
- *St. Julien,* which produces wines that are somewhat tannic and concentrated
- *Pauillac,* which produces wines called the classic clarets, because they live so long
- *St.-Estèphe,* which is the furthest north of the communes and produces the darkest black wines

Wines from the châteaux listed in the 1855 classification are designated *cru classé* (classified growths) on the front label. The *cru classé* designation is protected by wine laws and its use is limited to Bordeaux. Cru classé wines are also designated *Mis en bouteilles au Château* on the label, which means the wine was grown, produced and bottled at a real château.

If you cannot afford the high prices of the prestige reds in the 1855 Classification, you can buy their second labels (read the nearby sidebar) or buy wine produced at smaller estates from these same four red wine communes for a lot less money! When you go wine shopping, look for these famous red appelations, or AOCs. They have to be good, or they wouldn't be from the same commune as the great estates. You can also save money by buying the Cru Bourgeois red wines from the Médoc that were never classified in 1855 but received honorable mention—see Appendix E for a list of the best of these. Other districts of Bordeaux also produce great bargain wines.

SAVING MONEY WITH SECOND-LABEL WINES

Château owners use "second labels" to sell some of their great red Bordeaux wines that were made from younger vines or that weren't of high enough quality to bear the estate's classified main label. Second label wines are wonderful bargains. There has been an explosion of second labels in all areas of Bordeaux, but identifying these wines can be quite difficult. Often the only way to know for sure is to look up the names in Robert M. Parker's books, *Bordeaux* or *The Wine Buying Guide* (both published by Simon & Schuster).

Sometimes you can recognize second labels by the words *Société Civile du Château* in the fine print at the bottom of the front label, which tells who made the wine. For example, on the label of La Réserve du Général, which is the second label of Château Palmer, it actually reads "Société Civile du Château Palmer." Other famous châteaux use their top wine's name as part of the second label's name, such as Le Pavillon Rouge de Château Margaux, Pagodes de Cos (of Ch. Cos d'Estournel), or Lady Langoa (of Ch. Langoa-Barton). Most second labels cost half as much as main labels.

The One and Only: French Champagne

The Champagne region extends into the northeast of France from its border with Belgium. As you learned in Chapter 3, "Winemaking—The Six Basic Types of Wine," the world's most famous sparkling wine is Champagne—a title that can legally be applied only to wine made in the Champagne region, using the *méthode champenoise*.

In Chapter 3, we described the detailed *méthode champenoise* process, which results in the tiny bubbles of carbon dioxide that are trapped in the Champagne during a second in-the-bottle fermentation. Pick up any bottle of sparkling wine; if the label says "Product of France" and has the one word Champagne on it (the AOC), then it's real French Champagne.

France's great Champagne houses create their own "house blend," or style of Champagne, by blending Pinot Noir and Pinot Meunier black

note All wine writers have their favorite Champagnes. *Wall Street Journal* wine columnists Dorothy J. Gaiter and John Brecher wrote an article comparing vintages of Dom Perignon. *Wine Spectator* named Piper-Heidsieck 1995 as a "top 100 in 2004."

I think you should try Gosset 1996; it has delicious green apple and pear flavors and a classic Brut (dry) style. And certainly Veuve Clicquot Champagne **www.clicquotinc.com** is a "must have" for celebrations, especially their top-of-the-line vintage La Grande Dame Brut and Rosé, named in honor of the young widow (*veuve*) Clicquot. It was she who developed the process for removing the heavy sediment of yeast from Champagne in the nineteenth century. And Clicquot's elegant CEO, Mireille Guiliano, has written a best-selling (2005) book of diet secrets and recipes called *French Women Don't Get Fat: The Secret of Eating for Pleasure.*

grapes with the white grape, Chardonnay. To learn about the *méthode champenoise* and some of the great Champagne houses and vintages, see Chapter 3.

Champagne is an incredibly versatile wine. Despite claims to the contrary, Champagne is marvelous with smoked salmon and garnishes of diced boiled egg and onion. Salty, briny capers, too much soy sauce, or wasabi can overpower Champagne. Sushi/sashimi, Thai, or other Asian cuisines are terrific with Champagne, as are quiche, pasta salads, turkey, pork, fish meuniere, trout mousse, lob-

> **tip** Watch your wine and salt intake when drinking Champagne. Those bubbles seem to push the alcohol faster, and salty foods make you very thirsty.

ster, crab, shrimp, oysters, any mushroom dish, and St. André triple créme French cheese, which has the highest butterfat content (75%) of any cheese in the world. A little sip, a little taste—*magnifique*!

To do list

- ☐ Understand Burgundy's controlled appellations of origin or AOCs
- ☐ Learn to identify wines from each of Burgundy's wine-growing regions

Burgundy's Great Pinot Noir, Chardonnay, and Beaujolais Wines

By 1789, the French Revolution caused the division of the Burgundy vineyards among many small farmers. Then the Napoleonic Code of Inheritance gave every child an equal part of the estate upon the death of the parents. The resulting fragmentation of ownership of the Burgundy vineyards carries to the present day. Several famous vineyards have as many as 80 owners—all legally allowed to bottle wine under the name of the vineyard. To help you appreciate the extent of this fragmentation, consider that the average Bordeaux estate vineyard occupies about 200 acres and produces almost 24,000 cases of wine each year; in Burgundy, individual vineyards average 5–17 acres and produce fewer than 4,000 cases each year.

Burgundy is home to outstanding Pinot Noir, Chardonnay, and Beaujolais wines. Both white Chardonnay and red Pinot Noir Burgundy wines are aged in *Limousin oak* for added complexity and body. Both white and red Burgundies also go through *malolactic fermentation* to soften their acidity, make them more drinkable, and add a wonderful buttery quality to the Chardonnay.

The great Burgundies are worth every penny of their high prices. Fine Côte de Beaune white Burgundies from Puligny-Montrachet, for example, are vanilla accented, lemony, buttery rich, full-flavored wonders that fill every crevice of the palate and make a perfect marriage with elegant seafood such as lobster or crab. Fine Côte de Nuits red Burgundies from Chambolle-Musigny, on the other hand, are like bottled silk and satin with varietal aromas of roses, violets, and strawberries, with high acidity, smooth tannins, and a harmonious soft finish.

Understanding Burgundy's AOC Designations

Under French wine laws, Burgundy vineyards are rated *Grand Cru* for the best. *Premier Cru* is the designation for vineyard sites that are considered second best. The *Grand Crus* are single vineyards with the finest *terroir,* or conditions of soil, climate, and geography. The *Premier Cru* designation can be applied to single vineyards with second-best locations, or in the Côte Chalonnaise area of Burgundy, to villages or communes making wines that deserve this special rating. *Grand Cru* vineyards are rare. Only 7 exist in Chablis and 32 in the Côte d'Or. The wines they produce are expensive. *Premier Crus* number several hundred, but their wines are more affordable than *Grand Cru* wines and much better than regular village wines. Refer to Appendix E for a complete list of these vineyards.

It is easy to determine whether you are looking at a wine produced by a *Grand Cru* or *Premier Cru* vineyard. The AOC designation is listed on the bottle, as in *Appellation Chablis Grand Cru Contrôlée.* The name of the single vineyard rated *Grand Cru* will be printed above this in quote marks, as in *"Le Clos."* Do not confuse "Grand Cru Classé" châteaux in the Classifications of Bordeaux with *Grand Cru* single vineyards in Burgundy.

> **tip** The producer's reputation is your clue to the quality of the wine. The best Burgundy producers are Louis Jadot, Bouchard Père & Fils, Louis Latour, Joseph Drouhin, Domaine Leroy, Olivier Laflaive, Alain Gros, Faiveley, Prince de Merode, Marquis de Laguiche, Domaine de la Romane'e-Conti (abbreviated DRC) and the Hospices de Beaune (vineyards that support the local charity hospital).

Since most of the vineyards in Burgundy are divided up into small parcels, only those wines labeled *Mis au Domaine* are estate bottled. Very few Burgundy wines are domaine bottled, and even fewer are labeled *Monopole,* which means the entire vineyard is owned by one person or firm. Most small growers sell to large brokers in the city of Beaune. These brokers bottle the wine under their own labels.

Choosing Wines from Burgundy's Wine Growing Regions

Burgundy has five major districts, four of which are the original homes of Chardonnay and Pinot Noir:

- *Chablis,* a region of rich limestone soils that produces 100% Chardonnay whites

- *Côte d'Or,* which is divided into the *Côte de Nuits* area, where the greatest 100% Pinot Noir red Burgundies are made; and the *Côte de Beaune* area to the south, where some of the greatest 100% Chardonnay white Burgundy wines are made

- *Côte Chalonnaise*, where less expensive Pinot Noir and Chardonnays are produced

- *Mâconnais,* home of the famous 100% Chardonnay Pouilly-Fuissé

- *Beaujolais,* famous for dry but fruity, lighter style reds made from Gamay grapes planted in soils of granite or sand

The following is a brief description of the Burgundy districts and their best wines.

Chablis

Under the French wine laws, French Chablis can only be made from 100% Chardonnay grapes. The rare limestone soils in this area give its Chablis wines a mineral and lime quality, tart racy acidity, and flinty dry finish that make them one of France's most desirable seafood wines. Chablis is usually un-oaked (stainless steel fermented), except for the *Grand Crus*; but it retains its freshness and brilliance for several years of bottle aging.

The best Chablis comes from the *Grand Cru* single vineyards: Les Clos, Valmur, Vaudésir, Bougros, Les Preuses, Blanchot, and Grenouilles. The finest of the 40 *Premier Cru* single vineyards are Montée de Tonnerre, Fourchaume, Vaillons, and Montmains. Thank God, the Appellation Contrôlée on both types of labels will clearly say either *AOC Chablis Grand Cru* or *AOC Chablis Premier Cru*, with the name of the single vineyard above in quote marks. The greatest Chablis producers include Domaine Moreau, La Chablisienne, Michel Laroche.

Côte d'Or—Côtes de Nuits and Beaune

Home of the priciest red and white Burgundy wines, the *Côte d'Or* (meaning "slope of gold") is only 30 miles long and less than a mile wide. Wines produced by *Grand Crus* vineyards in the Côte de Nuits are more full-bodied and live much longer than other Burgundy reds. The same is true of *Grand Cru* whites from the Côte de Beaune, but their production is limited. The names of these *Grand Cru* single vineyards from both the Côtes de Nuits and Côtes de Beaune are listed in Appendix E. All of the wines have *Grand Cru* written in the AOC on the label, so you don't have to memorize the vineyards.

Many of the *Premier Cru* or even village wines from the Côtes de Nuits or Côtes de Beaune are much better values for money. The difference can be from $35 for a village wine such as Gevrey-Chambertin to $55 for a Gevrey-Chambertin *Premier Cru* to $150 for a wine produced by a *Grand Cru* single vineyard in that commune. To further the marketing of their village wines, Burgundy villages or communes in both parts of the Côtes d'Or hyphenate their commune name with the name of the most famous *Grand Cru* vineyard in their village. That's how we get Gevrey-Chambertin, for example.

Côte Chalonaise

South of the Côtes d'Or, the Côte Chalonnaise region has good white and red wines made from 100% Pinot Noir and Chardonnay grapes. The Chalonnaise region used to be the home of sparkling Burgundy; but the product lost its good reputation years ago, and little is made now. The region's most famous wines are Mercurey reds, Givry reds, and Rully whites and sparkling wines.

Mâconnais

Although it produces some red wines, Mâcon, which is the common abbreviated name for this region and its main town, (pronounced *maa' con*, not as in Macon, Georgia) is well known for its reliable, uncomplicated Chardonnay wines, the town of Chardonnay is located in the Mâconnais region, and its most famous commune or village and white wine is *Pouilly-Fuissé*.

Mâcon's clone of the Chardonnay grape is more melony in flavor; and white Mâcon wines receive little, if any, oak aging. The best domaine-bottled Pouilly-Fuissé is Château de Fuissé "Vielles Vignes" (old vines), produced by Vincent & Fils. Many Pouilly-Fuissé wines are a bit overpriced on restaurant wine lists, but they are mellower and age better than the less expensive and more ubiquitous *Mâcon Blanc Villages*.

Beaujolais

Furthest south in Burgundy, the Beaujolais region's climate is warm. Most Beaujolais wines are red and made from 100% Gamay grapes, which are big, grapey, and fruity. The best villages are the 10 *Cru Beaujolais* located in the granite soils of the northern part of the region. The *Crus* villages include Morgon and Moulin-à-Vent (the two most famous and richest); Chénas; Chiroubles; Juliénas; Fleurie; Brouilly; Côte de Brouilly; St.-Amour (called "holy love," it is popular for Valentine's Day); and Régnié. These Cru Beaujolais present excellent values for money, especially considering they only cost a few more dollars than an ordinary *Beaujolais Villages* (which is from the better villages and a higher grade than just AOC Beaujolais).

Well-known Beaujolais producer Georges Duboeuf uses a different wildflower on each of these Cru labels and imports some of the finest Cru Beaujolais estate wines, including *Fleurie "Domaine de Quatre Vents"* (of the four winds), owned by Dr. Daroze. His 80-year-old vines produce concentrated wines with aromas and flavors of roses, anise, and cassis or black currant flavors.

Beaujolais should be drunk young and fresh (within 3–4 years after the vintage) except for *Cru Beaujolais*, which lives longer. *Beaujolais Nouveau* is made very quickly in a few days by carbonic maceration (explained in Chapter 3). Each year's *Beaujolais Nouveau* is meant to be sold and consumed between Thanksgiving and the next spring, before it loses its grapey, yeasty, fruity quality. All Beaujolais can be served slightly chilled (five minutes in ice and water), especially in hot weather, because it has less tannin than most other red wines.

POLITICS, PATRIOTISM, AND HISTORY

After the Iraq war began in 2003, some of my fellow residents of Atlanta, Georgia, dumped French wines in the river. The next day I overheard two young women in a pancake house comment, "How dumb!" It was. And cruel, for thousands of small French grape farmers went bankrupt as a result of the drop in American sales. France has such a glut of low-end wine that much of it is being converted to alternative fuel for industrial use.

Despite this turn of events, sales of the great Bordeaux or Champagnes have never diminished, and for good reasons. More modern French wines are in the *Wine Spectator* "top 100 of 2004" list (not all of them expensive), including "Wine of the Year" (Ch. Rieussec 2001 Sauternes) than from any other wine-producing area except for California.

Of course, France is no stranger to the hardships of war. Some of France's oldest winemaking families suffered great hardships and performed incredible acts of heroism during World War II, as I learned when reading *Wine & War: The French, The Nazis & The Battle For France's Greatest Treasure* (by Don and Petie Kladstrup, Broadway Books, 2001). Not only did the French winemakers risk their lives to hide Jewish friends, but their sons were also forced to fight in the Nazi army. They lived in near starvation, saw their beautiful château homes converted into soldier barracks, and watched as their best wines were stolen. Any American who doubts the patriotism of the French people during WWII must read this book.

Loire Everyday Wines with Global Popularity

With half a million acres of vineyards, the Loire Valley is France's second largest wine region after Languedoc. The Loire Valley's red, white, Rosé, and sparkling wines are made to be drunk young and fresh as aperitifs before dinner, or with oysters (a specialty of the Loire) , other seafood, or chicken. Light, charming, reasonably priced Loire wines are produced in the following four districts:

- The **Central Region** produces two noteworthy dry white wines, *Sancerre* and *Pouilly-Fumé*, both made from 100% Sauvignon Blanc grapes. These wines share an herbal yet light citrus quality. In this district, the Sauvignon Blanc grape is known as the *blanc fumé*, which is how Robert Mondavi of California got the idea years ago to call his Sauvignon Blanc wines Fumé Blanc. The best producers include Henri Bourgeois, Lucien Crochet, and Pascal Jolivet.

- The **Touraine** district has some of the oldest vineyards in the Loire. Touraine's

> **note** Many people confuse 100% Sauvignon Blanc Pouilly-Fumé from the Loire with 100% Chardonnay Pouilly-Fuissé from Burgundy, but they are as different as their grape varieties.

most famous wine is *Vouvray,* made from 100% Chenin Blanc grapes. The Chenin Blanc gives Vouvray a medium-dry fruitiness, proving that not all French wines are bone dry. (See Chapter 5, "The Wine Label Decoder," for a description of Vouvray and its food partners.) Some rare, late-harvest, sweeter Vouvray is also made. Touraine has two famous medium-bodied reds made from Cabernet Franc grapes: *Chinon* and *Bourgueil.* Both are definitely worth a try.

- The district of **Anjou-Saumur** has two parts: the *Anjou,* known for fruity Cabernet Franc rosés and luscious Chenin Blanc whites; and the *Saumur,* famous for popularly priced sparkling wines made in the *méthode champenoise* (called *méthode traditionelle* anywhere outside the Champagne district) from white Loire grapes. One of the most famous producers of *Savennières,* a fabulous Chenin Blanc made north of Anjou, is Nicolas Joly, who literally wrote the book on biodynamic agriculture and owns two top estates: Domaines de Baumard and Coulèe de Serrant. Sweeter Chenin Blancs are made in *Coteaux du Layon, Quarts de Chaume,* and Bonnezeaux.

- The **Muscadet** (prounounced *moos cah day*) district around Nantes on the Atlantic is named for its renowned dry, white seafood wine, *Muscadet,* made from the Muscadet or Melon de Bourgogne grape. This grape is also grown in Oregon. Muscadet is light and slightly *pétillant* (spritzy) with a few tiny bubbles of carbon dioxide left from fermentation. The best Muscadets are labeled *Sevre et Maine* (names of the two rivers) and *sur lie,* meaning barrel-fermented and aged on the lees of yeast for a few months to make them creamier.

Alsace—White Wine Elegance

Alsace is on the French side of the Rhine River (*Rhin* in French and *Rhein* in German), opposite the Baden wine region of Germany. This explains why Alsace wines are the only French wines made with and named after German grapes, such as Riesling, Gewürztraminer, Pinot Blanc, Sylvaner, and Pinot Gris (same grape as Pinot Grigio in Italy), which is called *Tokay d'Alsace* in Alsace.

Alsace uses these flowery and fruity German grapes to make drier, higher alcohol, food-friendly, French-style wines. As French wines that name the grape variety, Alsace wines are 100% varietal. Most Alsace wines are AOC and their appellation is *Vin d'Alsace,* but some single vineyard wines are so great that they are classified as AOC Alsace Grand Cru. Great Alsace wines, though white, retain their freshness and elegance up to 10 years in the bottle.

The famous producers in Alsace include Hugel (featured in the book, *Wine & War*), Domaine Zind-Humbrecht, Domaines Schlumberger, and Trimbach, though every Alsace brand I've tried was good.

Riesling is considered the best white in Alsace, being dry, distinguished, fragrant, and perfectly balanced. Gewürztraminer (*Gewurz* means spicy) is next, offering a full, rich wine with a very recognizable perfumey bouquet of ripe tropical fruit or flowers. Gewürztraminer is good with quiche, patê, smoked fish, and curried chicken salad. *Reserve* wines are a special category for wines made from riper grapes that made more alcohol. Wines made from Botrytis "noble rot" grapes are called *Selection des Grains Nobles*. They are richer and much better selections than Vendange Tardive.

Alsace makes late-harvest wines, called *Vendange Tardive* in French, but these are not as sweet as German Spätlese. Most of the extra sweetness is turned into alcohol, leaving the wine dry to medium-dry.

Fine Wines of the Rhône Valley

The Rhône Valley is due south of Burgundy, following the Rhône River from Lyon to the city of Avignon. The grapes grown in the Rhône Valley's rocky soil bake in the sun and produce the highest alcohol wines in all of France—a minimum of 12.5%. This explains Rhône's reputation for robust, full-bodied red and surprisingly rich white wines. Sub-regions are divided between the elite northern and prolific southern Rhône.

The northern Rhône is noted for its concentrated, long-lived reds made predominantly from Syrah grapes. Syrah grapes give these low-yield northern Rhône reds an inky black color and aromas of black raspberry and peppercorns or cayenne—the main reasons Syrah (Shiraz) partners so well with Cajun/Creole, Indian, and other spicy cuisines as well as game, casseroles, and red meat. The most famous of these reds are *Côte Rôtie* (a collectors' item meaning "roasted slope," whose prestige single vineyards are named either *Brune* (brunette) or *Blonde* after the color of the soil), *Hermitage* (whose name is synonymous with Shiraz), *Crozes-Hermitage* (less expensive than Hermitage but also excellent), very rich *Cornas*, and *St.-Joseph*.

The famous producers are E. Guigal, M. Chapoutier (whose labels are in Braille for the blind), and Delas.

The northern Rhône is also the home of the incredible whites, such as *Condrieu* made from the wonderful white Rhône grape Viognier, which smells like tangerines, but tastes dry, full, and rich. The other Rhône white grapes are *Marsanne*, which is used in white Hermitage, and *Roussane*, used in white Château Neuf du Pape. In fact, a small proportion of white Rhône grapes is used in many Rhône reds.

The center of the southern Rhône is the city of Avignon where *Château Neuf du Pape* originated. The red version is the more famous, and it's composed of many different Rhône grapes including Syrah, Grenache, and Mourvèdre. Most Château Neuf wines have become pricier in recent years. Newer versions are a lot grapier as well. The best brands are Château de Beaucastel, Domaine de Pégaü, Clos des Papes, Ch. Fortia, Vieux Télégraphe, Domaine Charvin, and Mont–Redon.

> **note** The name *Château Neuf du Pape* means "new castle of the Pope" and refers to the fourteenth century, when the Pope (who was French) had to leave Rome and move to Avignon. Even today, the mitre and sceptre symbols of the Pope are embossed in the glass of estate-bottled Château Neufs, though the Pope has nothing to do with the wines.

Another very fine Rhône red wine made near Avignon is the deep, concentrated red *Gigondas*, and *Vacqueyras*. Two popular dry, orange/pink Rosé wines are also made in the nearby towns of Lirac and Tavel. And a distinctive, sweet white dessert wine called *Muscat de Beaumes de Venise,* made from Muscat grapes, is also made here. It is a VDN (*vin doux naturel*), or naturally sweet, wine made from late-harvest grapes; the wine is fortified to a minimum of 15% alcohol. (For other VDNs, see Languedoc.) Marinate fresh peach halves in it overnight in the fridge for a terrific dessert.

> **note** Recent developments in the Rhône include *Vin de Table* wines. These are made by famous producers who want to make modern wines from their own combinations of grapes outside their main appellation without having to abide by restrictive wine laws for *Vin de Pays*. *Vin de Table* wines are the lowest category for wine in the EU and cannot even carry a vintage year (but producers often use a code on the label).

The universal red blended wine of the Rhône region is called *Côtes du Rhône*. It represents very good value for money, and even connoisseurs drink it. The best have the word "Villages" in the AOC, meaning from the better villages. Your wine retailer can point out similar red Rhône blends such as *Côtes du Ventoux*.

Languedoc—Mediterranean Varietals

The largest grape-growing area in France, *Languedoc*, is located in the curve of the Mediterranean to the west of the Rhône River. Further west is its partner appellation, *Rousillon*. Languedoc produces huge quantities of wines named by grape variety (such as Viognier, Mourvèdre, or Syrah) that are called *Vin de Pays* (country wines) under the French wine laws. They are great values for money and can also be blends of several varieties. One of the most impressive of these reds is Mas de Daumas

Gassac, a collectors' item made from 75% Cabernet Sauvignon with Syrah, Cabernet Franc, Malbec, Pinot Noir, and Tannat.

Several other important Languedoc reds are AOC wines under the appellations o *Minervois*, *Corbieres*, and *Fitou* (my personal favorite). All are combinations of red Rhône grapes, are bargain-priced, and are best when three to five years old.

As for dessert wines, *Banyuls* is one of three well-known VDN sweet, late-harvest, fortified wines made in this region. *Banyuls* is a delicious sweet red that must be at least 50% Grenache; while a *Grand Cru* Banyuls must be 75% Grenache that's aged at least 2.5 years in oak. The other VDNs from Languedoc are sweet red *Maury,* made from 75% black Grenache grapes; and sweet white, tawny, raisiny *Muscat de Frontignan* that's terrific with ice cream desserts.

Provence Is Pretty in Pink—And Red

Nestled in the curve of the Mediterranean Sea in sunny southern France, east of the Rhône River, is *Provence.* Known for its cuisine and the beauty of its herb and wildflower vistas, Provence produces mostly pink rosé wines made from black Rhône grapes. These are the Rosés you'd sip on the beach in ritzy St. Barts. But the reds of the region have a superb reputation too.

The most famous Provence dry Rosé and red wines are made at Domaine Ott and Domaine Tempier, estates located in the prestige appellation of *Bandol*. Bandol reds are deep, rich, and spicy, being made from Rhône grapes that give the wines a tart red fruits character.

Cassis is another small Provence appellation known for its dry white seafood wine made from Sauvignon Blanc, Marsanne, and Ugni Blanc grapes. Don't confuse Cassis wine with the black currant liqueur, Créme de Cassis, made in Burgundy.

Summary

Americans who know French wines have never stopped buying them. But it is a shame that more new wine drinkers aren't taking the time to find French classics that will suit their lifestyles and palates. My hope is that these brief notes inspire you to learn some of the labels. Become the "few, the proud, and the brave" (as the Marines say) who venture into French wines.

In our next chapter, we take a whirlwind tour of Greece.

10

All Greek to Me

Four thousand years of wine culture have finally culminated in spectacular, interesting, and affordable Greek wines that have won the hearts and praise of experts and the public. We've mentioned Greek wines several times in previous chapters, including their appellations of origin and wine laws in Chapter 5, "The Wine Label Decoder." We also featured a Greek wine label at the end of that chapter.

In this chapter, you learn a bit about the wineries and wine regions where Greece's finest examples of native grapes and international varieties are grown. And let me entice you to seek some thrilling new-style Greek cuisine. Haven't you always wanted to sail around the beautiful Greek islands? Sun-bleached villages atop steep cliffs in a brilliant jewel blue sea call us to savor their very best products.

Best of all, none of the wine in this chapter is over $26 a bottle.

The Native Grapes of Greece

As you learned in Chapter 1, "Wine Is: History, Agriculture, Health, Food, and Joy," the Greeks invented wine appellations (place names of origin), and still use them. Greek winemakers often name their wines by grape variety. Here are Greece's three best white native grapes:

In this chapter:

* Managing the daily mail
* Learn about Greece's most important native red and white grapes
* Read about the wines being produced by some top Greek wineries and learn some fantastic Greek wine/food pairings

- *Moschofilero* is a pink-skinned grape considered to be Greece's best white variety. It makes citrusy, crisp, yet delicate dry white wine.
- *Malagousia* makes peach- and jasmine-scented dry whites such as the Gerovassiliou Malagousia 2003, whose wine label was featured in Chapter 5, "The Wine Label Decoder."
- *Assyrtiko* grapes make lovely lemony dry white wines with mineral finish.
- Greece's two native red grape varieties include
- *Agiorghitiko* (also called St. George), which makes elegant dry reds
- *Xinomavro,* which results in dark and concentrated wines with flavors of plum, cassis, and spice

These native grapes, and hundreds more, are grown nowhere else in the world but Greece.

THE IMPORTANCE OF GREEK WINES IN THE U.S.

In 2004, the hottest wine topic in national media and the most coveted U.S. wine events were Greek wine dinners and seminars. Sofia Perpera, director of "All About Greek Wines," and Chef Pano Karatassos of the top-rated "Kyma" Greek restaurant in Atlanta were responsible for conducting five prestige Greek wine and food events that year.

Sofia Perpera, a Bordeaux-trained enologist and a former director of the Greek Wine Federation, founded "All About Greek Wines" in the U.S. to teach Americans about Greek wines and to represent 23 of Greece's top wineries. Her website, **www.allaboutgreekwines.com**, offers a very detailed history of Greek wines, a colorful map of the Greek wine regions, explanations of dozens of native Greek grapes, and profiles/contacts for the best wineries.

Chef Pano Karatassos and his Kyma restaurant were acknowledged for outstanding Greek cuisine in both *USA Today* and *Wine & Spirits*. Chef Pano, who trained at the CIA (Culinary Institute of America) and in Greece, shares the name and heritage of his father who owns nine upscale Atlanta restaurants (learn more at **www.buckheadliferestaurants.com**). Most importantly, Kyma took the risk of opening with only Greek wines on the wine list; and diners were charmed by their quality and value.

To do list

- ❑ Learn about some of the best wines and wineries of Macedonia, in northern Greece
- ❑ Locate top wines and wineries near Athens, on the Peloponnese Peninsula
- ❑ Learn about fine wines produced on the islands of Santorini and Samos

Salute to Greek Wineries

Yiassou means "hello" in Greek, and *Stin-yiassou* means "cheers," what you say when you make a wine toast. With these two expressions, you are ready to travel Greece's wine route. And the first thing you'll notice is that there's water everywhere. Greece is a country of mainland peninsula and islands surrounded by two seas: the Mediterranean on the west and the Aegean on the east. Greece's ocean-tempered climate helps its vineyards produce grapes that result in great wines. But it wasn't until Greece joined the European Union in 1981 that its wine industry began to modernize.

The Wines and Wineries of Macedonia

Pioneering wineries, such as Ktima (Greek for "estate") Kir Yanni near the city of Naoussa in northern Greece's Macedonia wine region insisted on quality over quantity. Kir Yanni offers a dry white blend of native Greek grape Roditis, plus the international varieties Sauvignon Blanc and Gewürztraminer, in a splendid dry white wine called Samaropetra. This wine's flavors of white peaches and long, dry finish make it the perfect white for calamari, taramosalata, and prawns with *Ouzo*,

Greece's famous anise liqueur. Kir Yanni also produces superb red Ramnista, made with 100% Xinomavro grapes. This inky black, robust but soft red wine is wonderful with lamb. Kir Yanni also makes my favorite dry rosé (also from Xinomavro) named Akakies for the area's Acacia trees; it's a great sipping and brunch wine.

> **note** *Oenophile*, meaning a person who is a wine lover or aficionado, is from the Greek words *oenos* for wine, and *philo* for love. In American English, it is spelled *enophile*, and an enologist is a winemaker who has earned a degree in wine chemistry. Most of Greece's best winemakers are both.

Domaine Gerovassiliou is another prestige winery of Macedonia. With vineyards surrounded on three sides by the ocean, this winery is in the

appellation of Epanomi near the city of Thessaloniki. Gerovassilou's Malagousia (see its 2003 label in Chapter 5) is a fabulous dry wine from one of Greece's three best native white grapes. It's wonderful with any kind of seafood—the Greeks (especially Chef Pano) can even make grilled octopus taste so good people can't get enough of it. Ditto for dishes with eggplant or Kalamata olives.

Wines of the Peloponnese Peninsula

The Domaine Tselepos winery is acclaimed for Moschofilero and Merlot. Tselepos winery is located in the prestige wine area of Mantinia on the Peloponnese peninsula, southwest of Athens. Try the Tselepos Moschofilero 2003—Greece's greatest vintage year—with sautéed sea scallops and wild greens. The harvest was so good in 2003 that Tselepos used longer contact with the pink grape skins to give the juice more color and richer flavor.

> **note** Moschofilero is also used to make sparkling wine in Greece. This is one of Greece's only three pink-skinned wine grapes, the others being Gewürztraminer and Pinot Gris or Grigio.

And if you must have a dry white wine instead of red with your steak, I recommend the full-bodied Domaine Evharis Chardonnay/Assyrtiko 2003. Evharis's co-owner Eva Boehme is as bold as her wines. Located in a gorgeous area very near Athens, the Evharis estate also produces a terrific Syrah.

From Nemea, Palivos Estate's Agiorghitiko is one of the nicest examples of wine produced from Greece's other famous native red grape. Nemea, along with Mantinia and Argos, is the well-known wine district on the Peloponnese peninsula southwest of Athens. Nemea reds, which are invariably made from the *Agiorghitiko* grape, are Greece's answer to red Bordeaux. Try the Palivos Nemea with Greek lamb chops dressed with Feta cheese, allspice, and garlic, served with classic Greek roasted potatoes.

The Papantonis family makes a more traditional dry, oaky Agiorghitiko red called "Meden Agan." The Papantonis estate is in Argos, the third important wine district on the Peloponnese peninsula. Argos lies next to Mantinia and below Nemea. Like many established family wineries in Greece, it is adopting new vineyard and wine-making techniques. The estate owner's beautiful young and knowledgeable daughter, Lydia Papantonis, is leading them into a brighter future.

Some Wines from the Islands of Santorini and Samos

Finally, the lovely island of Santorini in the Aegean Sea beckons us. Santorini is a dormant volcano with such high winds that the grapevines are trained into baskets to help protect them from the winds. The only moisture the island receives is from fog and sea mist. The island's most famous white grape is Assyrtiko, and Domaine Sigalas is the finest wine producer on Santorini. Try any Sigalas white with wood-grilled, deboned, whole *lavraki* (a mild white fish of the turbot family that's flown in daily from Greece to top restaurants such as Kyma). Like all Greek-style grilled fish, *lavraki* is served with lemon, olive oil, and capers from Santorini.

> **tip** If this chapter has made you hungry, then check out any of the upscale Greek restaurants in the U.S., including Estiatorio Milos in New York, Black Olive in Baltimore, Kokkari in San Francisco, and Zaytinya in Washington. The websites of these restaurants include their wine lists.

Does Greece have any noteworthy dessert wines? Yes, the Greeks invented Vinsanto dessert wines. When the Venetians conquered Greece centuries ago, they became so fond of *Vin santo* that they decided to make their own version in Italy. My favorite Greek dessert wine is the Samos "Nectar." The island of Samos produces several golden sweet Muscat dessert wines that taste like candied orange and caramel. The very pretty etched glass half-bottles they use are worth more than the $11 price! Even the French import and drink Samos Muscat. Serve it as the Greeks do with homemade goat milk yogurt, Greek thyme honey, and walnuts. The other well-known Greek dessert wine is the sweet red Mavrodaphne.

Touring the Wineries of Greece

Almost everyone would start a tour of the Greek vineyards in Athens. The finest wineries closest to this Olympic city are Boutari (long-established but very progressive winemakers), Evharis (mentioned previously), and Katogi-Strofilia (gorgeous wines and location). Then it's a short hop southwest to the Peloponnese peninsula and its three major regions with their most famous wineries: Mantinia, where Tselepos and Domaine Spiropoulos make excellent Moschofilero; Nemea, where the great Gaia Estate, Palivos, and Domaine Skouras wineries make excellent Agioghitiko (St. George) reds; and Argos, where Papantonis winery also excels in St. George reds.

To the far north is the Macedonia region (**www.wineroads.gr**), home to the unforgettable wineries of Gerovassiliou and Kir Yanni, as well as Boutari's famous Naoussa red wine district estate. Flights or ferries can take you to the islands of Santorini, where Domaine Sigalas makes delicious Assyrtiko dry white wines; Samos, where divine Muscat dessert wines are made; Rhodes, where Emery winery makes fine sparkling wines; and Cephalonia, the Ionian island where the Gentilini winery is kissed by Mediterranean breezes. Finally, I must commend popular labels, such as Achaia Clauss and Tsantalis, which are widely available in casual Greek-American restaurants. They are really quite good, and you can't beat the price!

> **note** Fine Greek restaurants recommend serving Retsina, the ancient Greek wine flavored with pine resin, with sardines or sun-dried and salted small Greek fish similar to smelts. But Retsina is no longer considered a fine wine in Greece—not in comparison to any of the very modern Greek wines we've featured in this chapter.

Summary

Greece is not only the cradle of civilization, but it is also the origin of the golden, two-handled chalice of antiquity used for raising great wine in a toast to its great food. *Sto-kalo*—now you know how to say goodbye in Greek, and you are ready for your own explorations.

In our next chapter, we'll greet German and Austrian wines.

11

Sweet or Not Too Sweet— Wines of Germany and Austria

Everyone in the wine world acknowledges that Germany's elegant sun-kissed white wines are its greatest accomplishment. Produced in the coldest, northernmost climate in Europe, Germany's great white wines partner well with food and stand on their own as the purest examples of Riesling on the planet.

Germany's greatest wines are its sweetest and most expensive. *Wine Spectator* magazine (April 30, 2005) gave 100-point perfect scores to only 32 wines; several were these highest-quality German wines.

Austria also produces lush late-harvest wines, but they've made an effort to establish their reputation on drier whites such as Grüner Veltliner and dry reds from Blaufrankisch, a native variety some say is probably Gamay but appears to me to be heavier like Cabernet Franc.

To do list

- ❑ Understand Germany's system of classifying wine quality
- ❑ Learn what the six ripeness levels tell you about quality German wines
- ❑ Learn Germany's two new classifications for dry wines

Germany's Wine Designations

Vineyards have flourished in Germany's favorable river valleys of the Rhein and Mosel since Roman times. A famous statue in the Rheingau dated 1775 commemorates the monks who made the first sweet Spätlese wine from overripe grapes. Almost 200 years later in 1971, German wine laws established levels of quality based on the ripeness (natural sugar content) of the grapes at harvest. Increasing ripeness levels equate to increasing natural sugar content in the grapes. Increments of sweetness change the taste of the wines, from the drier basic quality level to the lush, golden, dessert-style sweetness of the highest quality level.

note Austria is the only other country in the world with similar wine laws.

The wine laws of Germany establish three quality levels for wines. The lowest quality level is *Deutscher Tafelwein*, German table wine (wines labeled simply Tafelwein can be made from juice that is not German), which is sold and enjoyed as everyday wine throughout Germany, but seldom exported. The remaining two categories, *Qualitätswein* and *Qualitätswein mit Prädikat*, separate quality wines into the former level that may have had sugar added during fermentation (called *chaptalization*) from the latter and higher level that never have sugar added. The wines in the latter category, the Prädikat wines, are further classified into six categories of ripeness. These categories and ripeness levels are described in the following sections and directly determine the natural sweetness and cost of the wines in those categories.

tip Since the sweetness level of German wine is also an indication of price, it is the most important information on the wine label.

note German wine labels can list the grape variety only if the wine contains 85% of that grape.

Qualitätswein: Germany's Quality Wine

Qualitätswein bestimmter Anbaugebiete (abbreviated QbA), is defined as "quality wine" from one of Germany's 13 designated wine regions. Although they are made from approved grapes and have a minimum alcohol content of 7.5%, QbAs can be chaptalized. The most popular QbA wines are Liebfraumilch from the Rhein and Zeller Schwarze Katz from the Mosel. Neither is labeled Riesling.

tip Chaptalization unbalances the aftertaste somewhat, but the QbA wines are quaffable bargains.

Qualitätswein mit Prädikat: Germany's Finest Wines

Qualitätswein mit Prädikat are Germany's top wines because they can never be chaptalized. The name means "quality wine with special attributes." The special attributes are the ripeness of the grapes at harvest and how they attained this ripeness—by late harvesting (longer time in the sun), or Botrytis "noble rot" shriveling of the grapes to raisins, or by picking grapes while frozen so that the ice crystals hold the water content out of the more concentrated juice. The higher the *Prädikat*, or ripeness level, the more rare and costly the wine becomes because it can be made only in exceptional growing seasons or vintage years when there extra weeks of sunshine or a hard frost that freezes the grapes. The six levels of ripeness are

- *Kabinett*, the driest Prädikat, makes an excellent aperitif before dinner with appetizers or cheeses and fruit. It also partners well with main courses of halibut, trout, cream soups, veal, and sausages. Fairly inexpensive, Kabinett is perfect for beginning wine drinkers. Serve all German whites chilled. Kabinetts from the Mosel taste like green apples because of high malic acid (the acid of green apples), are very pale in color and sometimes spritzy with tiny bubbles.

- *Spätlese*, meaning "late harvest," is made from riper grapes picked later than normal and costs a few dollars more than Kabinett. A Spätlese is medium-dry—just slightly sweeter than Kabinett—and is excellent with pork, ham, chicken, turkey, and scallops. A Spätlese from the Rheingau has aromas and flavors of white peaches or apricots.

- *Auslese*, meaning "select late harvest," is made by hand-picking the ripest bunches of the late-harvested grapes. A medium-sweet wine, only small amounts of Auslese can be made; so it's more expensive. Auslese partners with pound cake, butter cookies, flan, pumpkin pie, and spice cake.

> **note** You may be thinking "too sweet," but you'd be wrong! German wines, especially those labeled Riesling, are all tart/sweet, like biting into fresh, ripe green grapes. Later in this chapter, we explain that much drier versions of German wine (even Prädikat wines) are made. We also tell you how to recognize these by the designations on the label.

- *Beerenauslese (BA)*, meaning "berries or raisins of select late-harvest grapes," is rare and costly. Grapes that have been hanging in the sun so long that they shrivel to raisins are individually picked out of the bunch to make this rich, sweet dessert wine. BAs partner perfectly with pineapple upside down cake, cheesecake, or bread pudding. BAs are collectors' items whose price depends on the grape variety, reputation of the producer, and age. So little is made, it is sold in half-bottles.

- *Trockenbeerenauslese (TBA)*, meaning "berries or raisins of select late-harvest grapes shriveled by Botrytis," is the very rarest, sweetest, and most expensive of the six Prädikat levels. Only under ideal conditions of temperature and humidity in the greatest of Germany's sunny vintage years—such as 2001 and especially 2003—will the best vineyard owners make TBAs. Individual Botrytis-covered grapes are picked out of each bunch and placed in little red buckets to make a very limited amount of this rare dessert wine. The Botrytis gives TBA wonderful golden honeycomb color, aromas, and flavors, including royal jelly and beeswax. Its high sugar content allows a TBA to age well for many years.

- *Eiswein*, or "ice wine," is not made in sunny vintages, but rather in years when a hard frost freezes the grapes. (For a full description of how Eiswein is made, see Chapter 3, "Winemaking—The Six Basic Types of Wine.") Usually as sweet (and expensive) as an Auslese or BA, Eisweins (like other Prädikat wines) do not have to be made from Riesling, but can be made from other varieties, such as Scheurebe (an excellent cross between Riesling and Silvaner grapes).

New Classifications for Dry German Wines

In the past, Germany's driest wines were designated either Trocken (very dry) or Halb-Trocken (semi-dry). This applied even to the Prädikat wines, which confused consumers. To avoid this confusion, German winemakers created two new classifications for dry German wines in 2000. The *Classic* designation is used for dry varietal wines from typical regional vineyards. *Selection* is used to designate high-quality single-vineyard dry wines made from hand-harvested grapes.

caution Sparkling or Kabinett wines labeled Trocken are the driest versions of these wines. But beware of Auslese wines labeled Trocken. That means all the wonderful natural sweetness of the select late-harvest Auslese grapes has been fermented dry. What a waste!

VISITING THE GERMAN WINE INFORMATION BUREAU WEBSITE

You can read more about German wine-growing regions, grapes, wines, classifications, ripeness levels, touring Germany's wine country, studying at Germany's Wine Academy, and even get free booklets at the German Wine Information Bureau website www.germanwineusa.com (and .org) If you prefer writing, the address is 950 Third Avenue, New York, NY 10022. Telephone: 212-994-7600.

German Wine Regions and Producers

Germany has 13 wine-growing regions (see Figure 11.1). One of the most important of these is the *Mosel-Saar-Ruwer region*. Named for the Mosel (pronounced moe' zul) River and its tributaries, the Saar and Ruwer, this region has slate soil and a very cool climate. Most of its vineyards are planted in Riesling grapes. Most Mosel wines are easily recognized on store shelves because they're in tall green bottles. Wines from the Rhein River regions are usually in tall brown glass bottles. A few producers break tradition and make their wines stand out against the competition by using blue glass bottles.

FIGURE 11.1
German wine country.

Some of the best single vineyards in the Mosel face due east into the sun on steep slate hillsides. These vineyards have very recognizable names: Piesporter Goldtropfchen, Graacher Himmelreich, Wehlener Sonnenuhr, Bernkasteler Doktor, and Scharzhofberger. The best Mosel producers, in addition to Selbach-Oster (see Chapter 5, "The Wine Label Decoder"), include Joh. Jos. Prüm, Dr. H. Thanisch, Dr. Loosen, Egon Müller, and Von Kesselstatt.

Riesling also is the predominant grape grown in another important German wine region, the *Rheingau*. Several of the Rheingau vineyards are owned by German noble families, including Schloss (castle) Vollrads and Schloss Johannisberg. Other top Rheingau producers include Robert Weil, Schloss Schönborn, and Kesseler. All of these producers produce wines listed as "first growths" of the Rheingau.

Another important German wine region is the *Rheinhessen*, an area opposite the Rheingau with reddish sandy soil that produces sublime Niersteiner wines. The Rheinhessen has prestige producers such as Gunderloch who makes superb Nackenheimer single vineyard wines.

The *Pfalz region* (formerly Rheinpfalz) , below the Rheinhessen, is home to important producers such as Basserman-Jordan and Von Buhl, who have been making great estate wines for decades.

Germany's 2004 Vintage

A very good quality and quantity vintage year, 2004 surpassed expectations in Germany. Selbach-Oster in the Mosel reported being able to make Spätlese, Auslese, and a bit of Beerenauslese (with fortuitious Botrytis) as well. The wines are described as much sleeker than the previous three vintages, with more citrus and mineral qualities. Some producers were also able to make Eiswein in December 2004, with two opportunities to gather frozen grapes before Christmas. Though the Euro has caused pricing grief, consider what goes into a bottle of hand-crafted, old vine, steep-slope German Mosel Riesling. Today's consumer gets a unique piece of wine culture, a mouth full of complex flavors, and wines that can be cellared. They are worth every penny.

Germany's *Ahr region* produces a small amount of dry reds (or *rotwein* in German), the best being delicate Pinot Noirs, called Burgunder. The *Franken region* produces dry, fiery Silvaner whites in squat *bochsbeutel* bottles. And to distinguish full-bodied dry German Pinot Gris wines made in the *Baden region* opposite Alsace, burgundy-shaped bottles are used.

Austria's Wine Identity

The majority of Austrian wines are more like French than German wines, in that they're fermented dry and have higher alcohol content. Austria will never produce high volumes of wine because of its very rocky terrain and the very small size of its vineyards, all of which are located on the east side of the country, away from the colder Alpine regions to the west.

note Most of Austria's winemakers are young and very modern in their techniques. Austria's famous enology school established natural sugar levels from Kabinett to TBA and Eiswein, but some winemakers want to change these German terms.

Nearly one-third of all grapes planted in Austria are of the Gruner Veltliner variety. The Austrians use this native grape to make wine in both simple and complex styles, always with a white pepper finish. Usually dry, Grüner Veltliner wines partner well with many different cuisines, including vegetarian. Most tourists drink this wine from the vineyards of the *Wien district* around Vienna. One of the finest black grapes grown in Austria is Blaufrankisch, which can make spectacular, concentrated red wine that reminds me of Cabernet Franc (though some experts say it's probably the Gamay grape) in *Burgenland*, the district southeast of Vienna. This district includes the prestigious *Neusiedlersee* area, where humidity from the lake creates optimum conditions for Botrytis "noble rot" fungus, and luscious, sweet wines.

Several of Austria's finer wine regions follow the Danube River as it flows from Slovakia through the large northern *Weinviertel* area to Vienna and then on to the very famous *Wachau* district. Wachau is the most prestigious wine area in Austria, with ancient vineyards on rocky terraces dating back one thousand years. Wachau region wines have an enviable mineral quality and concentration due to long hang times and very late harvests. Nearby are the quality districts of *Kamptal* and *Kremstal*.

> **tip** Perhaps the greatest Austrian collectors' item is any wine from the great producer Kracher.

Summary

In this chapter, you've learned that Germany makes a wine for every occasion, cuisine, and budget. You just have to know how to read the ripeness levels to find your palate's pleasure. There are sweet wines, and then there are *German* sweet wines. No one does it better, Mr. Bond.

Austrian wines have even charmed the "good ol' boys" of Alabama retailers, as well as big-city restaurant sophisticates and London wine experts. Here you learned about some of Austria's top wine-growing regions and wines. In our next chapter, we experience *la dolce vita* of Italian wines.

Italy's Splendor in
the Glass

The ancient Greeks named Italy *Enotria*, the "land of wine," and it lives up to this name even today. Barolo, the oldest wine in Italy, has been continuously produced for at least 700 years. Today Italy's wine industry includes well over 25,000 different wine labels from 2,000 major wineries in 20 wine regions. Italy produces more than 1 billion gallons of wine a year, making it the world's largest wine producer. Italian wines are the #1 imports in the U.S. because there is much quality and value in this huge quantity of wine.

To help you sort through Italy's wealth of wine, this chapter provides a list of Italy's top 32 *DOCG (Denominazione di Origine Controllata e Garantita)* wines under the DOC (controlled name of origin) wine laws. This list also helps you learn Italy's most important wine regions and grape varieties. And we take a closer look at Italy's super-Tuscan, super-Venetian, sparkling, and dessert wines, while discussing some of the most delectable food partners to accompany them.

In this chapter:

* Learn about Italy's wine laws and wine categories

* Learn about the Italy's noble red and white grape varieties and best wine regions

* Understand what makes a wine "super-Tuscan" or "super-Venetian"

* Find out that Asti Spumante isn't Italy's only sparkling wine, and that Vin Santo isn't its only dessert wine

* Learn some of the best food partners for Italy's great wines

To do list

- ☐ Learn all about Italy's updated name of origin wine laws and their quality levels
- ☐ Learn about Italy's newest varietal wine designations and t their great values for your money
- ☐ Discover Italy's premier wine guide, wine event and wine centers

Italy's Updated Wine Laws—Bravo to the Best

Although the Italian government began regulating the labeling of Italian wines according to DOC, *Denominazione d'Origine Controllata* ("controlled names of origin") wine laws written in 1963, the first DOC wasn't approved until 1966. Now there are 310 DOC wines, with more achieving DOC status every year. Originally patterned after the French AOC (Appellation d'Origine Contrôlée) wine region categorization, Italy's wine laws go beyond those by adding aging requirements for each DOC. The top 32 DOC wines are called DOCG and are guaranteed by the producers. Italy's new varietal wine category is called IGT, and these bargain-priced wines are explained later in the chapter. Italy also produces lower level *vino da tavola* table wines.

Italy's IGT Varietal Wines

In 1992, Italy adopted a new wine law that designates a new category of wines called IGT, *Indicazione Geografica Tipica*. More than 200 Italian wines carry this designation. IGT wine labels abide by EU rules for varietal labeling, naming the grape if it accounts for at least 85% of the wine (just like French *Vin de Pays*, which you learned about in Chapter 9, "French Me!—Choosing Wines from the Great Wine Regions of France"), while indicating a non-DOC geographical origin. Two reasonably priced wines made from Italy's best-selling grape varieties—Pinot Grigio and Sangiovese—are among the most popular IGT designated wines.

IGT wines also rescued upscale blends made with non-traditional (international) grapes such as Cabernet Sauvignon, Merlot, or Chardonnay from their previous placement among the lowest quality level "vino da tavola" table wines without vintages, grape varieties, or geographical indications. For example, the Tuscan wine area on the Mediterranean Sea called *Maremma* has now achieved IGT status for its wines.

These updated regulations also permitted famous Italian wines such as *Sassicaia*, made in the Bolgheri coastal region of Maremma, to receive a DOC designation. Bolgheri Sassicaia is a pricey collectors' item. It's one of the first wines to be called a "super-Tuscan" by the *Wine Spectator*. (You learn more about these wines later in this chapter.) Moderately priced Sangiovese reds and Vermentino dry whites from the new Bolgheri DOC zone are obviously wines to look for, since they originate from such a prime growing area. Figure 12.1 shows where Tuscany and the other major wine areas in Italy are located.

FIGURE 12.1
Italian wine regions.

If you can't afford to buy Italy's DOCGs, remember the IGT varietals. You can purchase Tuscany IGT wines simply labeled "Sangiovese" starting at just $8 a bottle—Ruffino "Fonte al Sole" is an example. Another dark, rich, concentrated, yet elegant, example is the $10 Conti Contini IGT Sangiovese.

Italy's Top Wines—The DOCGs

Under Italy's wine laws, the DOCG (*Denominazione d'Origine Controllata e Garantita*) category is the highest quality category of Italian wines, with the G meaning "Garantita," or guaranteed by government-appointed commissions of wine producers. These DOCG wines are of particular reputation and worth, and only 32 had been named through July, 2005, including the newest DOCG, Dolcetto di Dogliani. The great red, Amarone—made in the Veneto region from mostly Corvina grapes—is predicted to achieve the DOCG rating it has always deserved in the near future, and Marsala Vergine is also pending as a DOCG.

The following table lists all wines that, as of the time of this writing, had been given the DOCG designation. This list can be a valuable learning tool. By studying it, you learn which of Italy's wine regions and native grape varieties account for the greatest number of the country's highest-quality wines. Italy's two best-quality wine regions, with the greatest producers and wineries, are Tuscany and Piedmont. This is why they are the top wine touring destinations in Italy and are the most popular types of Italian wine.

note Italian wine laws also govern other important wine terms on Italian labels. *Riserva*, meaning "reserve," is a term used to designate superior red wines from great vintages and vineyards. Riserva wines receive extended cellaring and aging in wood, which increases their complexity and life span. *Classico* designates wines from vineyards in the best, or "classic," area of a DOC zone. The term *Superiore* designates wines made from riper grapes (from sunny vintage years) that developed more alcohol during fermentation.

Without our list, however, it would be difficult to know which wines are from Tuscany or Piedmont because most wines are labeled according to the name of a grape-growing area within these regions. In addition, our list of DOCGs identifies the major grape varieties grown in these regions so that you can buy these famous native grapes—Sangiovese from Tuscany and Nebbiolo from the Piedmont—as less expensive varietal wines. In addition to helping you gain an understanding of Italy's wine regions and native grapes, this list also gives you a feel for the incredible range of wines, from dry white to red, dry sparkling to sweet, that Italy produces.

The following table of the 32 DOCG wines has the numbering provided to me by the Italian government. More than 32 wines actually exist because Roero, for example, has three versions (two reds and one white). Yet Roero is listed under dry red wines. There are exceptions to every wine rule in every country, especially in Europe. That is why I have taken the trouble to number the DOCG wines in this table. Also, to help you better understand this list, I have . divided the wines by type, in this order: 19 dry reds; 7 dry whites; 1 superior dry sparkling

note The names of the DOCG wines are most often derived from places, rather than grape varieties. Among the reds, the only exception is Brunello, which is the local name for the Sangiovese grape. But several of the dry white DOCGs are named by grape variety with the place of origin attached. These include Vernaccia, Albana, Greco, Fiano, and Vermentino. Brachetto red sparkling is also named for its grape

(white and Rosé); and 5 sweet wines (including 2 sweet white non-sparkling, 1 sweet white—Asti—that can be either sparkling or non-sparkling, and 2 sweet red sparkling wines). And percentages of grape varieties used in each wine can change from vintage to vintage, especially in Chianti Classico, where the consortium of growers participates in the decision and may include non-traditional grapes, such as Cabernet Sauvignon in the blend.

DOCG wines	Name	Region	Grape Variety
Dry Red			
1.	Barolo	Piedmont	Nebbiolo (100%)
2.	Barbaresco	Piedmont	Nebbiolo (100%)
3.	Gattinara	Piedmont	Nebbiolo (+10% Bonarda)
4.	Ghemme	Piedmont	Nebbiolo (+Bonarda etc.)
5.	Roero, Roero Riserva (Reds) and Arneis Roero (White)	Piedmont	Nebbiolo (or Arneis)
6.	Dogliani	Piedmont	Dolcetto
7.	Sforzato (Sfursat) di Valtellina	Lombardy	Nebbiolo (+5% other grapes)
8.	Valtellina Superiore	Lombardy	Nebbiolo (+5% other)
9.	Brunello di montalcino	Tuscany	Sangiovese (local clone called Brunello or Sangiovese Grosso)
10.	Carmignano	Tuscany	Sangiovese (+45% to 55% other)
11.	Chianti (includes 7 sub-districts, such as Rufina)	Tuscany	Sangiovese (75% to 100%)
12.	Chianti Classico	Tuscany	Sangiovese (80% to 100%)
13.	Vino Nobile di Montepulciano	Tuscany	Sangiovese (local clone called Prugnolo Gentile)
14.	Bardolino Superiore	Veneto	Corvina (+Molinara etc.)
15.	Cònero	Marche	Montepulciano (+ up to 15% other)
16.	Montefalco Sagrantino	Umbria	Sagrantino
17.	Torgiano rosso riserva	Umbria	Sangiovese
18.	Montepulciano D'abruzzo—Colline Teramane	Abruzzi	Montepulciano (+ up to 15% other)
19.	Taurasi	Campania	Aglianico
Dry White			
20.	Gavi	Piedmont	Cortese
21.	Soave Superiore	Veneto	Garganega (+ Trebbiano)
22.	Vernaccia di San Gimig nano	Tuscany	Vernaccia
23.	Albana di Romagna	Emilia-Romagna	Albana

DOCG wines	Name	Region	Grape Variety
Dry White			
24.	Greco di Tufo	Campania	Greco (Grechetto)
25.	Fiano di Avellino	Campania	Fiano
26.	Vermentino di Gallura	Sardinia	Vermentino
Superior Dry Sparkling			
27.	Franciacorta	Lombardy	Pinot Blanc (Bianco) Cabernet Franc
Sweet			
28.	Brachetto d'Acqui (sweet red sparkling)	Piedmont	Brachetto
29.	Vernaccia di Serrapetrona (sweet red sparkling)	Marche	Vernaccia (+ red grapes)
30.	Asti Spumante (sparkling) and Moscato D'Asti (non-sparkling)	Piedmont	Muscat (Moscato)
31.	Recioto di Soave (sweet white)	Veneto	Garganega (+ Trebbiano)
32.	Ramandolo (sweet white)	Friuli	Verduzzo Friulano

The Italian Trade Commission in New York has a really nice website for Italian wines and foods: **www.italianmade.com**. They also provide useful free booklets and vintage cards. Their main phone number is 212-980-1500. Ask for the Assistant Trade Commissioner for Food and Wine, Augusto Marchini; or his right-hand man, Fred Maripoti, at 212-848-0342. If you prefer e-mail: Augusto.Marchini@newyork.ice.it or Fred.Maripoti@newyork.ice.it.

THE KEY TO CHIANTIS!

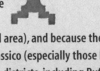

Chianti and Chianti Classico are listed as two separate DOCGs because they are from different viticultural zones (Chianti Classico is centered on the town of Castellina in Chianti, while regular Chianti is made in a much larger, less ideal area), and because they use different percentages of Sangiovese—the more robust and concentrated Classico (especially those labeled Riserva) having the highest percentage. The Chianti DOCG includes seven sub-districts, including Rufina, an area that also produces excellent Chianti Classico and Chianti Classico Riserva. The sub-district of Rufina should not be confused with the Ruffino winery, which makes wonderful Chianti Classico Riserva called gold label Ducale. Finally, you may be wondering about those straw bottle Chiantis. The best of them, including Castello Banfi's, are labeled "Classico."

Italy's Noble Grapes

The two noble native red grapes of Italy are the *Nebbiolo* grape of the Piedmont and Lombardy and the *Sangiovese* grape of Tuscany and Umbria. The Nebbiolo grape is used to produce the five great Piedmont DOCG reds: Barolo, Barbaresco, Gattinara, Ghemme, and Roero.

The name *Nebbiolo* derives from the Italian word *nebbia* for "fog" because the steep foothills of the Alps accumulate fog, which has a beneficial effect on the grapes in the Piedmont vineyards. Black cherry is one of the varietal flavors of wines made from the Nebbiolo grape. These great Nebbiolo reds are perfect with wild game, risotto, stews, cheeses, and casseroles that are prominently featured in the cuisine of the Piedmont. The newest DOCG, Dolcetto di Dogliani, is made from the red Dolcetto grape which makes a fruity but rich red wine similar to the best Beaujolais Crus. Dolcetto is a perfect partner for cheese fondue which, along with game and risotto, is a specialty of the Piedmont.

Five of the best Tuscany reds are made from Sangiovese grapes: Brunello di Montalcino, Carmignano, Chianti, Chianti Classico, and Vino Nobile di Montepulciano. The Sangiovese grape's varietal aromas and flavors include layers of violets, anise (licorice), and cherry. The name *Sangiovese* is the description of its color ("the blood of St. Jove"). Tuscany's very dry, sunny summers provide a perfect climate for Sangiovese (and the red Bordeaux grapes). Sangiovese reds are the ultimate food partners for Tuscany's famous grilled meats, wild boar, Porcini mushrooms, and Pecorino cheese.

Other premium Italian native red grapes include the smooth, rich *Montepulciano* (not to be confused with the town of Montepulciano in Tuscany) of Marche and Abruzzi; the *Corvina* of Veneto, used in making Bardolino Superiore and Amarone; and the *Aglianico* ancient Greek grape of Campania.

As for the traditional white Italian grapes, the delicate *Cortese* grape used to make DOCG Gavi in the Piedmont is considered a "noble" native variety. Two of my favorite native Italian white grapes appear in the DOCG list, as well: the light, citrusy *Fiano* (a Fiano from Settesoli in Sicily is featured in Chapter 5, "The Wine Label Decoder") and the full-bodied rival to Chardonnay, *Vermentino*, from Bolgheri in Maremma Tuscany and Sardinia. And finally, there is the ancient Greek white grape *Greco*, used to make the DOCG *Greco di Tufo* in Campania, whose greatest producer is Mastroberardino.

tip Speaking of Italian Chardonnay, Angelo Gaja's from the Piedmont is a vanilla-scented but never too oaky blockbuster, as are the barrel-fermented Pomino Bianco from Frescobaldi and Cabreo by Ruffino (both Tuscany). I know wine experts who thought they were such great Chardonnays that they never guessed they were Italian!

Italy's Super-Tuscan and Venetian Wines

Almost all of the French grape varieties are grown in Italy—even Syrah from the Rhône and Carmenère from Bordeaux. Nineteenth-century immigrants brought the grapes to Italy, and all have been doing exceptionally well in their adopted country. In particular, the red Bordeaux grapes have been used to add depth of color, fruit concentration, and flavor complexity to Tuscany's Sangiovese, creating world-renowned "super-Tuscan" wines. The most notable of these Sangiovese/Cabernet blends are made by the esteemed Tuscany wineries of Sassicaia, Frescobaldi, Riecine, Montevertine, Altessina, Cesani, Avignonesi, Tassinaia, Tenuta di Sette Ponti, Castello Banfi, and Antinori, among others. These particular brands of Super-Tuscan wines are all collector's items, but there are also inexpensive, early-drinking versions available for those of us on a budget.

Well-known producers from other regions also make outstanding blends of local native grapes with Cabernet Sauvignon. Angelo Gaja, producer of Barbaresco, makes one of the greatest Cabernet varietal wines. Veneto's "super-Venetian" producers (Alegrini, Boscaini, and Tommasi) blend Corvina and other native grapes with Cabernet to make more concentrated, modern-style wines.

Like the "super-Tuscans," the "super-Venetian" wines can be expensive ($45 to $100). They start at $22 per bottle and are every bit as good or better than similarly priced Bordeaux or California Cabernets. In fact, several California wineries struck gold by emulating the "super-Tuscan" Sangiovese blends, calling them "CalItal." Wineries doing this include Atlas Peak, which is co-owned by Antinori.

And as for "super-Venetian" substitutes, the best labels and bargains are Alegrini's Palazzo della Torre or any of Tommasi's reds, including Merlot; and the wonderful Valpolicella "Ripasso," whose wine label was featured in Chapter 5, "The Wine Label Decoder."

Italian Sparkling Wines

Italy also makes very admirable sparkling wines—white, red, and Rosé. Pinot Blanc (Bianco) and Pinot Noir (Nero) are used to make Italy's best sparkling wine, Franciacorta (pronounced *fran-shyah-KOR-ta*). This wine is made in the *metodo classico* (or *tradizionale*)

note   Italy's premier wine guide is Gambero Rosso, *Slow Food Guide to Italian Wines*. Every year the thick soft-cover guide rates almost 15,000 wines. The highest rating of *Tre Bicchiere* ("three glasses") was given to just 264 wines in 2004. Ten of these were from U.S. importer, Palm Bay Imports (**www.palmbayimports.com**), including Col d'Orcia Brunello di Montalcino "Poggio al Vento" DOCG 1997, and two wines from Feudi di San Gregorio in Campania (a Merlot and Grego di Tufo). The guide is available in English for $30. Gambero Rosso also has a magazine and a TV channel at their Rome wine center, called Città del Gusto. To order either, go to **www.gamberorosso.it,** or contact their NYC office, Telephone: 212-253-5653. If you travel to Italy, review our book's section on wine country touring.

technique, which is similar to the French *méthode champenoise* (a term that can be used legally to label only wines made in the Champagne region of France). Don't think these are sweet sparkling wines like Asti Spumante. They are Brut, very dry, *spumante* (the term for any sparkling wine in Italy).

In Chapter 5, "The Wine Label Decoder," we mentioned the bargain-priced Italian sparkling wines called *Prosecco* (starting at $11). These wines are produced in the Veneto DOCG region, north of Venice, using Prosecco grapes. Prosecco is very popular in the U.S. as a brunch wine. Mionetto vineyards now produce best-selling dry and delicious Rosé and red Proseccos (blended with Cabernet and Merlot), as well as dry and slightly sweet versions of the traditional white Prosecco. The handy thing about Prosecco is that it the bottles are closed with easy-to-remove metal crown caps like soda. Always served chilled.

ITALY'S BEST VINTAGES

The best Italian reds, especially the DOCGs, are not released until more than three years after the vintage because they are aged for several years in both barrel and bottle. Most Italian white wines are not barrel fermented or aged in oak. They are meant to be consumed young—within three to four years of the vintage date on the label.

Italy's best vintage years for the great reds are (exceptional years are marked with an asterisk) are: 1985, 1986, 1988, 1989, 1990*, 1991, 1993, 1994, 1995*, 1996*, 1997* (especially in Tuscany), 1998*, 1999* and 2000*, 2001*, 2003*, 2004.

Pairing Italian Wines with Food

The red wines of the Piedmont, including full-bodied reds such as Barolo or softer reds such as Dolcetto, are made to partner northwest Italy's cuisine of game, cheese fondue, and buttery, creamy risotto. Truffles are also used extensively in Piedmont cuisine since Alba, the capital city, is the source of white truffles.

Tuscany specializes in grilled meats (called *grillata mista*), Porcini mushrooms, pesto sauce, wild boar stews, Proscuitto, and Pecorino cheese—all of which are superb with Sangiovese wines. Tuscany's version of sweet white dessert wine, Vin Santo ("holy wine"), is almost always served with biscotti for dipping into the wine. The sweet white DOCG Ramandolo wine is served with everything from ham and salami to smoked trout and *zucotto* cake.

You can see the Italians love matching foods and wines. If you travel to Italy, your best chance to learn how to do this for yourself is to visit one of the many *enoteca*. These wine resource centers can include an extensive "library" of wines for tasting, a wine school, and a restaurant. They are found all over Italy. Keep in mind Italy's humongous annual wine tasting event, *VinItaly*, showcases thousands of wines and wineries and is open to the public. (Visit **www.vinitaly.com** for more information.)

Summary

This is the last, but not least, of our country chapters.

Americans often list Italy as the most desired travel destination. You can see why, from this brief overview of Italian wines, regions, and foods. I've escorted groups of my wine school graduates to both France and Tuscany. Everyone said France was the trip of a lifetime, but Italy was by far the better bargain: fabulous food, friendlier people, and more fun attitude. And they wanted to go back!

Part III

Buying, Serving, and Cellaring Wine

13

Serving Wine Correctly (When There's No Butler to Do It)

In this chapter:

* Learn simple rules for serving wine properly with a minimum of effort
* Learn the secrets of hosting a successful wine party

At several of the private wine parties I've organized, the host and hostess had the luxury of professional servers on staff. But what to do when you don't have a butler? Well, you learn to do it yourself. It's not that all of your guests really know the steps to proper wine service, but they've all had experience watching the wine steward in a fine restaurant. Let us teach you how to handle wine parties or wine dinners at home or at other venues where you might be in charge. You'll also learn trade secrets from keeping reds at proper serving temperature, to removing corks, choosing wine glasses, and preserving open bottles. After you read this chapter, you won't just look like a pro, you'll be one.

To do list

- ☐ Choose the correct glass for any wine
- ☐ Set your table for every wine occasion
- ☐ Remove wine corks elegantly and easily with the best openers
- ☐ Decant, pour, and serve wine like a pro
- ☐ Use simple, but effective, tools for saving leftover wine

Proper Wine Service—Rules of Engagement

Sometimes it's the little details that make or break the event. To prove this to you, I offer these funny stories of incorrect wine service by people who should know better. And I use these stories to introduce the first four wine service rules that you'll find in this chapter.

Horror Story #1: An hour before a lavish tasting, the "wine expert" arrived to verify the wines were in good condition. He opened each type, poured them into his wine glass, swirled, sniffed, and tasted. But then he proceeded to pour the wines that had just touched his mouth from his used glass back into the wine bottles to be served to the guests! As mystery author Janet Evanovich would write: "mental head slap." Hasn't this guy ever heard of germs? The wine company that hired him and the guests would have been appalled.

Wine Service Rule #1: Do not pour wine from your glass back into the bottle.

Horror Story #2: At festivals, wineries often display bottles in a big pan of ice. Some attendees dump wine from their glasses into the ice to get the next wine. The ice isn't sanitary to begin with since wine bottles are handled by many people. But this didn't stop one winery person from "rinsing" a customer's wine glass in the dirty ice and then giving it back for another pour!

Wine Service Rule #2: Ice used to chill the bottles is not to be used in the wine. And never use ice to rinse or chill a wine glass; it is unsanitary and it dilutes the wine.

Horror Story #3: Before teaching a wine class, I asked assistants to uncork the bottles. I didn't notice they had made the mistake of turning all the corks upside down and pushing the smaller (but moldy) tops of the corks into the bottles. Within a short time, the wines picked up the moldy smell from the corks and completely lost their aroma and flavor.

Wine Service Rule #3: Wipe off any visible green/black mold from the tops of wine corks before pulling them. Even if the corks have no mold from old cellars, never put the top of the cork into the bottle. All corks expand when they're extracted. If you can't squeeze the wine-stained end back into the bottle, cut the cork to fit or use a wine stopper made especially for storage. Many plastic corks can't be squeezed back into the bottle, nor can they be cut to fit.

Other common wine service mistakes are to "clank" the wine bottle against the wine glass when pouring or to put your fingers where guests will be putting their mouths. Since it's good manners to protect your guests, allow me to add one more rule.

Wine Service Rule #4: Do not touch the inside of a guest's wine glass with the top of the bottle as you pour. Don't put your fingers on the rim of clean glasses as you pick them up to hand to guests—always hold glasses by their stems, even dirty wine glasses that you are clearing from the table. And don't put your hand over the top of the bottle where the wine will flow; always hold bottles by the base.

As you read the other sections in this chapter, you'll discover the seven additional rules of wine service. It's my way of getting you to read a chapter whose topic may appear to be boring but is very important wine etiquette.

Things You'll Need

- ❏ Ice bucket and ice to achieve correct serving temperature
- ❏ Wine opener or corkscrew
- ❏ Decanter, strainer to remove sediment, and drip guard
- ❏ Wine glasses for each type of wine to be served
- ❏ Table settings, especially water, and appropriate foods
- ❏ Reusable wine bottle stoppers and gas preservative canister

Choosing Glasses and Wine Accessories

Don't be intimidated by the wide variety of wine glass shapes available today. Once you know how to match the shape of the glass to the wine being served, you can set a table that will make the most of the wine and occasion. If your budget won't allow an investment in a different style of wine glass for each type of wine served, you can use an all-purpose wine glass for all the wines. But, as you will read later, there is a reason why we have different shapes for wine glasses. And the way you arrange the glasses on the table matters, too, as you learn in this section of the chapter.

Finding the Perfect Glass

Wine glasses come in a variety of shapes—and not just for reasons of style and fashion. The shape of a wine glass can perfectly accentuate the aromas and taste profiles of each grape variety or type of wine. Some say it's the big-bowled beauty of the glasses that enhance a taster's perception, but the delicate shaping of each style has a physical purpose that works. This has been proven many times at Riedel "glass tastings" across the U.S. where each grape variety or type of wine is first served in the wrong shape glass and then tasted again in the correct glass. We may not know the physics behind this—though it has to do with the size and shape of the opening and the volume of air taken into the mouth along with the wine—but everyone at these tastings, wine experts included, remarks that the shape *does* make a difference. For more information about these glass tastings, go to **www.riedel.com**.

Figure 13.1 shows traditional and universal wine glass shapes for every type of wine from Port and Sherry to Champagne, sparkling and dessert wines, as well as dry white or Rosé and red wines.

FIGURE 13.1

Traditional and universal wine glass shapes for every type of wine.

White Wine   Brandy   Liqueur/ Dessert Wines

Champagne   Port   Sherry "Copita"   Red Wine

Wine glasses without stems are the hot ticket items today, especially Reidel "O" tumblers ($13 and up). Very innovative, these tumblers can also be used for fine Scotch, malt whiskey, or Cognac. Other trendy wine glass designs have indentations inside the bowl that more vigorously swirl/aerate the wine, or tiny imperfections in the glass itself to pick up the bubbles in sparkling wines.

Wine Service Rule #5: Always wash, repeatedly rinse, and dry all of your fine wine glasses by hand with linen tea towels. If your wine glasses are dishwasher safe, they will probably still need some hand rinsing and polishing before use. To save yourself a lot of trouble, take my tip and cover your clean wine glasses with a large piece of plastic wrap before putting them away in a cupboard. Then you can be sure they'll be dust and odor-free and ready for immediate use. Dusty glasses ruin great wine.

note Riedel wine glasses from Austria are the best-selling in the U.S. Their hand-blown, one-quarter lead crystal "Sommelier" collection has wine-specific shapes that complement individual types of wine, from Bordeaux or Cabernet to Burgundy or Chardonnay and Pinot Noir. You can buy Riedel at wine stores, from wine catalogs, or online at **www.surlatable.com**, which sells Sommelier for $55 to $85 per piece, and the more durable, machine-made Riedel "Vinum" line for $16 to $20 each. Riedel recently purchased another famous wine glass maker, Spiegelau.

Setting the Table

To properly set the table, the first-course wine glass (usually white or sparkling) is placed immediately above the knife and aligned vertically with it (knife is on the right, forks are on the left) in each place setting. If possible, each person's place setting is to be aligned with the one directly opposite on the table. Main course wine glasses, which are larger, are placed slightly inward and to the right of the first glass. Dessert wine glasses can be brought in later or are placed last.

To Chill or Not to Chill

Serving temperature is very important to your wine enjoyment. Many people serve Champagne or sparkling wines too warm. When the cork is popped, the wine foams all over the carpet. Considering the very high cost of some top-of-the-line French Champagnes, this is an incredible waste of good wine. If this happens to you in a restaurant, protest!

Wine Service Rule #6: White, Rosé, Champagne, and all sparkling wines (even red sparkling) are best served chilled to refrigerator temperature (42 to 45° F). It only takes 20 to 30 minutes in an "ice bath" of lots of ice and enough water to surround the bottle in an ice bucket to chill even the extra thick glass of sparkling wine bottles. The water is crucial; it hastens the chilling process while preventing possible freezing from ice alone. Alternatively, you can chill white, Rosé, or sparking wines in a refrigerator for two

caution   Never put wines in a freezer.

hours. Keep chilled bottles in an ice bucket or on the table in insulated wine holders that allow the wines to gradually warm up and release their flavors. If the wine is too cold for your taste, remove it from the ice bucket.

Wine Service Rule #7: Non-sparkling reds (especially light-bodied Pinot Noir and Beaujolais) are best served at wine cellar temperature, which is 55° F.—not room temperature, which is too warm. (Even air-conditioned room temperature is 72+° F.) To keep all reds at the optimum temperature outside the cellar, especially during hot summer months, fine restaurants use a "water bath" of lots of water and a couple of handfuls of ice in an ice bucket, which they bring to the table. Or you can request that any red be placed in ice and water for 5 minutes. Any colder (refrigerator temperature) and the reds will not reveal their fruit; if substantially warmer, the reds may taste "hot" from the alcohol.

Popping the Cork

Sommeliers or wine stewards carry compact "waiter's friend" wine openers, each with a handy folding knife to entirely cut off foil capsules over the cork or to remove plastic covering the cork. These professional corkscrews also have a smooth spiral corkscrew and metal lever to make it easy to open a bottle while holding it in front of guests. Practice with this type of corkscrew on empty bottles with the corks pushed back in until you are proficient.

Wine Service Rule #8: Always screw the spiral of the corkscrew all the way down until no more is showing before you place the lever against the top edge of the glass bottle and gently pull. Otherwise, the cork will break. If the cork does break and part remains in the bottle, put the point of the corkscrew in the middle of the cork; spiral down carefully and pull it out. If bits of cork fall into the wine, pour the first glass of wine containing the cork bits and dump it. Then use a clean glass for the next pour.

FINDING A GREAT CORKSCREW

Wine catalogs and online wine websites (www.wineenthusiast.com) are filled with every manner of wine accessory and corkscrew. One of the most popular corkscrews for home use is the "Rabbit" by Metrokane. It is handheld and can either extract the cork or fully re-insert it back into the bottle. Larger table-model corkscrews do both these tasks in one fluid motion, making it easy to open large numbers of bottles for wine parties. Of course, you don't need any corkscrew or stopper to open or reseal screwtop wines.

Decanting, Pouring, and Serving

Older wines, particularly vintage Porto, will have sediment and will need to be decanted. The easy way to do this is to buy a wine funnel with built-in strainer, place it in the decanter, pour the older wine through the funnel, and then serve the wine from the decanter at the table. Young tannic red wines also benefit from the aeration of being poured into a decanter. Older wines have more delicate aromas that fade away, so keep their stoppers in the decanters. Younger wines don't need stoppers inserted since they benefit from "breathing" time to open up. And those horizontal wine "baskets" for pouring have no real purpose other than presentation.

There's a reason for everything regarding table service. Professionals use "drip stops"—either circles placed around the neck of the bottle on the outside or curled foil inserts placed inside the open bottle—to prevent red wine from dripping onto clothing or tablecloths when poured. Many people say you can avoid drips by simply giving the bottle a slight twist as you finish pouring, but drip stops are safer.

Other useful wine accessories include Champagne "pliers" to muscle out difficult corks. Remember, Champagne and sparkling wines have corks that are jammed into the bottle to hold the precious bubbles inside; and some of them may be very hard to remove. You will see these wine pliers in wine catalogs—they look like a pair of small silver pliers. If you have nothing but your hands to remove the corks from

Champagne and sparkling wines, don't use your thumbs! Either hold the heavy bottom of the bottle steady while you ease out the cork by turning it gently until it pops (my preference), or turn the bottom of the bottle while holding the cork stiffly until it begins to come out.

Wine Service Rule #9: Servers pour wine (and remove dirty glasses) from the right of each guest, moving clockwise around the table. When serving wine to guests, do not fill glasses more than 1/3 full so they have room to swirl and sniff.

When deciding on the order of the wines for a wine tasting or wine dinner, serve from the lightest wines (in color, body and alcohol) wines to the heaviest, and from the driest to the sweetest. I actually look at the labels to find the alcohol content of each wine and then serve the highest-alcohol wines last. The order of wines for a typical wine tasting or wine dinner would be light, dry white wines; oak-aged, full-bodied dry white wines; Rosé wines; light, fruity, dry red wines; older red wines; rich, concentrated, higher-alcohol dry reds; and dessert wines.

You may also be wondering, who first tastes the wine at a dinner party? If the host or hostess is pouring, it is their obligation to have tasted the wine before it's brought to the table. If a server is pouring, the host or hostess at the head of the table receives the first sample to taste. Once he or she approves the wine, servers pour to all the other guests around the table first, and then come back to the host or hostess to give them a full pour. This is the exactly the same procedure as in a restaurant. If the server runs out of wine before serving all of the guests, he or she simply gets another bottle. In a restaurant, the host will be given a tasting sample of every bottle for approval before the other guests are served. Of course, this is impractical if it's a large dinner party with many tables. Then everyone takes it on faith the wine will be good until someone blows the whistle and says a particular bottle isn't.

Storing Leftover Wine

For years, consumers have tried various wine stoppers, as well as plastic pumps that suck out the air, to keep leftover wine fresh. The problem is that none of these work for long, and the pump doesn't work at all with sparkling wines. Storing leftover sparkling wines requires a special metal closure that screws down to form a tight seal over the bottle.

Blind tastings of a non-sparkling wine treated using vacuum pumps and more expensive restaurant systems concluded that the least expensive, easiest to use, and most effective way to save wine was the "Private Preserve" gas canister that's available in most wine stores and online at **www.privatepreserve.com**. This system requires that you spray the gas (an ideal combination of three inert gases) down into the partially full bottle, then recork or stopper the bottle and store it in an upright position (preferably inside the refrigerator). The canisters cost about $10 and contain 120 "sprays." The wine experts in this July 2005 study (see the *Beverage Journal* or **www.bevnetwork.com**) also concluded that, if you don't use any preservation system, refrigerating wine after opening kept the wine fresher.

Hosting a Wine Party

Hosting your own wine party can be lots of fun, but you'll enjoy the event much more if you enlist some help in preparation and serving. Hire or cajole the help you need to open bottles, pour wines, serve food, and continuously clean up. For large parties, borrow extra wine glasses or rent them from party suppliers. Have lots of non-sparkling bottled water on ice for party guests and encourage them to drink plenty of water. Other non-alcohol beverages are fine, but I recommend that you refrain from serving beer or liquor. Beer causes the men to leave their wives and congregate in a corner, while liquor gets everyone drunk too quickly. Don't put all of the food out at once or it will be gone in the first hour. And don't plug in the coffee pot until after the last wine has been served—the smell of coffee overpowers wine.

Wine Service Rule #10: Limit the number of wines to 5 or 6, or your guests won't remember what they drank. Be organized and have a printed menu of the wines with descriptions in the order they'll be served. Hire a wine speaker, or act as your own, to introduce and talk about each wine and answer questions. Chill wines ahead of time and provide dump buckets for excess wine. Always have extra bottles of both the reception wine (which is served while waiting for everyone to arrive), and the final blockbuster red.

Wine Service Rule #11: To estimate the total number of bottles needed for the evening, allow 1/2 bottle or 12 oz. minimum per person, plus extras. But don't open all the bottles; save some for door prizes or for your private stash. If guests complain of a bad bottle, take it away. Put the cork back in it and return it later to the wine store for a credit.

Greet guests at the entrance with a glass of Champagne or sparkling wine in tall flute glasses on silver trays. Then lead them to a pre-plated appetizer such as crab cakes or shrimp that they can eat standing up. This will set a very impressive tone for the evening. If this is a party or wine reception, set up wine and food stations such as a cheese display, pasta or bean salads, chicken satay, and beef

caution It is *not* a good idea to ask guests to each bring a bottle of wine to taste for a party. Each bottle will only serve 8 people, which means many guests at larger parties will never get to taste the wine that someone raves about. Besides, can you really trust people to bring a range of wines that showcase different grapes and countries?

tenderloin around the room or in different rooms. Open each station one by one as wines are poured. This will create a subtle "program" for guests to follow. Then enjoy the fun. Your guests will be wowed and very appreciative.

Summary

You don't need a butler to serve wine like a professional, especially if you practice the rules of wine service you learned in this chapter. You'll be able to hold your own with any group, including the wine snobs, and be jolly happy yourself while doing so.

In our next chapter we teach you to navigate any retail wine store and become a savvy wine shopper.

Being a Savvy Retail Shopper

Serving customers in the wine stores where I worked in London and the U.S. was always a thrill for me. The secret to creating satisfied customers was quizzing them first to find out what kind of wine they needed and at what price—and then putting the bottle in their hands. It didn't matter what I liked or what my bosses prodded me to sell. I knew the clientele would simply never return if I didn't do right by them.

Unfortunately, not all retailers have the palate to choose carefully among the overwhelming number of wines presented to them every week, nor do they have the backbone to say "no" to importers who choose mediocre wines for their portfolio. Wine is not worth any price, even a discounted price, if it tastes terrible. Using the suggestions in this book, you can work with your wine retailer to be sure you get the right wines for the right price.

14

In this chapter:

* Learn how to identify a good wine retailer
* Learn how to choose a perfect wine for any occasion

To do list

- ❑ Track wine preferences in your own wine "diary"
- ❑ Place special orders and purchase wine through direct shipping
- ❑ Find the best wine store in your area

What Customers Want—Stores Who Provide It

Our obligation as consumers is to know what we like, the reason for our purchase, and how much we're willing to pay. Sometimes we don't know the answers until the store's wine consultant asks, "What kind of wine have you had that you liked?" "Is $15 too much to pay, or can you go higher?" and "How many bottles do you need?" If buying a wine gift, you may not know what to ask for, though I make some wine suggestions for different occasions later in this chapter. But if you're buying wine for yourself, then you need to speak up and be honest with the clerk about your tastes, explaining whether you like your wine dry or medium-dry, light or full-bodied, fruit driven or more austere, low or high in alcohol content. Most stores display wines by grape variety and country, so stroll through the racks and read the labels.

Things You'll Need

- ❑   Notebook or other wine diary
- ❑   Computer and online access

Keeping Track of Preferences

Savvy wine shoppers keep notes in a "wine diary" or notebook they carry at all times, complete with each wine's vintage year, winery or brand name, grape variety, appellation or vineyard, and importer. Others use "Label-Off" clear adhesive sheets available in wine catalogs to strip off the label from the bottle and stick it in their cellar record books. (Trying to soak off the label never works.) If you don't have Label-Off, draw the label and copy all the prominent words. Memory alone is unreliable.

Keeping accurate records of your wine preferences is important if you want to rely on them for guiding your purchases. Recently I purchased a Petite Sirah for $10 that I really liked. A week later I saw the same brand on sale for only $7. That should have made me suspicious. But I took it home, and it tasted like vinegar. It was also one year older than the vintage I raved about. Normally that kind of difference doesn't exist between one vintage year and the next. But in this case, the close-out price was a red flag that it wasn't the same. Perhaps it had suffered in transport or storage.

Special Orders and Direct Shipping

Every retail store can try to "special order" a wine you've read about in some wine magazine, if it's distributed through normal channels in their area. But no one should expect a wine store to stock every wine request made by every customer. That's simply not possible or impractical, as a customer may not want a requested wine a second time. American wine retailers can check any wine's availability by looking it up. If you know the full name, the *Beverage Journal* they subscribe to lists brands that local wholesalers carry. Or you can do this before visiting a store by searching for the wine on the Internet. Larger winery websites list distributors by state. And any good retail store's wine consultant can recommend a wine that's very similar to your request.

WINE BY MAIL

On May 16, 2005, the Supreme Court of the United States ruled in favor of out-of-state wineries and their desire to ship directly to the public in Michigan, New York, Florida, Vermont, Massachusetts, Connecticut, Indiana, and Ohio. Other states were unaffected because they already allowed at least some shipping. But 16 states still do not allow any direct shipping: MT, UT, SD, KS, OK, AR, MS, AL, TN, KY, PA, ME, RI, NJ, DE, and MD. If you live in these states, you need to lobby your legislature. The ruling will help the 83% of U.S. wineries that are too small to distribute nationally and who only sell their wines from tasting rooms, their websites, or through third-party companies. For example, Winetasting Network (www.winetasting.com) uses their website to sell wine from 150 small wineries. Refer to *The Wall Street Journal*, May 17, 2005 for more details regarding this ruling.

Identifying the Best Wine Stores

The best wine stores track your wine preferences for you. Even suburban wine stores have software to register customer profiles so they can email you when they have tastings or a sale of your preferred wines. Other indications that you're dealing with a top retailer are wine clubs or frequent buyer discounts, websites, in-store wine con-sultants, rating cards from major wine magazines on selected wines, huge selection, and temperature control for the best wines, as well as cheeses, crackers, wine accessories, gift bags, and books.

The best wine consultants can educate you as you're shopping: they explain labels, name the most reliable importers and wineries, describe how wines taste, and discuss food partners. A good wine consultant can also pre-sell expensive wines even before they hit store shelves by calling customers in their database. Some small wine stores with fewer wine consultants arrange their wines with a color-coded or number system that distinguishes between light varietals or heavy, reds or whites, dry or dessert style so customers can help themselves. What most customers want first and foremost are the food and wine marriages.

note With 36 stores from New Jersey to South Carolina and annual sales of 1 million cases of wine, Total Wine (www.totalwine.com) is the largest independent wine retailer in America. Owners are brothers David and Robert Trone, who personally select wines and take lower mark-ups so customers save money.

The old saying was: "pink (Rosé) wines for pink foods such as ham; white wines for white foods such as fish; and red wines for red meat." But all wines are much more versatile than that. Pink or Rosé wines are also great with egg dishes and salads. White wines also partner vegetarian or rice dishes, white pizza, or pasta with white clam or alfredo sauce, pork, turkey or chicken. Light reds such as Pinot Noir are great with salmon, mushroom dishes, sushi, and hot pots. Heavier reds are perfect with any spicy or grilled cuisine. Think outside the box when matching wines to menus. When buying favorites, add some new wine for dinner tonight. It's the only way to learn what really pleases your palate.

To do list

- ❑ Choose sparkling wines for special occasions
- ❑ Choose red wines for gift giving

Finding the Jewels—Everyday and Celebration Wines

Before you invest in a case of wine, buy one bottle to try. If buying a mixed case of 12 bottles, ask for a discount. Return bad wines, with the wine in the bottles, for store credit. Ask for help with party planning; most stores are very experienced. Stocking up on wines may get you an invitation to free "trade tastings" where you can sample many wines from one wholesaler or importer.

Most people choose everyday wines by price point, palatability, and snappy labels. Special-occasion wines are chosen because of a particular holiday, celebration, or for gift giving. Here are my suggestions for finding the right wine among thousands.

Special Occasion Sparklers

Starting the calendar with New Year's, weddings, and Valentine's Day, the natural choice is top-of-the-line French Vintage Champagne in the $45 to $100+ price range. This will create just the right mood with a loved one or woo any boss at the holidays—just slip the gift into a fancy wine bag.

Save expensive Champagne for the bride and groom—but tell them don't fly it to the honeymoon, or it may explode. The best value in French Champagne is always Brut Non-Vintage, starting at just $20. If you have large groups to serve, try Spanish CAVA, California or Italian sparklers, especially rosé or Blanc de Noirs, which go so well with chocolate. Sweet red sparklers such as Bonny Doon's Freisa, Banfi's Brachetto, or Rumball sparkling Shiraz will elicit wows when served with premium chocolate cookies, biscotti, brownies, or cake. Wine and chocolate—now that's a great gift combination, including for Mother's Day.

Ruby Reds

If you know someone is a wine collector, then choose a really good red they can cellar. The best stores will have a list of elite red Bordeaux, Rhône, California Cabs, Italian Super-Tuscans, Vintage Porto, and Australia Shiraz. Buy highly rated recent vintages such as 2003 so they can save it for a future anniversary. Wine gift baskets—there are some great ones for sale at Christmas time in Sam's and Costco—contain fine chocolates and biscuits to accompany the wines. If you are creating your own gift basket and delivering it personally, you may also want to include terrific cheeses to partner great reds.

Father's Day reds might include wines made by famous golfers such as Greg Norman or former race car drivers such as Mario Andretti. If your Dad's more down to earth, then buying Cline's Red Truck will get a laugh. (It also tastes pretty good.)

And don't forget rare but affordable wines as hostess gifts, such as German Eiswein, "organic" wines for health nut friends (**www.organicwine.com**), and fantastic new kosher wines: from Yarden, Golan or, Barken Wineries in Israel; or from Herzog and Hagafen Wineries in California. Good kosher wines are also available from Argentina and several other countries.

When shopping for special gifts, turn to a reliable importer's collection.

Wine importer Wynn Pennington of Motovino (email: Wynn@motovino.com) has assembled a delicious roster of three mid-price brands—"Wishes" French varietals, "Vidanueva" Spanish wines, and "Crush Pad" Red from California. "Crush Pad" is already a hit in several states. Pennington travels extensively to do all his own selections; and his skill shows in the crisp whites, delightful Rosé, and jammy reds he makes available to his customers. The lively, attractive labels, designed by Wynn's artist wife Shannon, will also seduce you.

Summary

Each trip to the wine store gives you a chance to become an explorer—exotic locales beckon, beautiful artwork entices—as you escape into the sensual pleasure of holding the bottles and imagining how good the wines taste. In this chapter, you've learned some basic "shopping savvy" for finding a great wine store and choosing the best wines for any occasion. You've also learned some tips for working with your wine retailer and for logging your own wine notes, to help you in making future selections.

In our next chapter, we teach you to how to read a restaurant wine list and order wine like a pro.

15

Ordering Wine Like a Pro

Choosing wine from a restaurant's wine list typically requires a knack for finding the best selections among limited offerings. In this chapter, you learn how to find the "jewels" hidden among less interesting wines on the list. Whether traveling to Las Vegas, the #1 wine town in the U.S., hosting a private dinner or corporate wine party, or just eating in a restaurant, you need these "insider" tips and common sense recommendations. What follows are tips on reading any wine list, interacting with the wine steward or server, and choosing wines to complement the menu.

In this chapter:

* Managing the daily mail
* Learn how to "translate" a restaurant's wine list and work with the restaurant's server or sommelier
* Learn to choose wines for others at your table
* Understand how to pair wines with dinner themes and cuisines
* Learn the "ritual" of tasting wine in a restaurant

To do list

- ❏ Practice reading restaurant wine lists by category and by price
- ❏ Choose wines that will please everyone at your table and complement your dinner courses
- ❏ Learn proper technique for tasting wine, and how to send back a wine that doesn't pass the test

Restaurant Wine Lists and Service

When you walk into any restaurant, you can tell how serious they are about serving wine by the prominent presence of a wine display. It could be distinctive wine art that greets customers, dining tables made from old Champagne riddling racks, floor-to-ceiling glass wine vault with spiral staircase that the sommelier climbs to retrieve wines, or beautiful wine glasses at every place setting.

Engage servers in conversation about wines on the list. Properly trained staff must be able to discuss the origin, grape variety, and merits of any wine on the list and make wine suggestions for every menu item. You are there to relax with a loved one or entertain guests, so you do not want to get chatty with the server. But after you get the wine list, the server should ask if you need any help making a choice; so explain what kinds of wine you like and ask the server to point out the best examples on the wine list. Once you and your guest or guests decide what foods you want to order, you can again ask for a specific wine or wines to match the dishes. In fact, good servers will volunteer these wine and food pairings without you having to ask for them. And the best restaurants stay solvent by having trained staff who know wines and can sell them. Restaurants make much more profit on wine than on food.

To do list

- ☐ Order wines for multiple diners at your table
- ☐ Choose wines by the glass, or "samplers" of a series of wines

Satisfying Everyone at the Table

As a courtesy to your guests, don't wait until everyone has decided what foods they want to eat before getting them something to drink. Guests are thirsty when they arrive, and the first duty of any good host or hostess is to get them some wine. A table of four people will usually order a bottle of wine with appetizers and another bottle for the entrées, or a total of half a bottle of wine per person. If two guests want white wine and two want red, simply order one bottle of each at the beginning of the meal. You can also order a bottle of Champagne for everyone to share—that will

note In London wine bars, smart owners move expensive bottles that haven't sold with a little theater—they ring a bell and announce that a rare bottle of Guigal Côtes-Rôtie "Brune et Blonde" (brunette and blonde, meaning dark and light soil in the vineyard) will be opened if four glasses at $24 each are sold. This is a bargain to anyone who has never tasted these rare wines. But they will only sell if they are still in mint condition.

get the party started. Or let everyone order a wine by the glass. Each will get exactly what he or she wants and can share sips of stunning wines with table mates. Then everyone can relax and look at the menus.

The best restaurants have extensive by-the-glass lists or "highlight wines" available by the glass under every category, including fine wines. Wine lists also invariably start with Champagnes and sparkling wines for welcome toasts and celebrations. American diners don't mind paying $15 a glass (usually a 6 oz. pour in a restaurant) or $50 a bottle (about four 6 oz. glasses) and more for a great taste experience.

It is also the obligation of the host or hostess to make sure the wine arrives at proper serving temperature. Reds should be cool to the touch—yes, it's all right to actually feel the bottle. If reds are too warm, ask for ice and water in an ice bucket to chill them for five minutes.

You can also further your wine education by ordering a wine "flight"—small tasting samples or short pours of three or more wines served side by side for one all-inclusive price. The wine flight could include three types of Sherry from Spain, three Latin reds, three dessert wines, or wines made from three exotic

tip

Don't miss an opportunity to attend restaurant "wine dinners" or order special "fixed price" menus that include a different wine with each course—great ways to learn wine pairing. And pay attention to special wine pricing on week nights or at cocktail hours. Some restaurants discount wines as much as 50% during promotions.

white grape varieties such as Pinot Blanc from Alsace, Fiano from Italy, or Verdejo from Spain. Some restaurants may offer a smaller, less expensive "tasting size" of any wine available by the glass. Either way, this is truly comparison wine shopping because diners invariably order a full glass or bottle of their favorite.

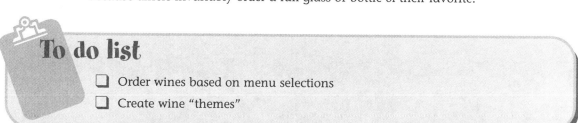

To do list

- ☐ Order wines based on menu selections
- ☐ Create wine "themes"

Choosing Wines by Theme and Cuisine

Customers who know a bit about wine seek variety in their passionate pursuit of palate pleasure. And they're the ones who spend the most money on wine in restaurants or for hotel events.

To find the best wine values on a restaurant by-the-glass or bottle list and on a hotel banquet wine list, choose wines that are just above the lowest-priced wines. These mid-price wines are often chosen with more care by wine managers and are a cut above mass-market wines.

Then narrow the wine choices to fit a theme or cuisine. Here are some examples of wine and food pairings that can satisfy everyone at your table:

- A sparkling wine to accompany appetizers such as crab cakes
- An elegant French Chablis to accompany Caesar salad
- Australian or New Zealand wines for drinking with Asian-inspired cuisine
- Smooth Italian red to partner with pasta or cheeses
- Latin reds for pork tenderloin or upscale Mexican or Southwest dishes
- California Cabernet to pair with beef tenderloin
- A late-harvest Riesling or Australian Muscat for a selection of desserts

note Why does the average American restaurant or hotel think that clients want a wine list with the same old inexpensive brand of Merlot and Chardonnay that they buy every day in grocery stores? They don't. Yet these easily identifiable wines not only take up valuable selling space on the list, but they also carry such exorbitant prices that clients think the entire wine list is overpriced. That cuts the client's appetite for wine, period.

tip If you're ordering wine for a large group or banquet, avoid choosing wines priced by the glass. That can add up to quite a bill when serving a crowd. (Also avoid selecting banquet food items sold by the piece for the same reason.) It's much less expensive to order young, rich tasting, but mid-priced wines by the bottle.

RESTAURANTS SET NEW STANDARDS FOR WINE OFFERINGS

Wine has a higher profit margin than food. (You wouldn't believe how much hotels and restaurants pay for top-quality ingredients from steak to strawberries, and there is so much waste. Wine is not as perishable and is often marked up more than three times its wholesale cost. Hotel markups are even higher). That's why servers must know wine. Bellagio Las Vegas wine director Rob Bigelow is not only a Master Sommelier himself, but he also trains and encourages his staff to become Master Sommeliers. Now that's the standard for hotels and restaurants to aspire to.

Trend-setting new Atlanta restaurant Two Urban Licks (**www.twourbanlicks.com**) whose talented chef is Scott Serpas, turned away from traditional wine service altogether. Instead, he serves good wines in carafes filled from taps connected to custom stainless steel wine "kegs" behind glass in a temperature-controlled room. Other innovative ways to promote wine include humorous wine list terms such as "second mortgage wines," and even "third mortgage wines" at chef/owner Kevin Rathbun's popular new Atlanta restaurant, Rathbun's (**www.rathbunsrestaurant.com**). Their easy-to-read wine list is printed with their menu and is organized by whites and reds in price categories: $22, $32, $42, $52, $62 and up per bottle; and by-the-glass wines marked $6.50 to $13+.

To do list

- ☐ Learn proper corking and pouring procedures
- ☐ Check wine appearance, aroma, and flavor
- ☐ Accept or reject wine gracefully

Tasting the Wine

It's what servers do at the table that determines the level of wine training in any restaurant. Waiters should never uncork wine before they bring wine to the table and present it to the customer who ordered it. This is for label verification. Customers need to be given the chance to determine that the wine and vintage year are correct, so they know they're getting the wine they ordered. The server then pulls the cork and places it on the table in front of the person who ordered the wine. The customer's part of the ritual is *not* to smell the cork—cork smells like cork—but rather to smell and taste the wine that's poured into a glass for judging.

The customer first swirls the wine gently in the glass, then sniffs the wine for off-odors. If the wine smells "corked" (overpowering mold and chlorine), tell the waiter so and refuse the bottle. My advice is to order some other wine to avoid a repeat disappointment. Other off-odors such as sulfur should dissipate as you swirl the wine. Sniff the wine again and take a good sip; roll the wine around on your tongue, then do the professional gurgle by sucking in air over the wine before swallowing. If the wine meets your approval, nod yes to the waiter. If a sommelier or wine steward is wearing a "tastevin" or silver wine cup, he or she may taste the wine at the same time as the customer. The sommelier will confirm the wine's condition.

This restaurant ritual is to be done very low-key; arrogant abuse of staff by customers is boorish. And vice versa: wine stewards are there to serve the customer, not bludgeon them with their expertise.

The 2004 Nobel Prize in medicine was won by two Americans who discovered how people recognize an estimated 10,000 aromas, from fine wine to perfume. Their research revealed odor-sensing proteins, called receptors, in the nose. They traced how the receptors send their information to the brain. Dr. Richard Axel and Linda B. Buck not only enhanced our understanding of the most enigmatic of our senses, but they also mapped it.

Thanks to them, we now know that people have 350–400 types of these receptors, each of which can detect only a limited number of aromas. When a person sniffs fine wine, a mix of different types of molecules flows over the receptors in the back of the nose. That activates an array of the receptors, but only those primed to respond to those particular molecules. The brain then notes which receptors are activated and interprets this pattern as the smell.

Since any given receptor can participate in more than one pattern, you might have both a flower and a cheese recognized by some of the same receptors. The two scientists showed that only one kind of receptor appears on each of the 5 million odor-sensing nerve cells in the nose, and that these cells are wired directly into the brain. No wonder we need to take a deep sniff of our wines!

Subject to Change—Prices and Vintages

Vintages are always subject to change on a wine list, so please cut restaurants some slack. Their suppliers make deliveries every week. And when they run out of one vintage, they send the next. Prices are also subject to change for the same reason, which is why smart restaurants print this disclaimer on their lists or computer generate their wine lists so they can be constantly updated.

What Makes an Award-Winning Wine List

Even budget-minded diners are voyeurs when it comes to a great wine list that makes them want to order something new or drool over elite wines. I just learned that the wine list I initially created for a new Latin restaurant, Mitra, opened by Sia Moshk of Sia's restaurant fame in Atlanta, received an Award of Excellence from the *Wine Spectator* in their August 31, 2005, issue. It was a very compact list with a distinct Latin wine flair, but I believe it won because of several innovations: flights of exotic Sherry, Reposado and An[td]ejo Tequilas; upscale rums from Venezuela and Nicaragua; dry white and red wine flights of unique grape varieties; 10 different "by the glass" wines from 10 different countries, plus 20 more; unusual sparkling wines, including dessert sparklers; and everything from organic Rioja and Monastrell from Spain to Petit Verdot from Australia and Pinot Noir from Tasmania. I kept prices under $62 a bottle. And when I couldn't afford big-name California Cabernets above that, I put them as half-bottles on the list. Where there's a will, there's a way. It took four months of tasting and revisions, but it greatly excited the customers.

Summary

Like retail stores, restaurants order their wines by country and grape variety. Since you've been studying diligently by reading previous chapters, you will have no trouble deciphering any restaurant or banquet wine list if you take it section by section. In this chapter, you've learned the restaurant "ritual" of wine service, how to interact with servers in restaurants, how to please everyone at the table, how to choose wines by theme and cuisine, and how to find the bargains on any wine list. Now you'll be able to order wine like a pro and hold your own with any sommelier.

In our next chapter, we explain everything you need to know about wine collecting and wine storage.

16

Collecting and Storing Wine

I f you're a casual wine drinker, buying wines for immediate consumption, then you can treat wine informally. Buy a simple wine rack to keep in a cool, dark kitchen pantry that's free from odors, mold, and vibration—or chill this week's bottles in the refrigerator. Just don't keep everyday wines too long, or you'll become one of the many people who proudly display old bottles of cheap wine that long ago turned to vinegar (and not good vinegar either). Even wine aficionados are guilty of the sin of keeping wine past its expiration date because they did not save famous labels or great vintage years or keep wines cool. This is the cardinal crime—to let good wine go bad without anyone having had the pleasure of drinking it.

Do not let wine snobs or pricey wines intimidate you. Anyone who has a few bottles of good wine at home is a collector. Knowing which bottles to buy, how to care for them, and for how long, brings wine distinction—and satisfaction. We hereby launch you on your journey to becoming a wine connoisseur. In this chapter, you learn how to create safe storage environments for your wine and how to pull together a collection you can enjoy for years to come.

Creating a Wine Cellar on Any Budget

Unlike antiques, which have a much longer shelf life, wine is a living, organic substance that improves and then dies in the bottle. Buying wine for investment purposes is much riskier than buying fine paintings, which can be restored if they deteriorate with age. But the principle is the same. Does the wine have a pedigree? Is it in good condition? Have the critics raved about it?

Bottles of wine drop in value when their fill level diminishes over time, a condition auction houses and wine experts refer to as *low ullage*. The condition of the bottle's label also affects value; old bottles without original labels are worthless unless the cork verifies the estate and vintage year. Even then, without labels, they are not valued as highly as bottles with intact, readable labels. That's why humidity control is important. If the humidity is too high, labels discolor or fall off.

Things You'll Need

- ☐ Storage space in cellar, kitchen, or dining area
- ☐ Tiles, racks, or cabinets for storage

Inexpensive Wine Storage Techniques

Terra-cotta drainage tiles stacked horizontally make nice, round cubby holes that are perfect for storing wine. When purchasing the tiles, take along the fattest squat wine bottle you can find to be certain the tiles are large enough to accommodate any bottle in your collection. Everyday wines can be stored in a wall of these terra-cotta tiles in the middle of a built-in bookcase or virtually anywhere, as long as the sun doesn't directly shine on the wine. Or the terra-cotta tiles can be used in a proper temperature-controlled wine cellar. Bear in mind that 75% humidity is ideal for wine cellars.

If you prefer wood racking, Apex Sauna and Wine Cellars (**www.apexwinecellars. com**) has reasonably-priced cedar and mahogany wine racks with bins and/or individual slots. The Apex website also has a Wizard feature to help you design your own cellar. And if you want Apex to install or create a permanent temperature-controlled wine cellar in your home (inside a kitchen closet or carved out of a basement area), their knowledge of vapor barriers (to prevent moisture or mildew from the humidity) is invaluable. Two other sources for racking include **www.winerack-shop.com** for do-it-yourselfers and Wine Cellar Innovations **www.winecellarinnovations.com**, which offers design services, lovely wine motif artwork, cellar doors, refrigeration, and kits.

note Most builders now realize homeowners want easy access in the kitchen for at least some of their wines, and they include wine storage areas in kitchen designs.

Storing Wine in Climate-controlled Cabinets

You will also find that culinary stores and showrooms such as Viking Range, Kitchen Aid, or Westye (which carries Wolf Sub-Zero appliances) feature top-of-the-line wine cabinets that are built-ins or under-the-counter units with both white wine (45° F. so whites are chilled and ready to serve) and red wine (55° F.) glass-fronted sections with digital read-outs that make your kitchen wine collection visible to visitors.

And for those with very upscale homes who can afford to pay from $30,000 to $200,000 for a showplace wine cellar (that's without the wine), there are people such as Keith Knupp of Wine Designs in Dallas, GA. He custom-crafts cellars using the finest materials, including travertine or limestone for floors, old brick or stone, and hand-cut beams. Typically, his wealthy customers know a lot about wine and attend auctions around the world or hire a wine expert to fill their cellar for them. No wonder rare wines are becoming so hard to find.

caution It is also possible to buy free-standing wine vaults or cabinets that are temperature- and humidity-controlled for $200 to $2,000. The price and size vary according to the appliance as well as the place where it is purchased. Although these small refrigerated units are handy to have behind your in-home bar, most suffer from short life spans. Everyone I've known to purchase one of these units has said that they've worked for only a year or so. So don't pay too much, and check out return or repair policies and warranties before buying.

A VALUABLE COLLECTION

On June 2, 2005, the *Atlanta Journal-Constitution* newspaper covered the story of the late Lee Kramer's basement wine cellar. It is considered to be the best single-owner collection in the U.S. The esteemed auction house, Christie's, is slated to sell the collection this year. What an inspiring story, since Mr. Kramer bought cases of good Bordeaux and Burgundy decades ago for $7 to $13 per bottle (impossible at today's prices) and his collection is now worth more than $1 million. The key was that he kept these 1947 Château Cheval Blanc and 1969 DRC Romanée-Conti wines in their original wooden cases (which have the great names burned into the wood) in a dark, humidity- and temperature-controlled wine cellar.

Things You'll Need

- ❑ Wine software
- ❑ Wine inventory log

Tracking Your Wine Inventory

If you have a large wine collection, keeping track of the wines in that collection is an important part of maintaining your investment. You can track your wine inventory using special software packages or by creating and maintaining your own inventory log or Excel spreadsheet. Wine cellar tracking software packages are available in most wine catalogs. Make sure to get a money back guarantee before purchase because some programs I've used in the past did not work well. Do your research first on the Internet. One source for wine tracking software is **www.imageryproducts.com**. Before buying, make sure the software provides updates on new vintages and can tell you when to drink which wines.

> **tip** Most connoisseurs measure their wine cellars in bottles: 1,200 bottles or 100 cases being average, 6,000 bottles or 500 cases being above average, and 12,000 bottles (1,000 cases) and up being a superior personal collection. A few Americans have cellars three times that size, and some restaurants have much bigger wine collections. For the rest of us, a few cases of prime wine is a fun start-up.

To do list

- ❑ Learn the basic rules of wine collection
- ❑ Build a beginning wine collection
- ❑ Grow your collection to intermediate status
- ❑ Form a connoisseur's collection
- ❑ Determine the value of your collection

Smart Wine Collecting

Anyone with a love of wine can take part in the enjoyment and investment potential of creating a wine collection. Whether you're interested in a simple "beginner's level" collection or would like to take your wine cellar to professional heights, the information in the following sections will help you choose wisely as you build your collection.

Ten Rules of Wine Collecting

When you're putting together your own wine collection, follow these simple rules to gain the most value and satisfaction from the experience:

1. Buy what you like to drink and share it with friends.

2. Always have everyday drinking wines on hand, or you'll end up using collectors' items in the spaghetti sauce.

3. If a wine does not have concentrated fruit character, it won't age well. Without it, aging will reduce tannins but expose nothing but acidity.

4. If a wine isn't phenomenal when young, it won't get much better with age; and it may not be worth a high price.

5. Research vintage year ratings for each type of wine you want to buy; even good wines from poor vintages don't last.

6. Consistent temperature throughout the year is better for your wines than sharp fluctuations of heat and cold.

7. Warmer storage conditions mature wines more quickly.

8. When buying wine "futures," do not pay until delivery (see Chapter 4, "Vintage Years/Vintage Wines").

9. To find out which wines are collectors' items, buy the latest editions of *Wine Spectator's Ultimate Buying Guide* or Robert Parker's *Wine Buyer's Guide*.

10. It pays to comparison shop at several wine stores before buying expensive wines. Markups and wholesale sources may differ, and you may find a bargain.

caution Be cautious about buying wine from estate sales or individual collectors. Not only is it against the law in some states to buy wines directly from individuals, but it may also be unwise. Wines from estate sales may not have been stored properly. Some families donate old family wine collections to charity instead of selling them, so they can claim a tax deduction rather than risking a low-value sale.

Putting Together a Beginner's Collection

To create a strong beginner's collection of wine, start with five cases, one case each of five wines you enjoy drinking. Always buy one bottle first to try before investing in a case because vintages differ. Make sure you buy young wines for cellaring—whites no more than two years old, and reds no more than two or three years old, so that they will age well for several more years. Most enophiles collect red wines because they live longer in the bottle. The longest-lived reds are usually Cabernet Sauvignon blends, whether from California, Chile, Tuscany, or Bordeaux. But if you prefer softer, less tannic reds, choose Merlot, Cabernet Franc, Petite Sirah, Zinfandel,

Pinot Noir, Beaujolais Cru, Spanish Garnacha or Monastrell, Australian or South African Shiraz, or Argentina's Malbec. But don't forget Champagne, Chardonnay, or White Burgundy, Loire or Alsace whites, German Riesling, and New Zealand Sauvignon Blanc, either.

All of these examples are dry wines, but you can add a few bottles of dessert wine too, such as Ports or Sauternes. For most American beginners, a California-grown wine collection (plus wines from your home state) is the easiest to acquire because labels are varietal and readable, and the wines are the most consistent in quality from bottle to bottle.

Your average bottle price will be about $15 to $25 for a starter cellar. But don't age wines at this price point longer than 3–5 years after purchase to be safe.

What's the sexiest collectible wine? It's made by California's Napa Valley winery, **Marilyn Wines**. Go to website **www.marilynwines.com** to view the most glamorous wine bottles ever made. Under special copyright licensing from her estate, gorgeous fashion photos of **Marilyn Monroe** grace the labels of Marilyn Merlots and Cabernets (the only types of wines they produce). Every vintage has a different art photo of Marilyn on the bottle, and the website says several of the earliest vintages that were purchased for only $20 to $35 per bottle have become collectors' items worth thousands of dollars. Their least expensive reds at about $11 are appropriately named "Norma Jean" (Marilyn's real name before she became a movie star).

I can believe people would want to save these bottles, though the wines are actually very good, because the photos of Marilyn Monroe are so beautiful. Look for that fabulous head shot of her in a big hat on the 2002 Marilyn Merlot. Be sure to click on the "Velvet Collection" because this new release is the very sexiest wine bottle of all. The 1.5 liter size bottle comes in its own wooden case for $200 and has a nude photo of Marilyn lying on her side that was taken by the famous photographer Tom Kelly for the 1949 launch of *Playboy* magazine. A discreet red sash overlay is used over the photo, but it can be peeled off once you get the bottle home. It proves once and for all that Marilyn Monroe was one of our great American beauties.

When you gain confidence, you can branch out to finer, more expensive wines.

If possible, buy at least one "reserve" or single vineyard wine in the $30 to $35 price range because it holds up better during longer cellaring of 5–8 years. When hunting for good value Cabernets and Chardonnays, look at the expensive versions first. If you see a winery selling its Cab or Chard for $60 or more, look for that brand name in the $20 to $25 price range. Almost all wineries do both. If you're still not sure, read wine magazines or ask the store wine consultant to explain which wines are the most collectible.

tip Taste at least a couple bottles out of each case every year to see how aging affects the wine. And remember that you can drink moderately priced wines while they're young without feeling guilty.

Creating an Intermediate-level Collection

If you want to seriously begin a wine collection that you can cellar and age for longer than 3–5 years, then you must purchase wines that are a minimum $25 to $35, up to $45. At this price, you will be able to find "reserve" Merlots, Meritage reds and Meritage whites (from California and other U.S. states), single-vineyard Chardonnays, perhaps some "artist labels," special appellation wines, classic French or Italian or German wines, or Vintage Porto and the best of the New World wines. Each one of our book's country chapters, Chapters 6–12, covers the top-rated wines and wineries to help you develop a list of the ones that interest you.

Even with rising prices, any intermediate collector will be able to find good values in Bordeaux (Margaux to St. Estephe to St. Emilion and Pomerol), Premier Cru white Burgundy from Chablis or Puligny–Montrachet, Piedmont or Tuscany reds, Super-Venetian reds, Vintage Champagne, great Latin or Southern Hemisphere reds and whites, German Beerenauslese, and Vintage Porto. Buy recent vintages and cellar for 5–8 years under temperature control.

Advanced Collectors

Serious collectors shop in the $50 to $75+ price range. They are looking for wines with a "name" or classification or top rating from great recent vintages. Opening these wines upon purchase will reveal great intensity of flavor—wines at this price are absolutely fabulous, even when young. These collectors not only have the know-how and confidence to purchase older vintages from the '80s or '90s— such as 1994 (Vintage Porto), 1995 (Vintage Champagne), 1996 (red Bordeaux or Burgundy or higher Prädikat German), 1997 (super-Tuscan reds or California Cabernets) and so on—they already have these wines in their cellar!

Putting a Value on Your Wine Collection

You should know the value of your wine collection for insurance or potential selling purposes. You can find the values of some wines by visiting an elite wine store in your area. It might have your wine for sale or be able to share their price list of obtainable Bordeaux and other fine wines.

Several online companies will price your wine collection for you, including **www.winebid.com**; **www.wineprices.com**, which sells *Vinfolio's 2005 Wine Price File*; **www.wineappraise.com**; **www.wine-storage.com**; and **www.internationalsommelier.com**. These sites compile wine prices from Christie's, Sotheby's, and many other auction houses. Specific vintage prices may also be available on winery websites.

Summary

In this chapter, you learned some basics for creating a beginning, intermediate, or advanced-level wine collection. You also learned some ideas for storing your collection, no matter what your budget allows. In our next chapter, we make your guests envious of your powers as acclaimed host or hostess as we entertain you with delicious wine menus and successful food and wine marriages.

17

Entertaining with Wine

Experience has taught me that wine events must be interactive to succeed. People need someone to jolly them along and get them very much involved in the "program," or they will make a quick exit. To get guests to participate in the fun, you need to plan ahead for every aspect and activity. But once the wine party or class begins, everyone can relax and enjoy the event.

In this chapter, you learn from my examples how to do innovative wine and food events that are exciting for guests but easy for the organizer. From wine "dinner classes," to sauce tastings, cheese tastings, or marriage of food and wine panels, you'll learn you have many options when it comes to entertaining guests with wine.

In this chapter:

* Learn how to host wine and food-tasting events

* Host a wine "dinner class" or informal series of marriage of food and wine tasting panels

Things You'll Need

- ❏ A guest list
- ❏ Appropriate foods and wines
- ❏ Printed menus with wine descriptions
- ❏ Adequate seating and wine glasses, plenty of water

Hosting Wine and Food Tastings

Guests never see the immense organizational effort beforehand, but without it the wine event has no polish or excitement. For example, it's great to prepare a food theme: premier chocolates and chocolate desserts; Champagne and sushi; an Italian menu of Tuscany white bean salad, Porcini mushroom pasta, veal, sautéed spinach, Pecorino cheese, and biscotti; or a Latin menu of fish tacos, chicken in mole sauce, and flan with Latin wines from Chile, Argentina, and Spain. Always choose wines to fit the theme. Another good idea is to invite a cheese expert to explain how each of the exotic cheeses pairs with the wines you've chosen.

Wine parties are also easy. Just select 5 or 6 wines and different finger foods to partner them, and serve them one at a time with commentary by a volunteer or guest speaker. Allow 20 minutes in between wines for people to talk, mingle, and eat. I've even done wine and food tastings with nothing but bottled sauces—Bella Cucina's Artichoke Lemon Pesto, or any gourmet barbecue, marinara, or pesto sauces; and Dijon mustard, capers, chopped onion, and egg or herbs. These are used as dipping sauces or to accompany tiny portions of grilled shrimp, chicken, pork, and beef with a range of wines. There's no limit to what can be done if you plan ahead and take the advice we present.

note If at all possible at wine parties, have enough table and chairs so guests can sit down comfortably while they are listening to the speaker. It is difficult to balance wine glasses and foods if your guests have to stand for long periods of time. And always have a printed menu, wine list, or lesson plan to help them remember what they tasted.

Igniting the interest of guests is incredibly easy when doing a cheese tasting. Clever hostesses make name tags for each cheese on a display. But to make a wine and cheese tasting truly interactive, place small, thin slices of eight different cheeses around a plate like the hands of a clock, positioning 12, 3, 6 and 9 o'clock first and then the other four slices in between.

My preference is to start at the top of the plate with delicate, fresh goat cheese such as Chèvre served with Pinot Blanc or similar white wine. Then an aged goat cheese such as goat Gouda with Sauvignon Blanc would be a good combination. I'd follow this with cow's milk cheeses such as Epoisses with Pinot Noir or red Burgundy; Jarlsberg or Gruyere with Merlot, and vintage cheddar or Cheshire with Syrah. Finally, I would complete the circle with sheep's milk cheeses such as Abbaye de Bellocq Trappist, Pecorino, or Manchego with Spanish, Chilean, Argentinean or Italian reds; and real French Roquefort bleu cheese with great Cabernet Sauvignon (or sweet Sauternes) or English Stilton blue cheese

tip Don't forget to include dessert cheeses such as Jacquin's Coeur de Berry—a creamy, heart-shaped French goat cheese—or Régal de Bourgogne, yummy soft white cheese covered in white raisins marinated in plum brandy that partner with white dessert wines.

with Vintage or Ruby Porto. White wine lovers may want to try Triple Crème or St. André cheeses with a rich, buttery, oak-aged Chardonnay, Asiago cheese with a Pinot Grigio, or Swiss cheese with Riesling.

READING UP ON CHEESES

Buying a cheese book brings an appreciation of the cheese possibilities, from world-famous grainy chunks of Parmagiano-Reggiano or Grana Padana from Italy that you can break into bite-size pieces and drizzle with Balsamic vinegar for an instant appetizer, to artisan or farmstead cheeses made in your own home state. Workman Publishing produces Steven Jenkins' *Cheese Primer,* covering almost every cheese I've encountered. There are other books, or let your fingers do the research on the Internet.

In France, Italy, and Spain "controlled name of origin" laws exist for cheese and olive oils, as well as wine. *Artisanal,* or hand-crafted cheeses, made on tiny farms with small herds of goats, sheep, or cows are also available from virtually every state in the U.S. Online shoppers can find many of these one-of-a-kind cheeses at **www.murrayscheese.com.**

And don't forget you can also do an extra virgin olive oil tasting as well.

Sales of olive oils in the U.S. have doubled in the last 10 years. In Napa, California, there are now olive oil tasting bars, just like wine bars. Studies show "extra virgin" olive oils contain more of the heart-protective and cancer-reducing antioxidants (called phenols, similar to the phenols in wine) than other types of olive oils that are heat processed. Chefs abbreviate these olive oils "evo" in recipes. To do an olive oil tasting, pour different oils into small bowls and provide cubes of crusty bread for dipping. The best olive oils from Italy, Spain, and even Chile reflect the *terroir* where they're grown and have strong, complex flavors with fruity, nutty, peppery, or evergreen overtones. This is another good training exercise for your palate, and olive oils are very compatible with wine.

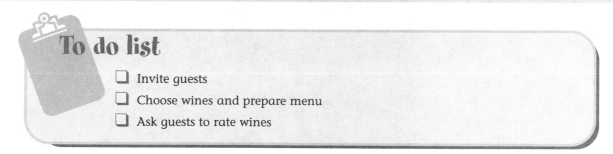

To do list

- ❑ Invite guests
- ❑ Choose wines and prepare menu
- ❑ Ask guests to rate wines

Creating a Wine "Dinner Class"

If you want to host a dinner that offers something beyond the usual dinner conversation, you might try holding your own "dinner class." Using the information you learned in this book, you can invite guests to a dinner designed specifically to highlight certain wines and their spectacular food partners.

Things You'll Need

- ❑ Wines and dinner menu offerings
- ❑ Printed menus/wine lists
- ❑ Seating and service for guests
- ❑ Index cards for wine ratings
- ❑ Door prizes

Creating a Dinner Class Menu and Wine List

A typical "dinner class" menu includes a sparkling or dry white reception wine and spicy hors d'oeuvres such as samosas, empanadas, or spring rolls. A first course, such as seafood risotto or scallops with classic French white Burgundy (or Chardonnay) follows. Then a refreshing heirloom tomato salad with Greek feta and basil vinaigrette with a Rosé or light red would be perfect. Angus beef tenderloin with red wine reduction sauce (don't add salt before boiling down the red wine sauce to reduce it or it will be as salty as the Dead Sea) with top-of-the-line California Cabernet, French red Rhône wine, or super-Tuscan Italian red would make a fabulous main course. A cheese course with an older red, such as Bordeaux, follows the main course. And finally, a dessert of cheesecake, apple tart, or pumpkin pie with white dessert wines would give everyone satisfaction. Or serve fine dark or semi-sweet chocolates with Zinfandel or even a Zinfandel port, or red sparkling wine.

Speaking of salt, that's another culinary item with many versions that taste and look completely different from each other. Rare sea salts can be white or gray, depending on their ocean origins and crystal structure. They are used as "finishing" salts, just before serving, after foods are cooked. If you cannot afford these exotic salts—though you should try them at least once because they do make a difference—then use kosher salt, which is the secret of many fine chefs.

To make your dinner class a true "class," be sure to give your guests information about the wines, the grapes they're made from, the area or estate where they're produced, or why you've chosen each wine to accompany specific courses of your dinner. You can feature wines from a single country or winery to match the theme of the cuisine. Or, if you feel up to telling your guests more information about the different wines at your party, you can choose wines from a variety of countries and vineyards.

Making the Event Special

You can use a number of low-cost ideas to make your dinner class more interesting and entertaining for your guests. For example, you can use index cards to get guests to vote for favorite wine and food combinations. Or you can offer a door prize (wine note cards or accessories) to anyone who can answer a question based on the information you offered them on the wines served at the event.

> **tip** You can help guests keep track of their glasses by using "wine circles" that fit over the base of wine glasses. "Wine circles" are made of donut-shaped paper with a slit to write guest names or wine names so there are no mix-ups or confusion. These are more useful than those jewelry rings. White place mats with numbered circles drawn to the shape of wine glass bases can also be provided for every seated guest to help them track the wines.

Summary

It is my sincere hope that, after reading this chapter, you are inspired to put this knowledge about hosting wine and food events into practice. Whether you create a wine "dinner class," wine party, marriage of food and wine tasting with finger foods, cheese tasting, or use simple sauces to discover their effect on wine, may they be delicious experiments in entertaining. What pleases your palate, and your guests', is always correct. Confidence comes from experience, so make wine entertaining a regular part of your social calendar.

Part IV

Appendixes

References and Resources

Many useful books, websites, wine organizations and sources for wines, maps, free booklets, recipes, wine accessories, and foods have already been referenced directly in the text of this book. The Internet has changed everything for the better for wine lovers and made it so much easier to find wine bargains; collector's items; appraisals of your wines; wine clubs to join; wine events to attend; sommelier societies; online wine education; wine and health research; wine tours; winery, importer, and distributor information; opportunities for working wine vacations; and ratings for recent and older vintages. Remember, you can "Google" any wine!

This is an additional list of books and websites you can draw upon to further expand your understanding and enjoyment of wine, including the author's own website, which has the answers to 100 wine FAQs (frequently asked questions). Que Publishing also has a web page for this book that posts the author's answers to your emailed wine questions. Go to **www.quepublishing.com**.

Final Note from the author: This is my only chance to say goodbye to my readers. I hope you've enjoyed this journey into the world of wine, and my company. It has been my pleasure to introduce you to the subject that has so enriched my life. I'm toasting your health, wealth, and happiness with a good red as I write this. And I very much look forward to meeting many of you in the very near future.

Books

Campbell, Christy. *The Botanist and the Vintner: How Wine Was Saved for the World.* Algonquin Books of Chapel Hill, 2005.

Clarke, Oz. *Oz Clarke's Encyclopedia of Wine, 2nd Edition.* Simon and Schuster, 1999.

Guiliano, Mireille. *French Women Don't Get Fat: The Secret of Eating for Pleasure.* Alfred A. Knopf Publishers, 2005. **www.mireilleguiliano.com**

Halliday, James. *Wine Atlas of Australia & New Zealand.* HarperCollins, 1998. **www.harpercollins.com.au**

Kladstrup, Donald & Petie. *Wine & War: The French, the Nazis, & the Battle for France's Greatest Treasure.* Broadway Books, 2001. **www.broadwaybooks.com**

Kochilas, Diane. *The Glorious Foods of Greece.* William Morrow publishers, a division of HarperCollins, 2001.

Kolpan, Steven; Smith, Brian H.; Weiss, Michael A. *Exploring Wine: The Culinary Institute of America's Complete Guide to Wines of the World, 2nd Edition.* John Wiley & Sons, 2002.

Laube, James. *California Wine, 2nd Edition.* Wine Spectator Press/M.Shanken Communications, 1995.

MacNeil, Karen. *The Wine Bible.* Workman Publishing, 2001.

McCoy, Elin. *The Emperor of Wine: The Rise of Robert M. Parker, Jr. and the Reign of American Taste.* HarperCollins Publishers, 2005. **www.harpercollins.com**

Platter, John. *South African Wine Guide.* KWV International. Newsome McDowall publishers, 2005. **www.platterwineguide.com**

Rayyis, Jamal A. *Food & Wine Magazine's Wine Guide 2005.* Food & Wine Books. (Distributor: Sterling Publishing) **www.foodandwine.com**

Robinson, Jancis. *Oxford Companion to Wine.* Oxford University Press, 1994.

Stevenson, Tom. *The New Sotheby's Wine Encyclopedia: A Comprehensive Reference Guide to the Wines of the World.* Revised & Updated Edition, 2001. Also, *Wine Report 2004* by Tom Stevenson. Both published by DK (Dorling Kindersley) of London and New York, a division of Pearson Education. **www.dk.com**

Turismo y Communicaciones S.A. *Guía de Vinos de Chile. Edición 2004.* Spanish/English. Francisca Sanchez, Editor. Email: **guiadelvino@terra.cl** and **infor@turistel.cl**

*Wine Spectator's Ultimate Guide to Buying Wine,
7th Edition*. M. Shanken Communications,
2000.

Zraly, Kevin. *Windows on the World Wine Book*.
Sterling Pubishing, 2000.

> **note** The Wine Appreciation
> Guild, San Francisco, CA,
> has an entire catalog of wine books.
> Elliott Mackey is the owner and director.
> Tel: 800-231-9463.

Websites

Wines and Accessories

www.wine.com: Probably the largest site for online wine shopping.

www.wineex.com: The Wine Exchange offers fine wines at great prices.

www.thewinestop.com: A good spot for finding unobtainable California wines.

www.winestuff.com: Sells Riedel glassware and other wine accessories.

www.discountmugs.com: Sells wine glasses with your logo or imprint.

www.wineenthusiast.com: Popular wine catalog. Also the magazine.

Wine and Travel

www.dolcetours.com: My favorite Italian tour guides, La Dolce Vita Wine Tours, based in New York City.

www.grapestoglasswinetours.com: Wine tours with an educational format.

www.wamagazine.com: New wine magazine for women launched July 2005. One of main focuses is on wine touring.

www.womenandwine.net: This website not only offers custom group wine tours for women, but also acts as a community message board, as a way for individuals to form or join a group and interact with other women who enjoy wine and travel.

Wine Clubs, Sommeliers, Wine Education

www.americanwinesociety.com: Among the myriad wine clubs to join is AWS, which has affiliates across the U.S. for both enthusiasts and professionals. They do the best job of organizing wine tastings that are truly educational.

www.aiwf.org: American Institute of Wine & Food was originally founded by Julia Child and Robert Mondavi. Now there are more than 30 active chapters across America. Their events are social occasions.

www.americansommelier.org: This website directs you to their New York chapter and other wine stewards working in the U.S.

www.bevnetwork.com: Beverage Media in New York City publishes the Beverage Journals for every city in the U.S., listing the local wine distributors and the brands they carry. If you are thinking of opening a wine store or restaurant, you will need a subscription.

www.ciachef.edu: The Culinary Institute of America, Greystone campus in St. Helena, California, offers many wine and food classes for public and professionals.

www.connectwithwine.com: The email monthly newsletter is very good, with timely reviews of newly released wines, winery profiles, and host Michael Bryan's extensive wine travel notes. He also directs the Atlanta Wine School.

www.copia.org: The American Center for Wine, Food and the Arts in the town of Napa, California. Ongoing classes taught by expert instructor. Lots of food and wine events.

www.erobertparker.com: Mr. Parker is the most influential wine writer and critic in America. He publishes *The Wine Advocate* newsletter, which rates many new wines. He has also authored books on Bordeaux, Rhône, and Provence, and a wine buying guide.

www.frenchculinary.com: The French Culinary Institute in New York City offers classes in French foods and wines.

www.frenchwinesfood.com: Foods & Wines of France in New York City offers online lessons on French wines and a free booklet with self-test in the back. If you complete the answers correctly, you get a diploma. Supervised by Sopexa, the global marketing arm for all French wines, spirits, and foods.

www.germanwinesociety.com: Devoted to the enjoyment of German wines, with regular tastings hosted by chapters in several U.S. cities.

www.internationalsommelier.com: Website of the International Sommelier Guild.

www.localwineevents.com: Eric Orange hosts this high traffic site that lists wine events by city. It is the best source of information for wine tastings all across the U.S.

www.mastersommeliers.org: The Court of Master Sommeliers in America offers study for internationally accepted credentials for the beverage service industry.

www.masters-of-wine.org: The Master of Wine (MW) designation began in England. Now Americans have earned this ultimate credential. This website tells you how to become one.

www.sherry.org: The Sherry Institute offers information about all types of Spanish Sherry, including the new categories of age-designated Sherries.

www.societyofwineeducators.org: The original, and still the largest, organization for wine educators. Offers certification courses and exams.

www.sonomawine.com: The website of the Sonoma County Grape Growers Association is a source for a DVD called *Exploring the Appellations of Sonoma County*, which was produced in conjunction with the Sonoma County Wineries Association. It highlights new Sonoma AVAs, such as Rockpile, and their wineries.

www.stratsplace.com: This is a very active wine website. Visitors post wine labels of their recent "finds." Much information is shared. The husband and wife team who launched this site several years ago never expected this success. Now they travel extensively to review wineries.

www.tastedc.com: Tasting Society International in Washington, DC, is run by Charlie Adler, who hosts classy wine events in beautiful venues, such as upscale restaurants and embassies.

www.wineschool.com: The Chicago Wine School website.

www.wset.org: Wine and Spirits Education Trust, which originated in London, offers several levels of wine certification. Its New York City headquarters supervises licensed instructors in American cities. In Atlanta, email **winewise2004@aol.com**.

www.winespectatorschool.com: Comprehensive online wine courses, including sales and service for the wine trade.

www.winelust.com: Wine School of Philadelphia offers courses and services to the public and the wine industry.

www.wine-women.com: This site features women in the world of wine.

www.womenforwinesense.com: Click on the health section of this site to find articles about wine and health.

www.wswa.org: Wine & Spirits Wholesalers of America represents all of the major wine distributors in the U.S. They are listed on this site by state.

For more information about author Anita LaRaia's Wine School, bio, references, wine parties, classes, consulting, tours, and wine FAQs, go to **www.anitalaraia.com**.

Wine Dictionary A-Z

ACETIC ACID—Vinegar is acetic acid. When old red wine turns to vinegar, it is said to have high volatile acidity.

ACIDITY—The tartness of a wine from tartaric, malic, and citric acids in grapes. Keeps wine fresh, balances sweetness, and makes some wines taste lemony (citric) or like green apples (malic).

APPELLATION (d'Origine) CONTRÔLÉE (Ah-pell-ah-see-own dor-ree-jeen Con-tro-lay)—The name of origin, and the highest quality level, of French wines controlled under their wine laws. Abbreviated AOC. Appellation in other countries also means a legally defined geographic zone where wines are made.

AROMA—Grape smells including fruit aromas associated with a particular grape variety, such as strawberry in Pinot Noir, melon in Chardonnay, or grapefruit in Sauvignon Blanc. See also BOUQUET.

ASTRINGENCY—A mouth-puckering sensation from the tannin in wine, especially in young red wine. It is the same texture, dry sensation, and bitterness experienced from the tannic acid of strong tea.

BLANC DE BLANCS (blawn d' blawn in French, but Americans add the hard c sound, as blawnk d' blawnk)—Costly French Champagne made from 100% Chardonnay. Elsewhere means white wine from white grape(s), not necessarily Chardonnay.

BODY—The thickness or viscosity of wine.

BORDEAUX (Bore-doe)—Wine region in southwest France on the Atlantic Ocean known for dry reds, which are combinations of five black grapes: Cabernet Sauvignon, Merlot, Cabernet Franc, Malbec, and Petit Verdot. See also MERITAGE.

BOTRYTIS CINEREA (bow-try-tiss sin-eh-ray-ah)—The "noble rot" fungus that under late-harvest conditions shrivels grapes to raisins, thus concentrating sugar, so grapes can be used to make sweet dessert wines. Creates a honey flavor in the wine.

BOUQUET—What you first smell in wine, that is, odors from the winemaking process. Good bouquet includes the fresh fruit smells of young wine or the raisin, cooked-fruit smells of bottle-aged wines called secondary characteristics. Bad bouquet includes the burnt match smell of sulfites, musty "cellar smells," moldy/chlorine smell of bad corks, or chemical smells and other "off odors."

BREATHING—Letting a wine have air, to open up its aroma and soften its tannin, by pulling the cork ahead of time; or better, pouring the wine into a decanter; or best of all, pouring the wine into wide surface area (big bowled) glasses that allow swirling.

BURGUNDY—Called "Bourgogne" (Boor-gon-yah) in French. It is the cool wine region of France, along with Champagne, where Chardonnay and Pinot Noir origi-nate. Also used to refer to some wines of the region: White Burgundies such as Chablis, Puligny-Montrachet, or Pouilly-Fuissé are 100% Chardonnay, and red Burgundies such as Chambertin or Vosne-Romanée are 100% Pinot Noir. The Burgundy region also includes Beaujolais.

CELLARING—Aging wine in a temperature and humidity-controlled wine cellar, usually 55° F. and 75% humidity.

CHAMPAGNE (Sham-pain)—French sparkling wine made in the méthode cham-penoise from Pinot Noir, Pinot Meunier, and Chardonnay grapes. The Champagne region is the Appellation Contrôlée of Champagne wine.

CHAPTALIZATION—Adding sugar to under-ripe grapes during fermentation to increase the alcohol content of the resulting wine. Used in cool regions of Burgundy, France, and Germany, chaptalization is not allowed or not needed in sunny climates of California, Italy, Spain, and Australia.

CHÂTEAU (shah-toe)—An estate in Bordeaux that has vineyards and a winery where they make and bottle their own wines, called château-bottled. The equivalent of estate-bottled, it is designated "mis en bouteilles au château" on Bordeaux wine labels.

CLARET (klar-et)—Any red Bordeaux wine. This term is also used for any red wine blended from Bordeaux grapes in California and other wine-growing regions.

CLASSICO—Better grade of Italian wine from classic vineyard area for that type, such as Chianti. Can be used with other terms such as SUPERIORE, meaning from riper grapes that make more alcohol; and RISERVA, meaning aged in oak barrels.

CLONE—Clones of specific grape varieties develop over time from vine cuttings and propagation in a particular area. Choice of clone is very important for Pinot Noir (since it mutates so easily), Chardonnay, and Merlot, and makes a significant differ-ence in the color, aroma, and taste of the resulting wine.

CORKED—Used to describe the moldy/chlorine smell and taste in wines with bad corks contaminated with TCA (trichloroanisole).

CÔTE (coat)—Slope or hillside of vineyards as in Côte d'Or (golden slope), the greatest wine district of Burgundy, France.

CRIANZA (cree-ahn-za)—Designation on labels of red Spanish Rioja wines indicating a minimum of 2 years of aging before release, of which 1 year must be in oak (casks). Spanish reds from other districts may have a shorter ageing requirement.

CRU (crew)—A level of quality in French wines, translated "growth" in English. As in "cru classé," meaning *classified growth*, in an official Bordeaux classification—or as in Grand (great) Cru in Burgundy, which are the finest single vineyards; or in Beaujolais Cru, which are wines from the 10 best villages.

DECANTING—The act of carefully pouring the clear wine off the sediment in the bottom of the bottles of older wines. Any benefits from decanting will derive from exposing the wine to the air and aerating it.

DENOMINAZIONE DI ORIGINE CONTROLLATA (Dee-nom-in-ah-zee-oh-nay dee Oh-ree-gee-nay Con-tro-lah-ta)—Abbreviated DOC; means "name of origin is controlled" by Italian wine laws. More than 310 quality traditional wines fall into this category.

EISWEIN (ice-vine)—Ice wine made from grapes frozen by a hard frost. As a result, German Eiswein or Ice Wine made in Canada, the U.S., or New Zealand is a rare and costly sweet white dessert wine.

ENOLOGY—The study of winemaking, the science of wine. Also spelled "oenology," from the Greek word *oeno* for wine.

ENOPHILE (ee-noh-file)—A wine lover. Also spelled "oenophile."

FERMENTATION—The process of turning grape juice into wine. Called *alcohol fermentation* because yeasts (from grape skins and added wine yeasts), act as a catalyst to the natural chemical process, converting grape sugar into equal parts of alcohol and carbon dioxide while releasing heat.

FINISH—The aftertaste of a wine, which is long, lingering, and pleasant in great wines and very short in lesser wines. Also called the "memory" of the wine.

FORTIFIED—Wines that are fortified by the addition of extra alcohol in the form of brandy or grain spirits. The five main types of fortified wines are Port, Sherry, Madeira, Marsala, and Vermouth.

FUME BLANC (Few-may Blawnk)—Another name for Sauvignon Blanc wines in California. First coined by Robert Mondavi, who inverted the French name for the grape, Blanc Fumé, to tell customers it is the same grape that makes Pouilly-Fumé in the Loire.

HANG TIME—American term for allowing red grapes to hang on the vines longer before harvest, making red wines more concentrated.

ICE WINE—See EISWEIN.

LANGUEDOC (lahn-guh-dock)—The Midi or Languedoc-Rousillon area of southern France in the arc from the Spanish border to the Rhône. Known for "vin de pays" country wines labeled by grape variety that are great values. Every grape is grown, including Marsanne, Mourvèdre, Syrah, and so on. The area also has several AOC wines such as Fitou and Corbieres.

LATE HARVEST—Sweet wine made from late-picked grapes that are extra ripe from longer exposure to the sun.

LEES—Residue of yeast that settles out of the wine after fermentation. Aging wine on its lees—called "sur lie" (sur lee-ay) in French—makes a white wine more complex. This technique is used extensively for great white Burgundy wines and the best types of Muscadet in the Loire.

MACERATION—The process of soaking the black skins of red grapes in their juice to extract the maximum amount of color, aromas, and tannins (and other antioxidants or phenols) during fermentation.

MADEIRA (mah-dare-a)—Fortified wine made on the island of Madeira in the Atlantic, 400 miles off the coast of Portugal. It's baked in rooms as hot as ovens for a couple of months to caramelize the sugars in the white wine.

MADERIZATION—The browning and oxidation of a wine caused by advanced age.

MERITAGE (mare-i-tij)—American trademark of the Meritage Association that is reserved for upscale wines blended like a great red or white Bordeaux. Meritage reds can be made from two or more of eight red Bordeaux grapes: Cabernet Sauvignon, Cabernet Franc, Merlot, Malbec, Petit Verdot, Carmenère, St. Macaire, and Gros Verdot. White Meritage wines can be any combination of two or more of the three white Bordeaux grapes: Sauvignon Blanc, Sémillon, and Muscadelle.

MéTHODE CHAMPENOISE (meh-toad sham-pen-wahz)—The Champagne method of France (used all over the world) to make the finest type of sparkling wines. The method involves many steps from blending the cuvée to second fermentation, riddling, aging, disgorging, final dosage, and bottling. Called "Fermented in This Bottle" in America and CAVA in Spain. See also CHAMPAGNE.

MICRO-OXYGENATION—The technique of introducing small amounts of oxygen into the wine through a tube as it ages in the barrel. It is used in Australia and worldwide by clients of Bordeaux enologist Michel Rolland to improve the fruit profile and richness of red wines while softening tannins. Though the technique is still controversial, very reputable wineries, including Chapoutier of France, are conducting experiments with and without it in some of their top wines.

NON-VINTAGE (Abbreviated N.V. or NV)—Not made from one vintage year, but rather a blend of years. The term is used in French Champagne and for other sparkling wines that are less expensive than a single vintage year. Also called multi-vintage.

NOSE—The smell or bouquet and aroma of a wine. Better wines with a good nose smell as wonderful as they taste.

NOUVEAU (new-vo)—Meaning a "new" wine made quickly, in just a few days, by carbonic maceration (explained in Chapter 3, "Winemaking—The Six Basic Types"). This accentuates the fruity, grapey properties of the wine. The term is used in Beaujolais, France, where a yearly contest is held to see who can get first Nouveau to Paris.

OAK—The wood used for most wine barrels. Oak barrels add complexity to wine, aromas of vanilla if they're new oak, especially if the barrels are toasted on the inside. Aging in oak barrels allows the wine to go through a slow, controlled process of maturation (oxidation).

OLD VINES—A wine made from very old grapevines, perhaps 80 to well over 100 years old, has greater intensity and concentration of flavor. These ancient vines must be in good health. It is common practice to replant vines after 30 years of age before they become prone to disease. The French call these old vine wines "vieille vignes" (vee-yay veen).

PHYLLOXERA (fil-lox-er-ra)—Plant lice or aphids that attack the roots of the grapevine and eventually kill it.

PORTO—The original Port from Portugal. A sweet, red fortified wine of four basic types: Vintage Porto from a single great year (a collectors' item because it lasts for decades) that must be decanted because of the heavy sediment that precipitates out of the wine as it ages in the bottle; LBV or late-bottled vintage Porto from single vintage years that have been kept in the barrel longer to throw their sediment; Ruby Porto from a blend of vintages that's been aged in wood for several years and throws no sediment in the bottle; and Tawny Porto, also a non-vintage blend whose original red color has turned tawny brown from many years of extra wood aging.

PRÄDIKAT (pray-dee-kaht)—Highest quality German wines that are never chaptalized or sugared because they're made from naturally ripe grapes.

RESERVE—This term usually means top-of-the-line wines from single vineyards in great vintages that get special oak aging and handling. In Italy (Riserva) and Spain (Reserva or Gran Reserva), the term cannot be used unless the wine meets strict legal aging requirements of so many years in the barrel and bottle. Spanish wine law definitions are given in Chapter 5, "The Wine Label Decoder."

RESIDUAL SUGAR—Natural grape sugar remaining in wine after fermentation.

RHÔNE (rohn)—Famous wine region in the south of France known for popular red wines, such as Château Neuf du Pape, Côtes du Rhône, Hermitage, and Côte Rôtie, made from Syrah, Grenache, Mourvédre, Carignan, Cinsault, and other red Rhône grapes. These red Rhône wines have distinct black/red color, full body, fairly high alcohol, aromas of pepper and black raspberry, and tannin in the finish. California, Australia, and South Africa make their own versions. White Rhône wines are also made here from grape varieties Viognier, Marsanne, and Rousanne.

ROSé (row-zay)—Deeper rose pink wine made from black grapes that are fermented with their skins for 24–36 hours.

SHERRY—True Sherry is the fortified wine from Jerez, Spain. The finest dry styles are made from white Palomino grapes grown on chalky soil in the best vineyards. Sweeter styles are made with white Pedro Ximénez grapes.

SOMMELIER (so-mel-yay)—The wine steward in a restaurant. May wear a "tastevin" silver wine cup on a neck chain, not only as a symbol of position, but also to taste wine to check quality.

SPARKLING—Wines that fizz or sparkle with bubbles of carbon dioxide trapped in the bottle. May be made in the méthode champenoise like French Champagne, the transfer method, or in the vat-fermented cuvée close method, which is the same as the Charmat or tank method, which is also the way Asti Spumanti (Spumanti means "sparkling") is made.

STICKY—Australian slang for sweet dessert wine.

SULFITES—Sulfur dioxide in wine. A small amount is produced by the fermentation of grapes—enough to be labeled "contains sulfites" in the U.S. The balance of the sulfur dioxide in wine is added in minute amounts to prevent oxidation and bacterial spoilage. Its use is limited by our government, but even more so by winemakers who don't want the smell of rotten eggs or burnt matches (sulfur) in their wines.

TABLE WINES—Wines with natural alcohol from fermentation of 7%–14%. The name means wines for use at the table with meals.

TANNIN—Natural preservative in wine that comes from the skins of black grapes or the wood tannin in barrels. Young red wines have the most tannin; but as the wine ages in the bottle, the tannin drops out as sediment, leaving the wine much smoother to the taste.

TARTRATE CRYSTALS—Cream of tartar crystals that precipitate out of a wine if it gets too cold. Though the crystals look like glass or salt or sugar crystals, they are tasteless and harmless.

TERROIR (tair-wahr)—The unique characteristics of a wine that are derived from the soil, geography, and climate of the vineyard where the grapes were planted. The term is used extensively in Burgundy, France, but has been adopted by other wine countries to make distinctions between wines from different appellations.

TROCKEN—Means dry in German. The legal definition on a wine label is that the wine is drier than normal and has 9 grams or less sugar per liter.

ULLAGE—The fill level of wine in the bottle. Loss of wine through evaporation, long cellaring, or extreme heat lowers the level and creates a large ullage or space from the end of the cork to the wine. A high fill or good ullage is looked for in older wines.

UNFILTERED—Wine that has not been filtered, though it will have been racked and gone through fining to remove small particles. Called *non-filtre* in French, wines labeled unfiltered may have a bit of sediment; but they are deeper in color and richness.

VARIETAL—Wine named for the grape variety or varieties used to make it.

VIN DE GARDE (van d'gard)—A more full-bodied and concentrated red wine suitable for aging.

VIN DE PAYS (van d' pay-ee)—The name translates to "country wines," the third level of quality under the French wine laws, below VDQS (quality wine from a delimited area), which is below Appellation Contrôlée. Vin de Pays wines are varietal wines from the regions in the south of France, such as Languedoc. Most Vin de Pays wines are moderately priced.

VINTAGE—The year of harvest (not the year the wine was made).

VITICULTURE—The agriculture of growing grapes.

VINIFICATION—The making of wine. Includes the study of pressing, fermentation, aging, fining, filtering, and so forth to get the best wine from the grapes harvested.

Wine Touring Tips

Strategic thinking will ensure the best possible outcome for your wine travels. Even if you have limited time and resources, you can find a way to spend a day in the wine country wherever you happen to be. Unlike other tours, wine trips have brought me lifelong friends and a greater appreciation for the bounty that comes from the land and from people who work the land.

In each of our previous country chapters, we featured trade associations, wine centers, wine ries, and website resources to assist you in planning your own domestic and international tours of the vineyards. Don't forget to reread the appropriate chapters in this book before you plan your tour for any of the wine regions we discuss in this book.

A recent American Express Platinum Luxury survey conducted by Pam Danziger, who wrote the book *Why People Buy Things They Don't Need*, discovered that fine dining was the first choice of respondents, followed by travel and entertainment. Creating memorable life experiences was the most important vacation criterion. And what better way to do so than traveling to the wine country, where nature restores your energy, good people and wines lift your mood, and fine restaurants (and hotels) nourish your body and soul?

To do list

- ☐ Visit Napa Valley wineries and restaurants
- ☐ Tour the wine areas of the Sierra Foothills and Livermore

Touring American Wine Regions

Before visiting any winery, avoid embarrassment by learning what kinds of wines they make. Search their website or the Internet. Don't ask for Pinot when they only do Cabernet Sauvignon! Plan your day ahead of time and mark rest stops, eateries, and hotels on the map you use to navigate. That way you'll know where to take a break and when to call it quits when you've had too much to drink.

2005 AMERICAN TOURING INFORMATION FROM THE *WINE SPECTATOR*

The Wine Spectator, June 15, 2005, (www.winespectator.com) had a comprehensive series of articles on "Wine Country Travel," covering six exciting "back roads" American wine regions: Charlottesville, Virginia; Willamette Valley, Oregon; Finger Lakes, New York; Texas Hill Country; Anderson Valley, California; and San Luis Obispo, California.

Useful maps and a list of the best inns, best places to eat, great wineries, and "must-see" local attractions for each region were provided. They chose well—Talley Vineyards and Hearst Castle in San Luis Obispo, CA; Dr. Konstantin Frank Vineyards on Lake Keuka, NY; Barboursville, 1804 Inn (www.barboursvillewine.com) and Thomas Jefferson's Monticello in Virginia; Domaine Drouhin in Dundee, Oregon; Becker Vineyards in Stonewall, Texas; and the Anderson Valley wineries of Mendocino County in Philo, CA.

Napa Valley Wineries and Restaurants

California wine country is not just Napa Valley. But if you do go to Napa, stop at the winery with two Hollywood connections—Niebaum-Coppola, owned by the famous film director Francis Coppola. Located on Highway 29 (called St. Helena Highway), Coppola's winery has dramatic gift shops and tasting rooms. Look for their top-of-the-line "Rubicon" single-vineyard Cabernet and the Sofia sparkling wine named for his film director daughter. St. Helena is the location of the Culinary

Institute of America's Greystone campus, which offers wonderful food and wine pairing classes. (Learn more at **www.CIAprochef.com**.) And in the town of Napa, its tourist center is staffed with people eager to arrange winery visits and the must-see COPIA wine center. To the east of Highway 29 and parallel to it is the Silverado Trail, where many prestigious Napa wineries are located, including its namesake, Silverado Winery.

One of the most popular new wine tourist areas in California is Lodi. Located 90 miles east of San Francisco, Lodi produces more wine grapes than Napa and Sonoma combined. Wine lovers linger in Lodi because of an attractive new $2 million Lodi Wine & Visitors Center, a revitalized downtown, and unpretentious tasting rooms. My winery picks for Lodi are Jessie's Grove and Michael-David Vineyards. The Mediterranean climate is ideal for exotic white grapes such as Viognier and Albariño, as well as some terrific Zinfandels, and so forth. For more info, go to **www.lodiwine.com**. Lodi is also the location of Mondavi's Woodbridge wines and one of *Consumer Reports'* favorite moderately priced wines, Napa Ridge.

Exciting new AVAs such as "Rockpile" in Sonoma County are home to well-known wineries. For a complete list of Sonoma AVAs and their wineries, go to **www. sonomawine.com**. Sonoma also has a very well attended Vintage Festival every year at harvest time. And the picturesque town of Sonoma itself is definitely worth a visit because Sebastiani and Buena Vista Wineries are located there. The town of Healdsburg is where Sonoma winemakers hang out, especially for breakfast.

Driving along the Pacific Coast Highway to Monterey's tasting rooms provides dramatic ocean vistas. The popular Bernardus Winery in Carmel Valley—said to have some of the most beautiful weather and scenery in the U.S.—also operates deluxe Bernardus Lodge (**www.bernardus.com**), whose glorious Marinus restaurant is open daily for dinner. Owner Bernardus "Ben" Pon drove race cars before he turned to winemaking. Just south in Santa Cruz, the top stop is Bonny Doon Vineyard, known for Rhône and Italian varietals, as well as the charismatic humor of owner Randall Grahm.

The movie *Sideways* also draws many visitors to Santa Barbara County, where former Hollywood actor Fess Parker has a winery and a Doubletree hotel under his name. Finally, don't miss a chance to visit Temecula, between Los Angeles and San Diego. Temecula's 24 wineries are concentrated in just 3 miles and their incredible wines can be discovered and purchased only there. The most notable wineries in Temecula include Hart Winery, Mount Palomar, Stuart Cellars, and Callaway.

It's easy to combine winery visits with restaurant dining when you map your itinerary. Next to Rutherford Hill Winery in Napa Valley's Rutherford is the elite restaurant (and hotel) Auberge du Soleil (**www.aubergedusoleil.com**). Try to make reservations for the sunset dinner on their mountainside patio with its awesome view. The little town of Yountville on Highway 29 in Napa is another favorite stop for diners and shoppers. It also hosts some lovely bed and breakfasts. Across the highway from the town is well-known Cosentino Winery, whose next-door neighbors are Mustard Grill and Brix restaurants. Both of them are busy at lunchtime, so call ahead for reservations. Several good restaurants are in the center of Yountville, including The French Laundry, which is booked months ahead.

WINE CRUISES, TOURING MAGAZINES, AND TOURS FOR WOMEN

Many cruise lines have theme voyages, including wine cruises. What better way to learn about wine than indulging in fabulous food, relaxing on the waves, and working off those extra calories in the sea air? A real wine cruise will have experienced wine teachers to educate you and will include special wine tastings in the price.

In 2005, Silversea Cruise Lines—whose Silver Wind ship travels from Rome to Palma de Mallorca—launched an Italian wine cruise hosted by Castello Banfi, one of the largest wine importers in the U.S. Options included an escorted land tour of Tuscany and Banfi's elite wine estate before departure. For more information about this sailing or others, contact Five Senses Exclusive World Tours, Tel: 866-282-5184.

Touring & Tasting magazine—the foremost wine touring magazine in the U.S. for travel to West Coast wineries—featured a "publisher's choice" wine cruise on the Radisson Seven Seas Voyager, hosted by British wine authority and Christie's wine director, Michael Broadbent. For more info about this sailing and other Radisson wine cruises, phone Fine Wine Travel, Tel 1-888-208-8338. And don't leave for California, Washington, or Oregon wineries without a copy of *Touring & Tasting* magazine in your hand (**www.touringandtasting.com**)!

Residents of Atlanta, Charlotte, and Birmingham can pick up a free copy of *The Wine Report* magazine, which also sponsors a wine cruise and always has helpful wine and travel articles (**www.winesimple.com**).

July 2005 was the launch date of the first wine magazine for women. Called *Wine Adventure*, its main focus is articles on wine destinations, wine and food pairings, and lifestyle enhancement. Cost is $30 for six issues, plus one bonus issue (**www.wamagazine.com**).

Women & Wine touring company was launched in 2005 to fill the need for custom group retreats for women who appreciate wine and travel. Their short trips can be accomplished in a weekend. I particularly liked their choice of winery visits for premier Cabernet country, Paso Robles, California. Backed by Omega Travel, the largest woman-owned travel company in the world, international destinations are also offered (**www.womenandwine.net**).

Touring the Sierra Foothills and Livermore

Between Sacramento and Lake Tahoe is the Sierra Foothills wine region. The two main counties in this famous viticultural area are Amador County and El Dorado County. This is called California's "Gold Country," which includes several exciting museums that showcase this important aspect of California's history. To view a map of the area, go to **www.sierraheritage.com/gold_country_map.htm**. Not far from Placerville is one of my favorite wineries, C. G. di Arie (**www.cgdiarie.com**), which specializes in fabulous Zinfandel and Syrah. Be sure to contact them to make an appointment since that is the only way to gain access. Owners are Dr. Chaim and Elisheva Gur-Arieh.

To the east of San Francisco Bay is the Livermore Valley, where Wente Vineyards Estate Winery is located. Wente offers a great wine tour, tastings in their wine bar, and exciting shopping in a wine-themed gift shop. Ten minutes away is the Wente Visitor's Center, which has a self-guided tour of the vineyards that lets you meander among the grapevines. A top-rated golf course is also on the property. From June to September, there are concerts in the natural theater formed by Italian cypress trees. For a special treat, make reservations at the Restaurant at Wente Vineyards, which offers exceptional wine and food matches. The annual Livermore Valley Harvest Wine Celebration is in September, and the annual San Francisco Bay Wine Auction is held at Wente. For more information, go to **www.livermorewine.com**.

To do list

- ☐ Learn how to get more out of a visit to Bordeaux, Burgundy, or France's exciting Rhône
- ☐ Discover the town in Tuscany that's home to three great wineries for an exciting overnight stay

Planning Tours in Europe

Americans seem to prefer traveling unscheduled and unstructured, but please take my advice to join a group, especially on your first trip to Europe. You will learn so much more and make wonderful new friends. Where and how to go are some of the tips I'm happy to share with you.

Attending a Cooking and Wine School in France and Beyond

Some of the great cooking schools in France are located in the wine country—especially prestigious schools such as LaVarenne, which has several programs in Burgundy, France, including three- to five-day trips with accommodations at the lovely Château du Fey. (For more information, visit **www.lavarenne.com**.)

In Bordeaux, a full-scale wine school can be found at beautiful Château Cordeillan-Bages in Pauillac (**www.relaischateaux.com/cordeillan**). This is a Relais Châteaux (elite chain of European hotels) property with an elegant hotel, a wonderful restaurant for the perfect wine country lunch (or dinner), and wine classes. It is owned by Jean-Michel Cazes of Château Lynch-Bages. Bordeaux hotels have colorful information cards on châteaux that are open to the public for tours. The lovely stone village of St.-Émilion is also worth a visit for homemade macaroons, an open-air lunch, cute little hotels, myriad wine stores, and the tiny train that takes you through the vineyards.

Experienced travel guide Walt Ballenberger has a wine tour company called Beaux Voyages that specializes in the Rhône region of southern France (**www.beauxvoyages.com**). Walt has a fabulous wine itinerary that includes meals, four-star hotels, two full days touring both the northern and southern Rhône with a certified enologist, two wine dinners, two nights in Château Neuf du Pape at a family hotel owned by a French master chef, and tours of the cities of Lyon and Avignon.

tip Having escorted groups to France and Italy, I also know that advance reservations are mandatory. The finest wineries require an appointment to gain entrance. That's why a tour guide is invaluable. And since most wineries are in rural areas that are dark and isolated at night, we had local drivers do the driving for us.

note ShawGuides (**www.shawguides.com**) publishes *The Guide to Cooking Schools 2005: Courses, Vacations, Apprenticeships and Wine Programs Throughout The World*. From New York to Singapore, Ireland, England, Spain, Italy, and France, ShawGuides provides details of both professional and recreational culinary and wine programs.

Enjoying *La Dolce Vita* of Italy Wine Tours

The best favor I can do anyone who wants to visit Italy is to recommend La Dolce Wine Tours, based in New York, NY (**www.dolcetours.com**). The owners are Claudio Bisio, a native Italian from the Piedmont, and his American wife, Pat Thomson. They know everything about Italian wines, food, art, hotels, restaurants, landmarks, and festivals. Detailed itineraries and prices for their 2006 tours of Tuscany (including the new area of Maremma), Piedmont, Cinque Terre, Sicily, and the Amalfi Coast are online.

The cost of Claudio's Dolce Tours to Italy is extremely reasonable when you consider it includes exceptional meals, hotels, and tastings of fine wines at famous wineries. Airfare is your responsibility, so you can try to use frequent flier miles. Their service is superb—Pat wrote every wine we tasted on our Tuscany tour in her PDA and then emailed us the list of wines. They also did all the driving (two minivans) for our group of 12 people. Dolce Tours can also be hired for private or custom tours.

The grandest restaurant in Tuscany is L'Enoteca Pinchiorri in Florence. It has the most extensive wine cellar, with 120,000 bottles stored below the restaurant and another 120,000 bottles in other cellars. Among the thousands of selections on the list are flights of Château Lafite and 100 grappas. Fixed-price menus are steep, but offer six outstanding courses. Be sure to save room for cheeses and dessert. Pinchiorri is closed for the late summer months, particularly August. Location: Via Ghibellina 87, 50122 Florence, Italy. Tel: (011) 39-055-242-7777.

The picturesque cobblestone hill town of Montepulciano is home to three famous Tuscany wineries. Across the plaza from the town's lovely Albergo (hotel) Il Marzocco are the 900-year-old caves of Avignonesi, top producers of upscale Merlot/super-Tuscan reds. Up the hill is winery Contucci, whose specialty is Vino Nobile di Montepulciano Riserva—incredible wine not available in the U.S. And on the square at the top of the town is respected Sangiovese producer Poliziano, whose wine cellars flow down three stories behind the walls. Every August, Montepulciano has a "wine barrel race. Food service is set up in sectors marked by colorful flags representing each of the 13 original Florentine families. The young people dress like the lords and ladies of old in heavy gowns and armor, and they don't even sweat in the 100° heat. Their flag-waving ceremony was featured in the American movie *Under the Tuscan Sun*, based on Frances Mayes's best-selling book.

Quick Tips for Touring Chile

Late February/early March is the best time to go for Chile's wine harvest. Two charming companions for a trip to Chile are Cynthia (Cindy) Hyman and her partner, Ralph Sarper. They own Atlas Travel, Inc. (**www.atlastravel.us**) and have personally toured the major wineries in Chile from Casablanca Valley to Santiago and Santa Cruz. Atlas Travel is organizing a special wine tour of Chile for Spring 2006. The tour includes fine hotels and dining, wine tastings, cultural museums, art galleries, and poet Pablo Neruda's home. There will also be an opportunity to fly to Mendoza, Argentina, to tour some wineries there.

Wine Spas, Working Winery Vacations, and Other Unique Touring Ideas

Wine spas in Bordeaux use every part of the grape to polish and rejuvenate the body. Just south of Bordeaux is the famous "Les Spas de Caudalie" (**www. sources-caudalie.com**), where Merlot body wraps, Cabernet scrubs, and facials are available. And in California's wine country, spa treatments are a thriving cottage industry. Touring is hard work, and lavish eating and drinking may require a bit of massage and pampering in order to detoxify.

How would you like to work with a winemaker for the day? Vocation Vacations (**www.vocationvacations.com**) gives you a chance to indulge in your dream job. Several wineries participate—including Eola Hills, two others in Oregon, and Lago di Merlo in Sonoma County, CA. While working in the Willamette Valley, you can also ask for an invitation to "Oregon Pinot Camp," held every June for the wine trade only. For a directory of participating wineries, go to **www.oregonpinotcamp. com**. Vocation Vacations has two other "on-the-job" wine experiences—working at a large wine store called Vineyard Express in Los Angeles or working directly with the owner of well-known New York restaurant, Ida Mae. Schedules are based on availability and the season. Prices start at $999 + tax (not including accommodations).

Each of Andrea Immer's "Simply Wine" television programs on American cable channel Fine Living (**www.fineliving.com**) contains very useful wine tasting and touring tips. For example, Andrea's May 31, 2005, show featured Whistler, Canada, in British Columbia (not far from Vancouver) as the starting point for a flying tour of the beautiful Okanagan Valley—Canada's premier western wine area.

David Mitchell Wine Group (**www.winesandtours.com**) offers flights to 90-mile-long Lake Okanagan ($380 U.S. + tax for a one-day "Magnum" wine tour for two people). See the wine country by plane, and then be whisked in a private car to wineries for tastings and a vineyard lunch—all included in the price. You'll taste fabulous Pinot Noir, Chardonnay, Meritage Red, Gewürztraminer, and Pinot Gris at the elite Canadian wineries of Cedar Creek, Gray Monk Cellars, Mission Hill, and Quails Gate. The town of Whistler has wine classes at the Fairmount Château Hotel and a patented snow-covered Champagne "Ice Bar" at Bearfoot Bistro. Whistler will host the Olympic Winter Games in 2010. For more information, call 1-800-WHISTLER.

Summary

This chapter has shared with you some of my favorite ideas for wine-country touring—both the traditional and non-traditional varieties! In our next chapter, we will discover how the butler did it! We'll teach you how to serve your guests properly, without the fear factor or snobbery.

Table of Varietal Wines

Grape Variety	Wine Name/Place of Origin
Whites: Dry and Light/Medium Body	
ARNEIS	**Arneis**/Italy/Oregon
ASSYRTIKO	**Assyrtiko**/Santorini (Greece)
CHASSELAS	**Fendant/Neuchatel**/Switzerland
CHENIN BLANC	**Vouvray**/Loire (France)/Varietal in CA
CHARDONNAY	**Chablis**/Burgundy (France)/ Un-oaked NZ
CORTESE	**Gavi**/Piedmont (Italy)
FIANO	**Fiano**/Compania (Italy)
GARGANEGA	**Soave**/Veneto (Italy)
GEWÜRZTRAMINER	**Gewürztraminer**/Germany/Alsace/ CA
GRÜNER VELTLINER	**Grüner Veltliner**/Austria
MACABEO	**CAVA sparkling**/Spain/**Viura**/Spain
MOSCHOFILERO	**Moschofilero**/Martinia (Greece)
MUSCADET	**Muscadet**/Loire (France)/**Melon**/ Oregon
PALOMINO	**Fino/Amontillado Sherry** (Spain)
PINOT BLANC	**Pinot Blanc**/Alsace/Oregon/CA
PINOT GRIGIO	**Pinot Grigio**/Italy
PINOT GRIGIO	**Pinot Gris**/Alsace/Oregon
RIESLING	**Riesling**/Alsace (France)/U.S.
RIESLING	**Kabinett**/Germany/Austria

Grape Variety	Wine Name/Place of Origin
Whites: Dry and Light/Medium Body	
SAUVIGNON BLANC	**Pouilly-Fumé**/Loire (France)
SAUVIGNON BLANC	**Graves**/Bordeaux (France)
SAUVIGNON BLANC	**Sauvignon Blanc**/New Zealand/U.S.
SAUVIGNON BLANC	**Fume Blanc/Meritage White**/CA/U.S.
SERCIAL	**Sercial**/Madeira
SEYVAL	**Seyval**/New York/Virginia/GA
SILVANER	**Silvaner**/Germany/**Sylvaner**/Alsace
TOCAI FRIULANO	**Tocai Friulano**/Friuli (Italy)/CA
TORRONTES	**Torrontes**/Spain/Argentina
TREBBIANO	**Orvieto/Frascati etc.**/Italy
VERDELHO	**Verdelho**/Madeira/**Verdejo**/Spain/Australia
VERNACCIA	**Vernaccia**/Tuscany (Italy)
VIDAL	**Vidal**/USA/Canada
Whites: Dry and Full-Body	
ALBARIÑO	**Albariño**/Spain/**Alvarinho**/Portugal
CHARDONNAY	**Meursault etc.**/Burgundy (France)
CHARDONNAY	**Chardonnay**/U.S./Australia/Chile
MARSANNE/ROUSANNE	**Marsanne/R.**/Rhône (France)/Australia/CA
SÉMILLION	**Graves**/Bordeaux (France)
SÉMILLION	**Meritage White**/California
SÉMILLION	**Sem-Chard**/Australia
VERMENTINO	**Vermentino**/Italy
VIOGNIER	**Condrieu**/Rhône (France)/Varietal in U.S.
Whites: Sweet and Light-Medium Body	
FURMINT	**Tokay Aszu**/Hungary
GARGANEGA	**Recioto di Soave**/Veneto (Italy)
GEWÜRZTRAMINER	**Spätlese**/Germany/**RT**/Alsace/**Ice**/NZ
MUSCAT	**Moscato**/Asti (Italy)/**Muscat**/Greece/CA
MUSCAT	**Beaumes de Venise**/Rhône (France)
MUSCADINE	**Muscadine**/Georgia
MALVASIA	**Malmsey**/Madeira
PEDRO XIMÉNEZ	**Cream Sherry/Pedro Ximénez**/Spain
RIESLING	**Auslese**/Germany/**Late-Harvest**/U.S.

Grape Variety	Wine Name/Place of Origin
Whites: Sweet and Light-Medium Body	
SÉMILLON	**Sauternes**/Bordeaux/Australia
TREBBIANO	**Vin Santo**/Tuscany (Italy)
VIDAL	**Ice Wine**/Niagara (Canada)
Reds: Dry and Light/Medium Body	
BARBERA	**Barbera**/Piedmont (Italy)/CA
CABERNET FRANC	**St. Emilion**/Bordeaux/**Chinon**/Loire (France)/Varietal/U.S.
CORVINA etc.	**Valpolicella**/Veneto (Italy)
DOLCETTO	**Dolcetto**/Piedmont (Italy)
GAMAY	**Gamay Beaujolais**/California
GAMAY	**Beaujolais**/Burgundy (France)
MALBEC	**Malbec**/Argentina/France
MERLOT	**Merlot**/CA/Washington/Chile etc.
MERLOT	**Pomerol**/Bordeaux (France)
MONTEPULCIANO	**Montepulciano**/Abruzzi & Marche (Italy)
PINOTAGE	**Pinotage**/South Africa
PINOT MEUNIER	**Pinot Meunier**/Oregon
PINOT NOIR	**Pinot Noir**/California/Oregon
PINOT NOIR	**Beaune etc.**/Burgundy (France)
SANGIOVESE	**Chianti**/**Brunello**/Tuscany (Italy)
SANGIOVESE	**Sangiovese**/California/Italy
TEMPRANILLO	**Ribera del Duero**/**Rioja**/ etc./Spain
Reds: Full-Body	
AGIORGHITIKO	**Nemea**/Greece
AGLIANICO	**Taurasi**/Campania (Italy)
CABERNET SAUVIGNON	**Haut-Médoc**/Bordeaux (France)
CABERNET SAUVIGNON	**Meritage Red**/U.S./**Varietal**/Worldwide
CORVINA etc.	**Amarone**/Veneto (Italy)
GRENACHE	**Rhône**/France/**Varietal**/Worldwide
MOURVÈDRE	**Rhône**/**Monastrell**/Spain etc.
NEBBIOLO	**Barolo**/Piedmont (Italy)
PETITE SIRAH	**Petite Sirah**/California
PETIT VERDOT	**Bordeaux**/France/**Varietal**/Australia

Grape Variety	Wine Name/Place of Origin
Reds: Full-Body	
SYRAH	**Hermitage**/Rhône (France)
SYRAH	**Shiraz**/Australia/**Varietal**/Worldwide
ZINFANDEL	**Zinfandel**/California
Reds: Sweet	
BLACK MUSCAT	**Black Muscat**/California/Italy
BRACHETTO	**Brachetto**/Italy
CONCORD	**Concord**/New York/U.S.
CORVINA	**Recioto della Valpolicella**/Veneto (Italy)
FREISA	**Freisa**/California
GRENACHE	**Banyuls**/Languedoc (France)
MAVRODAPHNE	**Mavrodaphne**/Greece
TOURIGA etc.	**Vintage, LBV & Ruby Porto**/Portugal
ZINFANDEL	**Zinfandel Port**/California

Bordeaux Classifications and Burgundy Vineyards

Bordeaux Classifications

1855 Classification of the Haut-Médoc
"Grand Cru Classé en 1855"
(All Haut-Médoc wines are red).

	Commune/Appellation
Premier Crus (First Growths):	
Château Lafite-Rothschild	Pauillac
Ch. Mouton-Rothschild	Pauillac
Ch. Latour	Pauillac
Ch. Margaux	Margaux
Ch. Haut-Brion (Pessac)	Graves
Deuxième Crus (Second Growths):	
Ch. Rauzan-Ségla	Margaux
Ch. Rauzan-Gassies	Margaux
Ch. Léoville-Las-Cases	St.-Julien
Ch. Léoville-Poyferré	St.-Julien
Ch. Léoville-Barton	St.-Julien
Ch. Durfort-Vivens	Margaux
Ch. Gruaud-Larose	St.-Julien
Ch. Lascombes	Margaux
Ch. Brane-Cantenac (Cantenac)	Margaux

	Commune/Appellation
Seconds Crus (Second Growths):	
Ch. Pichon-Longueville-Baron	Pauillac
Ch. Pichon-Longueville-Comtesse-de-Lalande	Pauillac
Ch. Ducru-Beaucaillou	St.-Julien
Ch. Cos d'Estournel	St.-Estéphe
Ch. Montrose	St.-Estéphe
Troisième Crus (Third Growths):	
Ch. Kirwan (Cantenac)	Margaux
Ch. d'Issan (Cantenac)	Margaux
Ch. Lagrange	St.-Julien
Ch. Langoa-Barton	St.-Julien
Ch. Giscours (Labarde)	Margaux
Ch. Malescot-St.-Exupéry	Margaux
Ch. Boyd-Cantenac (Cantenac)	Margaux
Ch. Cantenac-Brown (Cantenac)	Margaux
Ch. Palmer (Cantenac)	Margaux
Ch. La Lagune (Ludon)	Haut-Médoc
Ch. Desmirail	Margaux
Ch. Calon-Ségur	St.-Estéphe
Ch. Ferrière	Margaux
Ch. Marquis d'Alesme-Becker	Margaux
Quatrièmes Crus (Fourth Growths):	
Ch. Saint-Pierre	St.-Julien
Ch. Talbot	St.-Julien
Ch. Branaire-Ducru	St.-Julien
Ch. Duhart-Milon	Pauillac
Ch. Pouget (Cantenac)	Margaux
Ch. La Tour-Carnet (Saint Laurent)	Haut-Médoc
Ch. Lafon-Rochet	St.-Estéphe
Ch. Beycheville	St.-Julien
Ch. Prieuré-Lichine (Cantenac)	Margaux
Ch. Marquis-de-Terme	Margaux
Cinquièmes Crus (Fifth Growths):	
Ch. Pontet-Canet	Pauillac
Ch. Batailley	Pauillac

	Commune/Appellation

Cinquièmes Crus (Fifth Growths):

Ch. Haut-Batailley	Pauillac
Ch. Grand-Puy-Lacoste	Pauillac
Ch. Grand-Puy-Ducasse	Pauillac
Ch. Lynch-Bages	Pauillac
Ch. Lynch Moussas	Pauillac
Ch. Dauzac (Labarde)	Margaux
Ch. d'Armailhac	Pauillac
Ch. du Tertre (Arsac)	Margaux
Ch. Haut-Bages-Libéral	Pauillac
Ch. Pédesclaux	Pauillac
Ch. Belgrave (St. Laurent)	Haut-Médoc
Ch. Camensac (St. Laurent)	Haut-Médoc
Ch. Cos Labory	St. Estéphe
Ch. Clerc Milton	Pauillac
Ch. Croizet-Bages	Pauillac
Ch. Cantemerle (Macau)	Haut-Médoc

1855 Classification of Sauternes

Grand Cru Classé

Château d'Yquem   Sauternes

Premier Crus (First Growths):

Ch. La Tour Blanche (Bommes), Lafaurie-Peyraguey (Bommes), Clos Haut-Peyraguey (Bommes), Rayne-Vigneau (Bommes), Suduiraut (Preignac), Coutet (Barsac), Climens (Barsac), Guiraud (Sauternes), Rieussec (Fargues de Langon in Sauternes), Rabaud-Promis (Bommes), and Sigalas-Rabaud (Bommes).

Deuxième Crus (Second Growths):

Including Ch. Doisy-Daëne (Barsac), Doisy-Dubroca (Barsac), Doisy-Védrines (Barsac), Filhot (Sauternes), d'Arche (Sauternes), de Malle (Preignac), Caillou (Barsac), and Suau (Barsac).

1959 Classification of Graves

(Red and White wines).

Cru Classé:

Château Bouscaut (Cadaujac), Ch. Carbonnieux (Léognan), Domaine de Chevalier (Léognan), Couhins-Lurton (Villenave—white only), de Fieuzal (Léognan), Haut-Bailly (Léognan—red only), Haut-Brion (Pessac), La Mission-Haut-Brion (Talence—red only), Latour-Haut-Brion (Talence—red only), La Tour-Martillac (Martillac), Laville-Haut-Brion (Talence—white only), Malartic-Lagraviére (Léognan), Olivier (Léognan), Pape-Clément (Pessac—red only), and Smith-Haut-Lafite (Martillac—red only) .

1996 Classification of St.-Émilion

(All St.-Émilion wines are red).

Premier Grand Cru Classé (Class A):

Château Ausone and Ch. Cheval Blanc

Premier Grand Cru Classé (Class B):

Ch. l'Angélus, Beau-Séjour Bécot, Beauséjour (Duffau Lagarosse), Belair, Canon, Figeac, Clos Fourtet, la Gaffelière, Magdelaine, Pavie, and Trottevieille.

Grand Cru Classé (72 Châteaux):

Including: Ch. l'Arrosée, Bellevue, Canon-la-Gaffeliére, Clos des Jacobins, Corbin, la Dominique, Fonplégade, Fonroque, Tertre Daugay, la Tour Figeac, and Troplong Mondot.

Top Cru Bourgeois of the Médoc

(All Médoc wines are red).

Including Château d'Agassac (Haut—Médoc), Ch. Belle—Rose (Pauillac), Fourcas-Hosten (Listrac), du Glana (St.-Julien), Greysac (Médoc), Haut-Marbuzet (St.-éstephe), La Cardonne (Médoc), Lalande-Borie (St.-Julien), Larose-Trintaudon (Haut—Médoc), de Marbuzet (St.-éstephe—second label of Cos d'Estournel), Maucaillou (Moulis), Meyney (St.-éstephe), les Ormes-de-pez (St.-éstephe), Phélan-Ségur (St.-éstephe), Potensac (Médoc), Sociando-Mallet (Haut—Médoc), and La Tour de By (Médoc).

Pomerol

Never classified. (All Pomerol wines are red).

Best include: Château Pétrus, Ch. Le Pin, La Conseillante, L'Evangile, Lafleur, Trotanoy, and Vieux Château Certan.

Burgundy Vineyards

Grand Cru Vineyards—Côte d'Or Burgundy

Côte de Nuits (*Red Wines—100% Pinot Noir*):

Commune/Village	Grand Cru Vineyard
Fixin	None
Gevrey-Chambertin	Chambertin
	Chambertin Cloz-de-Bè
	Chapelle-Chambertin
	Charmes-Chambertin
	Griottes-Chambertin
	Latriciéres-Chambertin
	Mazis-Chambertin
	Ruchottes-Chambertin
Morey-St.-Denis	Clos de La Roche
	Clos-St.—Denis
	Clos de Tart
	Clos des Lambrays
	Bonnes Mares (overlaps next commune)
Chambolle-Musigny	Musigny (also white)Vougeot Clos de Vougeot
Vosne-Romanée	Romanée-Conti
	LaTâche
	Richebourg
	La Romanée
	Romanée-St.-Vivant
	La Grand Rue
Flagey-Echézeaux	Grand Echézeaux
	Echézeaux
Nuit-St.-Georges	None

Côte de Beaune (White Wines—100% Chardonnay):

Commune/Village	Grand Cru Vineyard
Aloxe-Corton	Corton (also red)
	Corton-Charlemagne
Pernand-Vergelesses	None
Savigny-Les-Beaune	None
Beaune	None

Commune/Village	Grand Cru Vineyard
Pomard	None
Volnay	None
Monthelie	None
Auxey-Duresses	None
Meursault	None
Puligny-Montrachet	Montrachet
	Bâtard-Montrachet (overlaps next commune)
	Chevalier-Montrachet
	Bienvenues-Bâtard-Montrachet
Chassagne-Montrachet	Montrachet
	Criots-Bâtard-Montrachet
Santenay	None

Index